OECD-FAO
Agricultural Outlook
2011-2020

OECD

ORGANISATION FOR ECONOMIC
CO-OPERATION AND DEVELOPMENT

FOOD AND AGRICULTURE ORGANIZATION
OF THE UNITED NATIONS

This work is published under the responsibilities of the Secretary-General of the OECD and the Director-General of FAO. The views expressed and conclusions reached in this report do not necessarily correspond to those of the governments of OECD member countries, or the governments of the FAO member countries. The designations employed and the presentation of material in this information product do not imply the expression of any opinion whatsoever on the part of the Food and Agriculture Organization of the United Nations concerning the legal or development status of any country, territory, city or area or of its authorities, or concerning the delimitation of its frontiers or boundaries.

Please cite this publication as:
OECD/FAO (2011), OECD-FAO Agricultural Outlook 2011-2020, OECD Publishing and FAO.
http://dx.doi.org/10.1787/agr_outlook-2011-en

ISBN 978-92-64-410675-8 (print)
ISBN 978-92-64-10676-5 (PDF)

Periodical:
ISSN 1563-0447 (print)
ISSN 1999-1142 (online)

Foreword

*T*he Agricultural Outlook *is prepared jointly by the Organisation for Economic Co-operation and Development (OECD) and the Food and Agriculture Organization (FAO) of the United Nations. The main purpose of the report is the attempt to build consensus on global prospects for the agriculture, fisheries and food sectors, and on emerging issues which affect them. Accordingly, the projections and assessments provided in the report are the result of close co-operation with national experts in OECD countries as well as some key non-OECD countries and agro-industry organisations, reflecting the combined knowledge and expertise of this wide group of collaborators. A jointly developed modelling system, based on the OECD's Aglink and FAO's Cosimo models facilitates consistency and analysis of the projections. The fully documented outlook database, including historical data and projections, is available through the OECD-FAO joint internet site www.agri-outlook.org.*

This annual report provides market projections for biofuels, cereals, oilseeds, sugar, meats, dairy products and, for the first time, fish and seafood over the 2011-20 period. The market assessments are contingent on a set of underlying assumptions regarding macroeconomic factors and the continuation of domestic agricultural and trade policies. They also assume normal weather conditions and long-term productivity trends. As such, the Outlook presents a plausible view on the evolution of global agricultural markets over the next decade and provides a baseline for further analysis of alternative economic or policy assumptions.

Underpinning this Outlook are expectations that world economies will continue recovering from the 2009 global crisis; that population growth will continue to slow; and that energy prices will trend upwards. The setting for these projections is one of high and volatile commodity prices in recent years with new price hikes again in 2010 and early 2011. A good harvest this year will be critical in bringing more stability to commodity markets. However, many of the drivers of price volatility – weather, yields, stocks, energy prices – may themselves be more volatile in the future. Agriculture and fish production and trade will continue to grow, led by the emerging economies, while growing food deficits are expected in Sub-Saharan countries.

An important message from this report is the need for both shorter term measures to help manage and mitigate the risks associated with volatility and for further investment to enhance the productivity and resilience of the global food and agriculture system. The implications of high and volatile prices for food insecurity have become a central issue for the G20 and new proposals for action are to be considered at the June 2011 meeting of G20 Agriculture Ministers.

Acknowledgements

This *Agricultural Outlook* is jointly prepared by the OECD and FAO Secretariats.

At the OECD, the *Outlook* report was authored by the Agro-Food Trade and Markets Division of the Trade and Agriculture Directorate: Wayne Jones (Division Head), Céline Giner (*Outlook* and baseline co-ordinator), Pavel Vavra, Linda Fulponi, Ignacio Pérez Domínguez, Garry Smith, Gregoire Tallard and Shinichi Taya. Additional Directorate contributions were provided by Claire Jolly (International Futures Programme), Kevin Parris (Agricultural Policies and Environment Division) and Carl-Christian Schmidt (Fisheries Policies Division). The OECD Secretariat is grateful for the contributions provided by Pierre Charlebois, Brooke Fridfinnson and Nathalie Hamman of Agriculture and Agri Food Canada and Stefan Tangermann of the University of Gottingen. Research and statistical assistance were provided by Armelle Elasri, Alexis Fournier, Gaëlle Gouarin and Claude Nenert. Meetings organisation and document preparation were provided by Christine Cameron. Technical assistance in the preparation of the *Outlook database* was provided by Frano Ilicic. Many other colleagues in the OECD Secretariat and member country delegations furnished useful comments on earlier drafts of the report.

At the FAO, the team of economists and commodity officers from the Trade and Markets Division contributing to this edition consisted of David Hallam (Division Director), Merritt Cluff (Team Leader), Holger Matthey (Baseline Coordinator), Abdolreza Abbassian, El Mamoun Amrouk, Pedro Arias, Concepcion Calpe, Denis Drechsler, Adam Prakash and Peter Thoenes. Marcel Adenäuer and Arno Becker from Bonn University joined the team as consultants. Hansdeep Khaira and Doussou Traore contributed from the Statistics Division. Stefania Vannuccini and Audun Lem contributed from the Fisheries and Aquaculture Department, with technical support from Pierre Charlebois. Research assistance and database preparation were provided by Emily Carroll, Claudio Cerquiglini, Barbara Ferraioli, Berardina Forzinetti, Marco Milo and Barbara Senfter. Secretarial and publishing services were provided by Rita Ashton and Valentina Banti.

Finally, the assistance and cooperation of the Executive Director, Peter Baron, and staff of the International Sugar Organisation (ISO) in London, in reviewing the country level projections and providing information on the market outlook for sugar and key emerging issues is gratefully acknowledged.

Table of Contents

Tables

"Online": follow the Statlink for the tables available online

Figures

This book has...

StatLinks

A service that delivers Excel® files from the printed page!

Look for the *StatLinks* at the bottom right-hand corner of the tables or graphs in this book.
To download the matching Excel® spreadsheet, just type the link into your Internet browser, starting with the *http://dx.doi.org* prefix.
If you're reading the PDF e-book edition, and your PC is connected to the Internet, simply click on the link. You'll find *StatLinks* appearing in more OECD books.

Acronyms and Abbreviations

ACP	African, Caribbean and Pacific countries
AI	Avian influenza
AMAD	Agricultural Market Access Database
ARS	Argentinean peso
AUD	Australian dollars
AUSFTA	Australia and United States Free Trade Agreement
BN	Billion
Bnl	Billion litres
BRIIC	Emerging economies of Brazil, Russian Federation, India, Indonesia and China
BRL	Real (Brazil)
BSE	Bovine Spongiform Encephalopathy
Bt	Billion tonnes
CAD	Canadian dollar
CAFTA	Central American Free Trade Agreement
CAP	Common Agricultural Policy (EU)
CCC	Commodity Credit Corporation
CET	Common External Tariff
CIS	Commonwealth of Independent States
CN	Combined Nomenclature
CNY	Yuan (China)
COOL	Country of Origin Labelling
CMO	Common Market Organisation for sugar (EU)
CO_2	Carbon dioxide
CPI	Consumer Price Index
CRP	Conservation Reserve Program of the United States
Cts/lb	Cents per pound
Cwe	Carcass weight equivalent
DDA	Doha Development Agenda
DDG	Dried Distiller's Grains
Dw	Dressed weight
EBA	Everything-But-Arms Initiative (EU)
ECOWAP	West Africa Regional Agricultural Policy
ECOWAS	Economic Community of West African States
EISA Act	Energy Independence and Security Act of 2007 (US)
EEP	Export Enhancement Program (US)
EPAs	Economic Partnership Agreements (between EU and ACP countries)
ERS	Economic Research Service of the US Department for Agriculture
Est	Estimate
E85	Blends of biofuel in transport fuel that represent 85% of the fuel volume
EU	European Union
EU15	Fifteen member states of the European Union

EU12	Ten new member states of the European Union from May 2004
EU27	Twenty seven member states of the European Union (including Bulgaria and Romania from 2007)
EUR	Euro (Europe)
FAO	Food and Agriculture Organization of the United Nations
FCE Act	Food, Conservation and Energy Act of 2008 US Farm Bill
FDP	Fresh dairy products
FMD	Foot and Mouth Disease
FOB	Free on board (export price)
FR	Federal Reserve (US central bank)
FSRI ACT	Farm Security and Rural Investment Act (US) of 2002
G10	Group of ten countries (see Glossary)
G20	Group of 20 developing countries (see Glossary)
GATT	General Agreement on Tariffs and Trade
GDP	Gross domestic product
GHG	Green House Gases
GMO	Genetically modified organism
Ha	Hectares
HFCS	High fructose corn syrup
Hl	Hectolitre
HS	Harmonised commodity description and coding system
IBRD	International Bank for Reconstruction and Development
IDA	International Development Association
IEA	International Energy Agency
IFAD	International Fund for Agricultural Development
IMF	International Monetary Fund
INR	Indian rupees
IPCC	Intergovernmental Panel on Climate Change
JPY	Japanese Yen
Kg	Kilogrammes
KORUS	Korean-US Free Trade Agreement
KRW	Korean won
Kt	Thousand tonnes
L	Litre
La Niña	Climatic condition associated with the temperature of major sea currents
Lb	Pound
LDCs	Least Developed Countries
LICONSA	Leche Industralizada
Lw	Live weight
MERCOSUR	Common Market of South America
MFN	Most Favoured Nation
Mha	Million hectares
Mn	Million
MPS	Market Price Support
Mt	Million tonnes
MTBE	Methyl tertiary butyl ether
MXN	Mexican peso
NAFTA	North American Free Trade Agreement
NZD	New Zealand dollar
OECD	Organisation for Economic Cooperation and Development

OIE	World Organisation for Animal Health
p.a.	Per annum
PCE	Private consumption expenditure
PPP	Purchasing power parity
PROCAMPO	Mexican Farmers Direct Support Programme
PRRS	Porcine reproductive and respiratory syndrome
PSE	Producer Support Estimate
Pw	Product weight
R&D	Research and development
RED	Renewable Energy Directive in the EU
RFS2	Renewable Fuels Standard in the US, which is part of the Energy Policy Act
Rse	Raw sugar equivalent
Rtc	Ready to cook
RUB	Russian ruble
RUK	Russian Federation, Ukraine and Kazakhstan
Rwt	Retail weight
SFP	Single Farm Payment scheme (EU)
SMP	Skim milk powder
SPS	Sanitary and phytosanitary measures
T	Tonnes
T/ha	Tonnes/hectare
THB	Thai baht
TRQ	Tariff rate quota
UHT	Ultra-heat treatment is the partial sterilisation of food by heating it for a short time
UN	The United Nations
UNCTAD	United Nations Conference on Trade and Development
UNICEF	The United Nations Children's Fund
URAA	Uruguay Round Agreement on Agriculture
US	United States
USD	United States dollar
USDA	United States Department of Agriculture
v-CJD	New Creutzfeldt-Jakob Disease
VAT	Value added tax
VHP	Very high polarization sugar
WAEMU	West African Economic and Monetary Union
WFP	World Food Programme
WMP	Whole milk powder
Wse	White sugar equivalent
WTO	World Trade Organisation
ZAR	South African rand

Outlook in Brief

Commodity prices rose sharply again in August 2010 as crop production shortfalls in key producing regions and low stocks reduced available supplies, and resurging economic growth in developing and emerging economies underpinned demand. A period of high volatility in agricultural commodity markets has entered its fifth successive year. High and volatile commodity prices and their implications for food insecurity are clearly among the important issues facing governments today. This was well reflected in the discussions at the G20 Summit in Seoul in November, 2010, and in the proposals for action being developed for consideration at its June 2011 meeting of Agriculture Ministers in Paris.

This *Outlook* is cautiously optimistic that commodity prices will fall from their 2010-11 levels, as markets respond to these higher prices and the opportunities for increased profitability that they afford. Harvests this year are critical, but restoring market balances may take some time. Until stocks can be rebuilt, risks of further upside price volatility remain high. This *Outlook* maintains its view in recent editions that agricultural commodity prices in real terms are likely to remain on a higher plateau during the next decade compared to the previous decade. Prolonged periods of high prices could make the achievement of global food security goals more difficult, putting poor consumers at a higher risk of malnutrition.

Higher commodity prices are a positive signal to a sector that has been experiencing declines in prices expressed in real terms for many decades and are likely to stimulate the investments in improved productivity and increased output needed to meet the rising demands for food. However, supply response is conditioned by the relative cost of inputs while the incentives provided by higher international prices are not always passed through to producers due to high transactions costs or domestic policy interventions. In some key producing regions, exchange rate appreciation has also affected competitiveness of their agricultural sectors, limiting production responses.

There are signs that production costs are rising and productivity growth is slowing. Energy related costs have risen significantly, as have feed costs. Resource pressures, in particular those related to water and land, are also increasing. Land available for agriculture in many traditional supply areas is increasingly constrained and production must expand into less developed areas and into marginal lands with lower fertility and higher risk of adverse weather events. Substantial further investments into productivity enhancements are needed to ensure the sector can meet the rising demands of the future.

Main messages:

- Agricultural production is expected to increase in the short term, assuming normal weather, as a result of an expected supply response to current high prices. Commodity prices should fall from the highs of early 2011, but in real terms are projected to average up to 20% higher for cereals (maize) and up to 30% for meats (poultry), over the 2011-20 period compared to the last decade. Increases in commodity prices are now moving down the commodity chain into livestock commodities.

- As higher prices for commodities are passed through the food chain, recent evidence indicates that consumer food price inflation is currently rising in most countries, contributing to higher aggregate consumer price inflation. This raises concerns for economic stability and food insecurity in some developing countries as the purchasing power of poorer populations is reduced.

- Global agricultural production is projected to grow at 1.7% annually, on average, compared to 2.6% in the previous decade. Slower growth is expected for most crops, especially oilseeds and coarse grains, which face higher production costs and slowing productivity growth. Growth in livestock production stays close to recent trends. Despite the slower expansion, production *per capita* is still projected to rise 0.7% annually.

- The global slowdown in projected yield improvements of important crops will continue to exert pressure on international prices. Higher production growth is expected from emerging suppliers where existing technologies offer good potential for yield improvements, although yield/supply variability may be higher. The share of production from developing countries continues to increase over the outlook period.

- The fisheries sector, which is covered for the first time in this *Outlook*, is projected to increase its global production by 1.3% annually to 2020, slower than over the previous decade due to a lower rate of growth of aquaculture (2.8% against 5.6% for 2001-10) and a reduced or stagnant fish capture sector. By 2015, aquaculture is projected to surpass capture fisheries as the most important source of fish for human consumption, and by 2020 should represent about 45% of total fishery production (including non-food uses). Compared to the 2008-2010 period, average capture fish prices are expected to be about 20% higher by 2020 in nominal terms compared with a 50% increase for aquaculture species.

- *Per capita* food consumption will expand most rapidly in Eastern Europe, Asia and Latin America where incomes are rising and population growth is slowing. Vegetable oils, sugar, meat and dairy products should experience the highest increases in demand.

- The use of agricultural output as feedstock for biofuels will continue its robust growth, largely driven by biofuel mandates and support policies. By 2020, an estimated 13% of global coarse grain production, 15% of vegetable oil production and 30% of sugar cane production will be used for biofuel production. Higher oil prices would induce yet further growth in use of biofuel feedstocks, and at sufficiently high oil prices, biofuel production in many countries becomes viable even in the absence of policy support.

- Trade is expected to grow by 2% per year, which is slower than over the previous decade, with only modest production increases by traditional exporters and higher domestic production by importers. The fastest growth will come primarily from emerging exporters in Eastern Europe, Central Asia and Latin American countries. Growing food deficits are expected in Sub-Saharan countries as population driven demand outpaces rising domestic production.

- Stochastic analysis demonstrates the uncertainty of the price projections, which are highly dependent on the underlying assumptions, and suggests the risk of higher prices is greater than lower prices. This analysis also confirms that yield induced production fluctuations in major crop exporting countries have been a prime source of international price volatility. Last year's drought and fires in the Russian Federation and the Ukraine, and excess moisture in the United States illustrated how quickly market balances can change. Weather-related crop yield variations are expected to become an even more critical driver of price volatility in the future.

Price volatility

The *Outlook* takes a look at the key forces driving price volatility, which create uncertainty and risk for producers, traders, consumers and governments. Price volatility can have extensive negative impacts on the agricultural sector, food security and the wider economy in both developed and developing countries.

- *Weather and climate change* – The most frequent and significant factor causing volatility is unpredictable weather conditions. Climate change is altering weather patterns, but its impact on extreme weather events is not clear.

- *Stock levels* – Stocks have long played a role in mitigating discrepancies in short term demand and supply of commodities. When accessible stocks are low relative to use, as they currently are for coarse grains, price volatility may be high.

- *Energy prices* – Increasing links to energy markets through both inputs such as fertiliser and transportation, and through biofuel feedstock demand, are transmitting price volatility from energy to agricultural markets.

- *Exchange rates* – By affecting domestic commodity prices, currency movements have the potential to impact food security and competitiveness around the world.

- *Growing demand* – If supply does not keep pace with demand, there will be upward pressure on commodity prices. With *per capita* incomes rising globally and in many poor countries expected to increase by as much as 50%, food demand will become more inelastic such that larger price swings would be necessary to affect demand.

- *Resource pressures* – Higher input costs, slower technology application, expansion into more marginal lands, and limits to double-cropping and water for irrigation, are limiting production growth rates.

- *Trade restrictions* – Both export and import restrictions amplify price volatility in international markets.

- *Speculation* - Most researchers agree that high levels of speculative activity in futures markets may amplify price movements in the short term although there is no conclusive evidence of longer term systemic effects on volatility.

Policy challenges

This *Outlook* highlights both significant challenges to addressing global food insecurity and the major opportunities for food and agricultural producers arising from the higher average prices projected over the coming decade. The policy challenge is to promote productivity growth, particularly for small producers, that improves market resilience to external shocks, and that reduces waste and increases supplies to local markets, at affordable prices. Public sector investments are required in agricultural research and development, institutions and infrastructure to increase sector productivity and resilience towards weather/climate change and resource scarcity. Investments are required to reduce post harvest losses. Recognising that volatility will remain a feature of agricultural markets, coherent policies are required to both reduce volatility where possible and to limit its negative impacts.

- *Mitigating volatility* – Enhanced market transparency can reduce price volatility. Greater efforts are required to improve global and national information and surveillance systems on market prospects, including better data on production, stocks and trade in sensitive food security commodities. Removal or reduction of policy distortions, such as restrictions on imports and exports or biofuel subsidies and mandates, can also reduce price volatility. Information and transparency in futures markets should be improved recognising the importance of harmonising measures accross exchanges.

- *Managing volatility* – Social safety nets can assist the most vulnerable consumers when food prices rise while producer safety-nets can offset low incomes, thereby maintaining their ability to purchase inputs and maintain production. Emergency food reserves for targeted assistance to poor people are useful to lessen the impact of high prices. Greater efforts are required to make market-based risk management schemes, including the use of forward contracting and commodity futures exchanges, available to smaller producers. Governments can also adopt certain risk management strategies such as insurance to finance food imports when poor weather reduces domestic production or option contracts to lock in future food import purchases.

Chapter 1

Overview

Introduction

The *Agricultural Outlook* is a collaborative effort of the Organisation for Economic Co-operation and Development (OECD) and the Food and Agriculture Organization (FAO) of the United Nations. Bringing together the commodity, policy and country expertise of both Organisations and input from collaborating member countries, it provides an updated annual assessment of the medium-term development of global commodity markets, using the Aglink-Cosimo model[1] to generate a consistent set of commodity projections and for the analysis of issues. The baseline projection is not a forecast about the future, but rather a plausible scenario of what can be expected to happen under a certain set of assumptions, such as the macroeconomic environment over the coming ten years, as well as current agricultural and trade policy settings around the world. The projections of production, consumption, stocks, trade and prices for the different agricultural products described and analysed in this report cover the years 2011 to 2020. This year's edition contains for the first time a chapter on the outlook for the fisheries sector. The final section of this Overview outlines risks and uncertainties in the baseline projection, and in particular, the sensitivity of the projections to changes in some of the more important assumptions that underlie it. This aspect of uncertainties is addressed comprehensively in the special feature on the drivers of market volatility in the second chapter of the report.

The setting – high and volatile prices dominate markets

Agricultural commodity prices have experienced considerable volatility in recent years starting with the price surge of 2007-08. As Figure 1.1 illustrates, there has been substantial co-movement among primary commodity prices during this period with most commodity prices having shown increased variability. After three years of turbulence, commodity markets seemed to return to calmer conditions up to mid-2010 when weather-related supply shocks occurred and the resulting price movements demonstrated that agriculture remains susceptible to extreme volatility. A severe drought took a heavy toll on grain crops in the Russian Federation, Ukraine and Kazakhstan, leading to an almost 5% decline in world wheat production, the largest fall since 1991. Maize yields in the United States were negatively affected by a hot and wet summer. Floods in Pakistan and other parts of Asia lowered rice harvests which impacted regional markets. As a result, wheat and coarse grain prices surged and approached their 2008 highs by early 2011. The developments on international cereal markets also impacted on other food commodities such as meat, where higher feed costs contributed to price increases. In the case of dairy markets, a combination of strong demand in the Russian Federation and South East Asia, and constrained supplies from Oceania contributed to strong price increases. Sugar markets also went through a period of renewed volatility with prices experiencing a succession of peaks and downward corrections in 2010 before surging to a 30-year high in February 2011, as a rundown in global stocks to their lowest level in 20 years, helped to underpin higher and more volatile prices.

Figure 1.1. **Commodity price variability has increased since 2006**

International commodity price indices

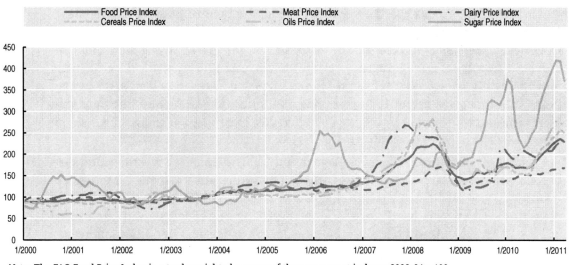

Note: The FAO Food Price Index is a trade weighted average of the component indexes 2002-04 = 100.

Source: GIEWS (2011).

StatLink 🔗 http://dx.doi.org/10.1787/888932425935

Figure 1.2. **Lower production leads to a drawdown in global stocks**

Annual change in world net agricultural production, 2005-2010

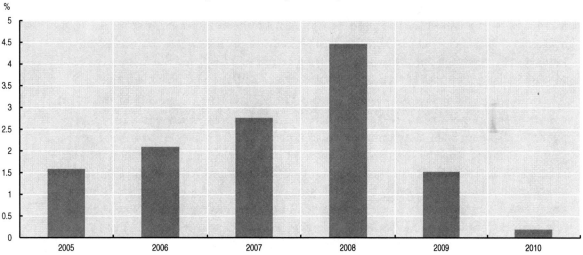

Note: The net agricultural production is calculated by weighting agricultural production of commodities and countries included in this *Outlook* with base international reference prices averaged for the period 2004-06, with deduction for feed and seed used for this production to avoid double counting in the livestock and grains.

Source: OECD and FAO Secretariats.

StatLink 🔗 http://dx.doi.org/10.1787/888932425954

The increase in some crop prices in 2010 was particularly steep because of production shortfalls which became evident in the latter half of the year. International stocks, which are critical to market volatility, were too low to effectively off-set such a production shortfall in the crop sector (Figure 1.2). While record yields in 2008 and 2009, especially of cereals, helped to gradually refill warehouses, hopes of a reversal of the negative trend in the stock-to-use ratio[2] were quickly disappointed. Stable agricultural production (with a change of merely 0.1% in 2010) coupled with a drawdown in stocks – a combination that also characterised the period prior to the 2008 crisis – clearly contributed to the price surge.

In addition to factors specific to each commodity, a number of other developments played a role in driving up commodity prices recently. In many emerging and even some least developed economies, especially in those well integrated to the world market, economic growth has resumed apace following the financial and economic crisis. Demand for virtually all commodities has resumed the strength that has been evident in the last ten years, and appears resistant to higher prices. Oil prices are rising and fluctuate with increased uncertainty concerning the sustainability of supplies as political instability spreads across countries in the Middle East region.

Exchange rates have also fluctuated significantly, and have affected the competitiveness of countries in trade. The depreciation of the US dollar with respect to many currencies has increased dollar denominated prices of agricultural products. The resort to *ad hoc* policy measures such as trade restrictions by some exporting countries has further curtailed supplies and aggravated price rises for cereals, in particular. In addition, increased financial funds investment in commodity markets has been a persistent feature during the period, although their influence on commodity price movements remains unclear and would require further research.

Growth resumes in consumer food prices

In reflection of these commodity price developments, FAO's index of international food commodity prices reached its highest recorded level in February 2011. Food price increases as measured by the food component of the consumer price index (CPI) accelerated in most developed and developing countries in the twelve months ending in January 2011, reversing the downward trend in food prices in 2009 and the first half of 2010. In general these increases continued to outpace overall inflation in most countries.

In looking at the past year from January 2010 to 2011, three-quarters of the OECD countries experienced retail food prices increases of 5% or less, while in six they rose by over 5%. Two countries, Korea and Estonia, experienced increases of over 10%. Brazil, China, Indonesia, and the Russian Federation all had double digit rates of food inflation this past year. These rates represent a significant acceleration from the previous year of single digit inflation. For those other developing and least developed countries that were examined, a similar picture of accelerating food price inflation emerged. Nonetheless, a few countries continued to experience a slowing in price increases, these include Ghana and Kenya. In Rwanda, prices actually decreased by about 2%.

The contribution of food prices increases to inflation has been small in OECD countries over the past twelve months, not only because food price increases were relatively moderate but also because the share of food in consumer expenditures is small. For the emerging economies the contribution was greater than in OECD countries, because of higher food price inflation and the fact that food constitutes a larger share of the total consumption basket. The largest contribution of food prices to inflation was found in some Asian countries. Box 1.3 on retail food prices, to be found at the end of this chapter, provides additional details on the recent evolution of food prices in a number of OECD, developing and least developed countries.

Box 1.1. **The main assumptions underlying the baseline projection**

The *Outlook* is presented as one baseline scenario that is considered plausible given a range of conditioning assumptions. These assumptions portray a specific macroeconomic and demographic environment which shapes the evolution of demand and supply for agricultural and fish products. Developments in other sectors, especially the energy sector, may also significantly affect both the supply and demand for these products. Technology and innovation remain the key to longer term market balances, as is its acceptance by both producers and consumers. Policy interventions influence agriculture and the fish sectors, in the form of regulations, taxes, subsidies or market price support. These general factors are described below. The Statistical tables, at the end of the chapter, provide more detailed data for these assumptions.

Economic growth in developing countries resumes at a quick pace

The economic environment underpinning the *Outlook* for OECD countries and some large emerging economies is based on assessments made at the OECD, supplemented by information provided by its Member countries. For other countries, projections from the World Bank (Global Economic Perspectives, January 2011), have been extended to 2020 using its longer term poverty projections. The projections suggest that around the world, economies are gradually recovering from the 2009 financial and economic crisis, albeit at different paces. For OECD countries, annual growth rates in the short and medium term are expected to be around 2% *per capita*. Economic growth outside the OECD area continues to be dominated by China and India, with annual rates of 7.4% *per capita* and 5.5% *per capita* respectively. These rates are above the average of developing countries as a group (around 3.8% *per capita*), but lower than in the previous decade when both countries lifted the group's average to more than 4% p.a. Brazil and the Russian Federation are also expected to show a strong performance with annual growth rates averaging above 4% p.a. as do some other developing and least developed countries that are rich in raw materials such as metals and oil (Figure 1.3).

Figure 1.3. **GDP growth resumes a quicker pace**

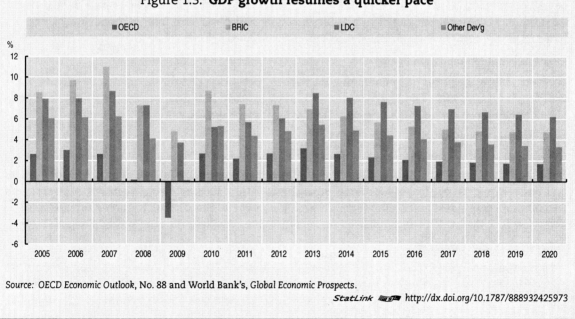

Source: *OECD Economic Outlook*, No. 88 and World Bank's, *Global Economic Prospects*.

StatLink http://dx.doi.org/10.1787/888932425973

Box 1.1. **The main assumptions underlying the baseline projection** *(cont.)*

Table 1.1. **Population growth to decline in coming decade**

	Annual growth rate in %	
	2001-2010	2011-2020
World	1.21	1.05
Africa	2.34	2.18
Latin America and Caribbean	1.19	0.91
North America	0.97	0.88
Europe	0.11	0.09
Asia and Pacific	1.23	1.01
China	0.65	0.55
India	1.51	1.17
Oceania Developed	1.13	0.93

Source: UN World Population Prospects (2008 Revision).

StatLink ▇▇▇ http://dx.doi.org/10.1787/888932427474

Population growth continues to slow

World population growth is expected to further slow to 1.05% annual growth between 2011 and 2020, compared with 1.2% p.a. in the previous decade. The slowdown in the growth rate is manifested in all regions, however with significant differences between developing and developed countries.

While slowing, population development patterns will continue to differ between developing countries and the developed world. Populations in OECD countries have mostly stagnated (*e.g.* many European countries) or even experienced declines in some countries (Japan, with a negative growth rate of 0.28% p.a.). Within the OECD area, Turkey, Mexico, Australia and the United States show the highest projected population growth rate. Net additions to population are anticipated to fall significantly during the outlook period, particularly in Asia, while they continue to rise in Africa which is projected to grow at over 2% p.a. An additional demographic dimension is urbanisation, which will continue to reshape consumption patterns toward higher value processed products and convenience foods (Table 1.1).

Inflation is held to moderate levels

Despite increasing prices of commodities, inflation is expected to remain subdued in most parts of the world. Inflation in OECD countries is assumed to average around 2% p.a. over the next ten years, while higher inflation rates, in the 4-8% range are anticipated for high growth emerging economies.

US dollar remains weak

The depreciation of the US dollar since 2002 has had important impacts on commodity prices (see Chapter 2 for further analysis). Currency movements among countries have altered competitiveness and trade prospects, particularly for large exporting countries such as Brazil, Australia, Argentina and Canada. For many developed and some emerging countries, the *Outlook* assumes further modest depreciation of the US dollar in the short term, and thereafter, constant exchange rates in nominal terms.

Energy prices trend upward

The energy sector which has displayed high volatility in recent years has become increasingly critical to agricultural markets. The level and volatility of crude oil prices are reflected in fertiliser and energy related input costs. The world oil price assumption underlying this *Outlook* was formed in February 2011, based on the analysis of the International Energy Agency, and has been assumed to be constant in real terms over the Outlook period. In nominal terms, this means that it will increase from an observed price of USD 78 per barrel in 2010 to USD 107 per barrel by 2020 (Figure 1.4).

Box 1.1. **The main assumptions underlying the baseline projection** (*cont.*)

Figure 1.4. **Crude oil prices projected to rise steadily to 2020**

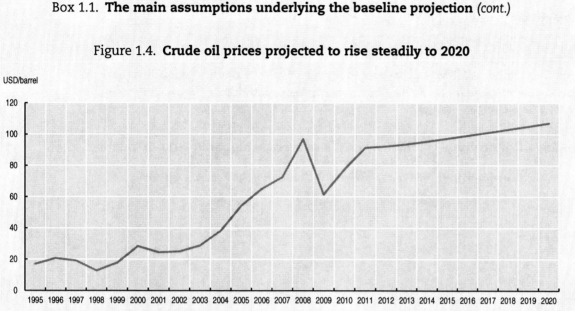

Note: Brent crude oil price.

Source: OECD Economic Outlook, No. 88 and the Energy Information Administration.

StatLink 🔗🔗🔗 http://dx.doi.org/10.1787/888932425992

Crude oil prices also affect the demand for agricultural feedstocks such as maize, sugar, cassava and vegetable oils and fat residues used to produce biofuels. The demand side link through biofuels has been increasingly important in determining crop prices at the margin, and in keeping stocks of feedstock commodities low. The risks and uncertainties section of this chapter outlines assessments, which are more extensively discussed in the special feature of Chapter 2 of how sensitive the projection is to both higher and lower oil prices.

Against the backdrop of rising production costs there is an apparent slowdown in productivity growth in agriculture. For example, while there remain large yield gaps among countries, crop yield growth, measured in percentage growth, has been slowing in recent years. This *Outlook* assumes that crop yields will continuously increase to 2020, but the rate of these improvements declines. Chapter 2 provides evidence suggesting that historical yield variability explains an important share of world commodity price variability for some crops such as coarse grains.

Policy considerations

Policy has long been recognised as an important influence in agricultural as well as fisheries markets. Policy reforms of the past decade or so have changed the shape of markets in many cases. The introduction of more decoupled payments and progress towards the elimination of direct price supports mean that policy measures are having less direct influence on production decisions. However, policies still loom large in many developed economies, while the recent application of export taxes or bans (these were exclusively in emerging and developing countries) has also had important impacts. This *Outlook* assumes that policies will continue to be applied in line with existing legislation. A conclusion to the Doha Development Agenda of multilateral trade negotiations, that include trade in agricultural products, is not anticipated in this baseline.

Global agriculture in perspective

Commodity prices are likely to remain high and volatile

The major assumptions underlying the baseline projection are discussed in Box 1.1. Given the current setting and these conditioning assumptions, two key questions arise from this *Outlook*. Will prices continue to remain high over the next decade and are price surges likely events in the light of future market prospects? The answer indicated by the *Outlook* is yes to both questions.

Figure 1.5. **All agricultural commodity prices to average higher in 2011-20 relative to the previous decade**

Percent change of average nominal prices in 2011-20 relative to different base periods

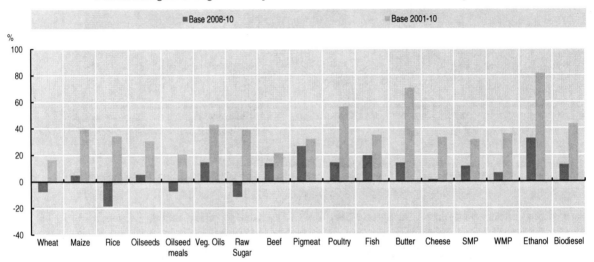

Source: OECD and FAO Secretariats.

StatLink ⬛ http://dx.doi.org/10.1787/888932426011

In a nutshell, this *Outlook* anticipates that the recent increase in prices and a return to normal yields will generate a short term supply response that will cause commodity prices to fall from current highs. However, consistent with the view of the past three editions of this *Outlook*, prices, on average, are projected to remain on a higher plateau compared to the previous decade in both nominal and real terms (Figures 1.5, 1.6 and 1.7). A slow growing supply set against expected high demand underlies the projection of high and more volatile agricultural commodity prices. Critical drivers on the supply side include high and increasing energy and related inputs and feed costs. These are mainly driven by high oil prices, but resource pressures, in particular those related to water and land are also increasing. These higher costs will limit production increases and result in slower yield growth. Relatively slower rates of agricultural production growth will also slow the replenishment of stocks, which will make commodity markets more susceptible to high price variability. On the demand side, growing populations and rising incomes in the large emerging economies such as China and India will sustain strong demand for commodities. Rising incomes will also drive a shift in diets from staple foods to more value-added and higher protein products, especially for consumers in emerging economies who will increasingly demand meat and dairy products in their consumption choices. These developments, coupled with the implementation of biofuel mandates have increased demand and made processors and consumers much less responsive to high commodity prices. The baseline view presented above is highly conditional on the

Figure 1.6. **In real terms, average 2011-20 cereal prices up to 20% higher; livestock prices up to 30% higher, relative to the previous decade**

Percent change of average real prices relative to different base periods

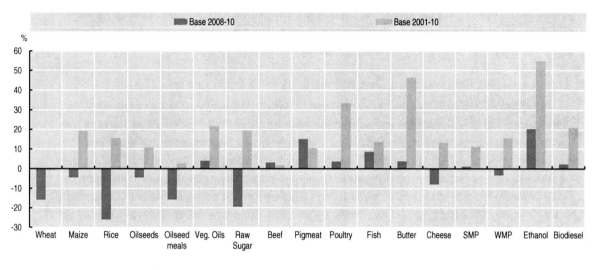

Source: OECD and FAO Secretariats.

StatLink 🔗 http://dx.doi.org/10.1787/888932426030

Figure 1.7. **Price trends in nominal terms of agricultural commodities to 2020**

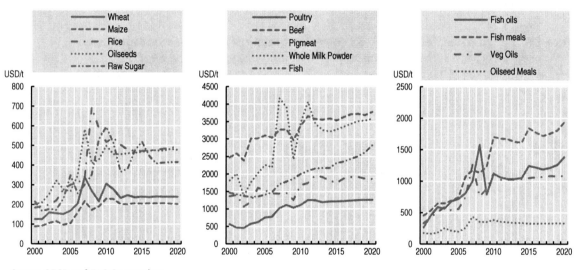

Source: OECD and FAO Secretariats.

StatLink 🔗 http://dx.doi.org/10.1787/888932426049

assumptions described in Box 1.1, and as such should be interpreted with considerable caution. The section on "Risks and uncertainties" presents a number of scenarios that illustrate the impact of a range of driving factors. Chapter 2 provides detailed explanations on the sensitivities and policy challenges.

All commodity prices in nominal terms will average higher to 2020 than in the previous decade. In real terms, cereal prices are anticipated to average up to 20% higher for maize and 15% higher for rice, compared to the previous decade, while for wheat, prices may remain at the same level. For meats, real poultry prices may average more than 30%

higher in the next decade, while pigmeat prices in Pacific markets may be some 20% higher, and Pacific market beef prices may remain at the same high level. Prices of meat are adjusting as higher costs of feedstuffs are factored into prices. Reflecting the fact that prices have moved sharply higher recently, prices of wheat, rice, oilseed meal and sugar will average lower compared to the past three year average, while prices of some meats, dairy products and maize will show a rise above this benchmark period.

Production costs on the rise with higher energy and feed costs

In addition to the effects of robust demand in developing and emerging economies, the increasing costs of some inputs are as well factored into the higher price projections in the medium term. Prices for nitrogen fertilisers and other farm chemicals are closely related to the crude oil price, so rising oil prices translate into increasing production costs. While the *Outlook* projects nominal commodity prices to remain on a higher plateau, when adjusted by costs of production, profitability in some input intensive production systems is not expected to improve significantly (Figure 1.8). Strong production responses are therefore expected in countries where production is less input intensive. This applies both to crop and livestock sectors. An exception is the United States, for which exchange rate depreciation may help to sustain the competitiveness of its agricultural and food sectors on world markets.

Oil prices also impact on commodity markets through the diversion of crops for feedstocks in biofuel production. Depending on the respective policies, an increase in oil prices could bid up feedstock prices as demand for ethanol or biodiesel increases. Such impacts are elaborated further in the last section of this Overview chapter.

Figure 1.8. **Maize price deflated by US cost of production index has not increased**

International maize price expressed in nominal terms divided by US cost production index

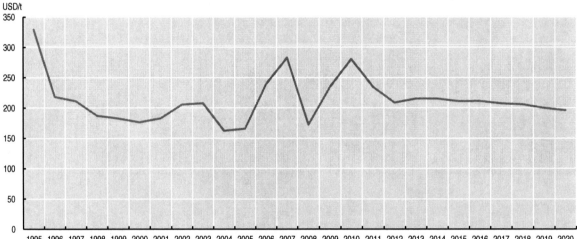

USD/t

Source: OECD and FAO Secretariats.

StatLink 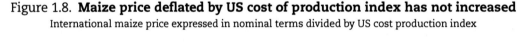 http://dx.doi.org/10.1787/888932426068

Agricultural production to continue to grow, but at a slower rate

The production projections for agricultural commodities included in this *Outlook* indicate a slowing of growth to average 1.7% p.a., down from 2.6% average annual growth of the previous decade. Developed and the large emerging developing countries in particular are projected to enter a period of lower productivity improvements for most crops. Oilseeds, palm oil and coarse grains experienced very strong growth in the previous decade based on the emerging demand for biofuels and the acceleration of feed demand. The livestock sectors are expected to maintain a more even development in the period to 2020, with a notable slowdown in the rate of growth only projected for poultry production. These developments reflect rising energy and feed costs and slower growth in crop yields. The implications for world price, consumption, stock and trade are manifold and these changes are described in the subsequent sections.

The projections confirm the continuation of the gradual shift in agricultural market share from developed to developing countries. Latin America, the growth engine of recent years, is expected to be joined by Eastern Europe making these two regions increasingly important suppliers of agricultural markets in the coming decade. Their crop area and yields are both expected to increase and livestock inventories to expand. Fuelled by investments and improved efficiency through structural reforms, the Russian Federation and other former Soviet republics may play an increasingly significant role in export markets for wheat and coarse grains, regaining some of their historic importance as a bread basket for the world. Despite the end of spectacular growth in soybeans, Argentina and Brazil, as relatively low cost producers, will continue to exhibit solid growth in oilseeds, cereals and livestock production. Production prospects appear to be equally strong in Sub-Saharan Africa. However, much of this growth originates from a relatively low production base, and is driven mainly by high population growth in rural areas and by higher investment. *Per capita* production increase is low in this region, growing about 0.5% per year in this projection. Sub-Saharan Africa continues to be characterised by low productivity and domestic markets which face low transmission of price signals from international markets.

North America is the only high income region that is expected to expand its agriculture significantly, led by the United States. The highly mechanised, capital and input intensive agricultural industries will grow mainly from intensification and efficiency gains and will benefit from a depreciated US dollar. The crop area is projected to remain largely stable, but livestock herds rebuild over the projection period in response to strong export demand for high quality meat.

Agriculture in Asia is encouraged by strong local demand as more and more people are moving into income brackets where they can afford higher value products. This is particularly the case for China which continues to benefit from rapid economic growth and development. Agriculture in the region is expected to grow mainly from expansion of the livestock sector. For example, rice production growth is expected to slow to 1% annually while poultry output continues its high growth at almost 3% p.a. Asia is a major deficit region for other crop products such as sugar and certain cereals. Area and water constraints are limiting factors in Asian agriculture, and these may induce increased food imports to meet rising consumption requirements.

The high income countries in Western Europe and Oceania are expected to exhibit very slow growth throughout the outlook period, similar to the previous decade. Environmental concerns, high input costs, limited additional arable land, on-going policy reforms and reduced competitiveness because of strong currencies keep agricultural sectors of the main Western European producers roughly at their current levels, barely higher than peak production in 2008. These mature markets will reduce area planted to many crops. Production growth in crop and livestock will increasingly come from efficiency gains. This is the consequence of a process of economic reforms, especially the EU CAP reforms designed to increase the market orientation of production. Growth in Australia and New Zealand is mostly driven by higher demand for livestock products, primarily beef and dairy products, but high currency values also limit their competitiveness.

While higher prices can be expected to lead to increased production, productivity growth, as measured by growth in crop yields, has been on a downward trend over the past ten years. Crop production per hectare continues to increase at a relatively fixed quantity per year, resulting in significant production increases over the outlook period. Although it declines as a percentage of trend yield, as the rate of increase is falling. Main factors for the slower growth include limited input application because of high costs and the expansion of planting into less suitable areas. Albeit, some increases in land under high cost irrigation will also be undertaken, water constraints may tighten in other regions.

Area expansion and a higher yield growth potential sustain the shift that has been underway for some time in market share from developed to developing regions. This trend towards the increasing importance of emerging countries, where use of inputs such as fertiliser may be lower and yield variability higher due to more variable weather conditions, is one of the factors behind the expectation of increased price volatility. Apart from yield improvements, which have been the main source of increasing crop production in the past several decades, growth in arable land will continue but at a slower pace. Some expansion of land under high cost irrigation is also expected, while in other regions water constraints continue to tighten. Developing countries will account for an increasing share of global agricultural production and experience the fastest growth in output in the coming decade. However, traditional suppliers in developed countries, with their high productivity will also continue to expand production, albeit at a slower rate than in the past, to remain large suppliers for a range of products.

Figure 1.9. **Net agricultural and fish production by region**
Net agricultural production index, base 100: 2004-06

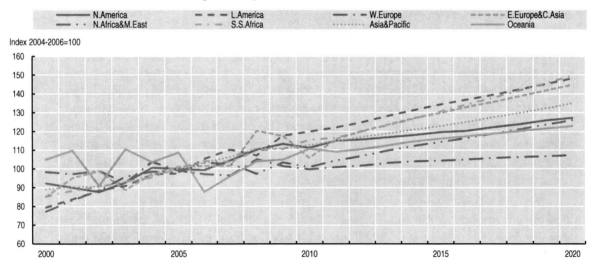

Note: The net agricultural production index is calculated by weighting agricultural production of commodities included in this Outlook by base international reference prices for the period 2004-06, with deduction for feed and seed used for this production to avoid double counting in the livestock and grains sectors.

Source: OECD and FAO Secretariats.

StatLink ⧉ http://dx.doi.org/10.1787/888932426087

Global fish production driven by aquaculture

World fisheries production is projected to increase by 14.7% over the next ten years, mainly driven by aquaculture which will contribute around 45% of total fishery production by 2020. Fish production is larger than any of the single meat categories. Aquaculture, although expanding more slowly than in the previous decade, is one of the fastest growing commodity sectors of this *Outlook* at an annual growth rate of 2.8%. Slower growth in the coming decade is attributable to increasing production bottlenecks mostly associated with location of fish farms. Over 80% of world aquaculture production is located in the Asian region, with China alone accounting for over 60% of production (Figure 1.9). El Niño should affect catches in South America, in particular Peru and Chile, in 2015 and 2020. World capture fisheries production has peaked around 90 Mt and is not likely to grow much further in the future (Figure 1.10).

Figure 1.10. **Rising fish production driven by aquaculture as capture fisheries stagnate**

Evolution of world fish production

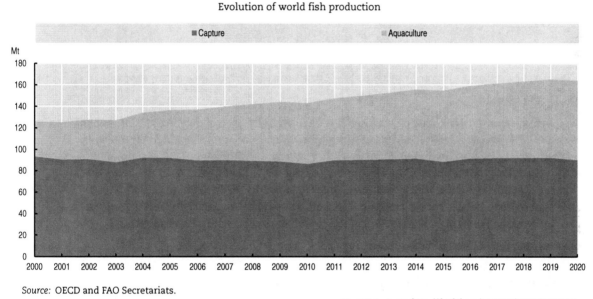

Source: OECD and FAO Secretariats.

StatLink 🖾 http://dx.doi.org/10.1787/888932426106

Food consumption growth is strongest in developing countries

Population growth and rising incomes will drive up demand for commodities over the projection period, especially in developing countries. Although slower than in previous decades, population growth is still particularly high in many developing and especially least developed countries, with rates of increase in excess of 2%, (compared to 0.2% in developed countries). These developing regions also display the highest *per capita* income growth, with increments of 3.7% and 4.7%, respectively. Growth in food demand is particularly high in countries with low but increasing incomes since a greater portion of additional income is devoted to improving diets in these countries.

Aggregate food consumption *per capita* is anticipated to expand most rapidly in Eastern Europe and Central Asia, where income growth is projected to be firm, and

Box 1.2. **The impact of the Japanese earthquake and tsunami on agriculture and fisheries**

Earthquake and tsunami

A major earthquake followed by a destructive tsunami hit the coastal area of north east Japan on 11 March 2011. It was the largest earthquake recorded in Japan, registering 9.0 on the Richter scale. The death toll of the event has already reached 15 000 with about 9 000 of people still missing as of 19 May 2011. This natural disaster severely damaged the Fukushima Daiichi nuclear plants, generating a nuclear incident now classified at level 7 by the Japanese government. The total area of flooded land by the tsunami is estimated at 561 000 ha. The possible impacts of the earthquake/tsunami on heavily affected prefectures of Japan and for Japanese agriculture and fisheries are still highly uncertain, as are the impacts of radiation leaks from the damaged nuclear power plants.

Table 1.2. **Profile of heavily damaged prefectures**

	Population (million)	Total area (km^2)	Flooded area (km^2)	GDP (Billion USD)	Value of agricultural production (Billion USD)
Iwate	1.3	15 278	58	38.2	2.6
Miyagi	2.3	6 862	327	70.5	2.0
Fukushima	2.0	13 782	112	66.3	2.6
Japan	128.1	377 946	561	4 419.7	88.9

Sources: Ministry of Agriculture, Forestry and Fisheries; Cabinet Office; Geospatial Information Authority of Japan.

Macroeconomic effects

Japan released an initial estimate of between JPY 16 trillion to JPY 25 trillion yen (USD 183 billion to USD 286 billion) in damages to fixed capital (infrastructure, houses and machinery) in the area, or the equivalent of 3 to 5% of annual Japanese GDP. The negative impact on GDP is estimated to reach JPY 0.5 trillion (USD 5.7 billion) in 2011, and lowering GDP growth for 2011 from 1.6 to 1.4% (IMF projections). These figures imply that the economic impact is likely to be rather limited. The impact on food consumption should be limited as well. The impact of electricity shortages is one of the significant but as yet unknown factors in the overall macroeconomic assessment.

Temporary shortage of food and responses

The unprecedented magnitude of the damage from these events had initially raised fears of food shortages with a rundown of stocks in many stores. But retailers quickly responded by replenishing their supplies of basic foods and necessities by two or three times normal volumes. The Japanese Ministry of Agriculture, Forestry and Fisheries (MAFF) released an assessment of the supply and demand situation for rice. According to the announcement, Japanese total annual rice food demand is estimated some 8.1 Mt in brown rice basis, while rice supply is estimated 10.1 Mt, ensuring an ample supply. Lending of feed grains is made available without fee and collateral and 340 000 ton has been distributed to growers through this scheme by 12 April. As a result of timely supply responses and information dissemination, it was quickly understood that the temporary shortage of food was related more to the disruption of transportation. MAFF also reported that supplies and retail prices of vegetables, meats and eggs had quickly returned to pre-crisis levels.

Agricultural and fisheries sector impacts

MAFF has released an assessment of damage to cultivated land. The total area of flooded farmland is estimated at 23 600 ha over six coastal prefectures as of March. In Miyagi prefecture, one of the hardest hit, 11% of its total agricultural land is damaged. As the total affected land represents only about 1% of Japanese cultivatable land, the loss to agricultural production directly caused by the tsunami is assessed as not being very large.

> Box 1.2. **The impact of the Japanese earthquake and tsunami on agriculture and fisheries** *(cont.)*
>
> The rice harvest for 2010 was completed well before the tsunami struck. With only around 1.2% of Japan's paddy rice fields directly affected, the damage to rice production is considered quite limited. No information on the damage to livestock is available yet. Since less than 3% of the total agricultural land was flooded in the six coastal prefectures, the tsunami damage to the livestock sectors is not expected to be significant. The main production areas of meat and dairy products in Japan are Hokkaido with 56% of the national dairy herd and Kyushu with 37% of the beef herd and 31% of hogs. Estimates of damage to production capacity are not large from a national perspective as major production areas were largely unaffected and the tsunami damage was limited to coastal regions. That said, the impact is tremendous from the viewpoint of local economies. In some towns, more than 75% of total farmland was flooded. Significant financial supports are necessary for recovery of agricultural and fisheries infrastructure and efforts are being made both in the public and private sectors.
>
> MAFF has released a preliminary report on the impact on fisheries which states that the fishing boats and port facilities in Iwate, Miyagi and Fukushima prefectures, including several major fishing ports located along the northern eastern Pacific coast, have been devastated. These three prefectures in aggregate account for 11.7% (513 kt) of Japan's total capture fisheries production (4.4 Mt) in 2008.
>
> Following detection of radioactive materials, the government immediately took action to ensure food safety, instructing restrictions of consumption and shipments of several products originating from the affected regions. The coverage of restrictions is updated in accordance with the ongoing monitoring, with some having already been lifted. As of 20 April 2011, bans are placed on several vegetables including spinach, on raw milk, shiitake mushroom and one species of fish. The planting of rice in the evacuation zone (a 20 km radius of the power plants) and neighbouring regions is restricted.
>
> **Trade**
>
> Many countries have taken restrictive measures on exports of agricultural and fisheries products from Japan due to the concern of possible radioactive contamination. Given the relatively small quantities of exports of these products by Japan, the impact on world trade will not be large. On the import side, Japan is one of the largest traders. Its import shares of world trade are: 4.2% for wheat, 17.4% for coarse grains, 10.3% for beef and 19.9% for pigmeat, respectively. As significant reductions in consumption and domestic production are not foreseen, large changes in imports by Japan are not expected either.

population growth is limited or declining. Growth is also high in Latin America and in Asia largely due to solid income growth. Food consumption growth is projected to be less robust in Sub Saharan Africa, where relatively strong income growth remains unequally distributed across the population of the region and previously has not led to strong food consumption growth. In contrast, growth in food consumption in this *Outlook* is stagnant or falling in many high income countries where markets are saturated for many of the commodities included in this *Outlook* (Figure 1.11).

The global food basket is slowly changing toward higher value products

With additional income to spend on food, consumer demand will also continue shifting from staple foods towards more processed and prepared food products that contain a greater proportion of animal protein. Global consumption on a *per capita* basis of wheat, for example, is projected to decline over the next ten years, while poultry as a relatively inexpensive livestock product will gain in importance, especially among poorer

Figure 1.11. **Per capita food consumption stagnant in developed countries but rises elsewhere**

Net agricultural *per capita* food consumption index by region

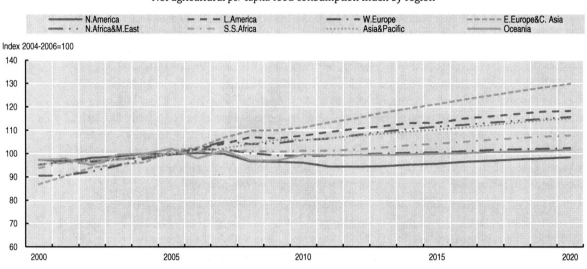

Note: Indices are calculated to measure aggregate volume changes in food consumption of commodities in this Outlook. The index weights commodities by international reference prices in the period 2004-06.

Source: OECD and FAO Secretariats.

StatLink 🔗 http://dx.doi.org/10.1787/888932426125

populations. However, the picture looks slightly different for rice, which remains a primary staple in Asian diets, and will still respond to high income growth in Asia (Figure 1.12).

Despite increasing demand from the biofuel industry, cereals continue to be used predominantly as food or as feed. Roughly two-thirds of wheat production is currently used for direct human consumption, but over the projection period, growth from this segment of demand is anticipated to slow down. On the other hand, rice and coarse grain food

Figure 1.12. **Value-added products show the strongest growth in *per capita* consumption**

Growth in *per capita* consumption of food products (2008-10 to 2020)

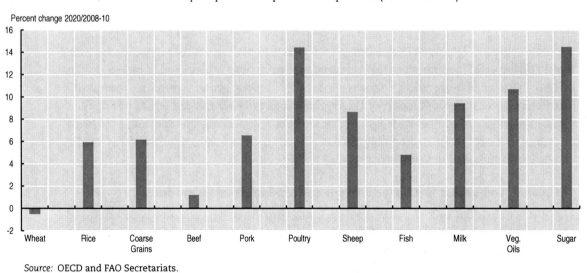

Source: OECD and FAO Secretariats.

StatLink 🔗 http://dx.doi.org/10.1787/888932426144

consumption will grow more vigorously because they remain the main staples in many countries of Asia, Africa and parts of Latin America where consumers still struggle to satisfy their daily energy requirements.

Due to higher projected prices of sugar in real terms over the next decade, growth in sugar consumption will be less rapid than in the previous decade, but still one of the fastest growing commodity sectors with a growth of 2.2% p.a., 14% in *per capita* terms. Almost all this growth is occurring in developing regions, as sugar consumption in most developed regions has already reached saturation levels and may even decline in response to diet and other health-related concerns.

World meat consumption continues to experience high rates of growth among major agricultural commodities. Significant *per capita* consumption growth is projected for large economies in Asia, the Middle East and some Latin American economies. Poultry meat consumption, due to its relatively low price, is expected to expand the fastest (14%), reaching parity with pigmeat consumption by the end of the projection period. *Per capita* fish consumption is projected to increase by only 5% over the next decade, largely because Asian consumers shift their preferences more toward meats, but also due to limited growth in the availability and higher prices of capture fish as well as of fish raised in aquaculture. The increase in prices for farmed fish is mainly due to higher costs resulting from the strong growth in fish meal prices. Nonetheless, fish consumption is projected to increase in all regions, with Oceania and Europe displaying a particularly dynamic picture.

Demand for milk and dairy products is expected to remain strong, particularly in richer developing regions, such as North Africa, the Middle East and East Asia, but also in mature markets for dairy products such as the European Union, the United States and the Russian Federation. Driven by continuing urbanisation, lifestyle changes and rising income levels, consumption of dairy products in developing regions is expected to increase vigorously by some 30% between 2010 and 2020. However, on a *per capita* basis there are still significant differences between countries. While people in least developed countries consume less than 50 kg per person per year, the rate is 100 kg per person in developing countries and more than 200 kg per person per year in the developed countries of Europe and North America.

Representing 80% of total use, consumption for food is expected to continue driving vegetable oil demand in developing countries, with China being the world's leading vegetable oil consumer. In the least developed countries, vegetable oil consumption is stagnating due to persistently high prices in recent years. The negative consumption trend in these countries since the 2007/08 food price crisis is expected to be overcome with positive income growth, but not before 2020.

Non food use continues to rise

Food use has been declining slowly as a share of total use from over 50% in 2000, and is projected to be around 47% by 2020. Feed use of cereals and coarse grains in particular, is projected to pick up its growth in the coming decade based on expansion and intensification in the livestock sector. More than 120 Mt of additional feed grains are expected to be consumed by 2020. Non-food or industrial use of cereals, wheat and coarse grains, as a feedstock for the growing biofuel sector is projected to reach a 9% share of total utilisation by 2020. A more striking pattern is seen for vegetable oils, where industrial use is projected to absorb about 15% of total use, up from 6% in 2000 (Figure 1.14). In the

Member States of the European Union and Argentina, biodiesel production will represent an increasing share of vegetable oil use by 2020, exceeding 50% and 70%, respectively. For sugar, and sugar related products, the rise in industrial use is even more important, and constitutes a major demand driver for this sector. For example, the use of sugarcane for ethanol production is rising rapidly, and will exceed 30% of total sugarcane use by 2020 (Figure 1.13), and double this share in the case of Brazil.

Figure 1.13. **Food and feed use dominate cereal consumption**

Main uses of cereal production (2004 to 2020)

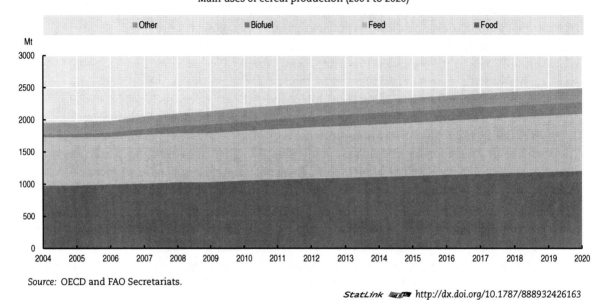

Source: OECD and FAO Secretariats.

StatLink http://dx.doi.org/10.1787/888932426163

Figure 1.14. **Biodiesel share of vegetable oil use to continue to grow rapidly**

Main uses of vegetable oil (2004 to 2020)

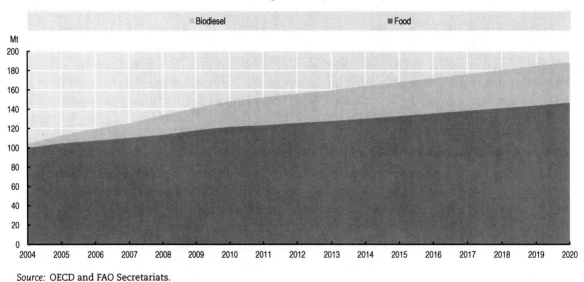

Source: OECD and FAO Secretariats.

StatLink http://dx.doi.org/10.1787/888932426182

Biofuel demand for agricultural feedstocks driven by policies

Biofuel production has been the largest source of new demand in recent years, and has tied agricultural markets closer to the much larger energy sector which exhibits demand characteristics quite unlike those for food. Policies in place in the US and in EU Member States with mandated use of biofuels in transportation fuels are expected to continue as key drivers of the growth of ethanol and biodiesel markets during the projection period. The growth in Brazilian ethanol production will be conditioned by gasoline pricing policies and blending provisions. However, ethanol and biodiesel production are also expected to grow considerably in other countries to meet blending requirements using a variety of feedstocks such as cassava (Thailand) and jatropha (India). Global ethanol production is anticipated to grow to over 150 bnl by 2020, an increase of almost 70%, when compared to the base period of 2008-10. Biodiesel production is projected to expand by almost 140% over the same period, from 18 bnl to 42 bnl.

Figure 1.15. **Ethanol from sugar cane to expand rapidly**
Main uses of sugar cane production (2004 to 2020)

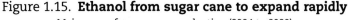

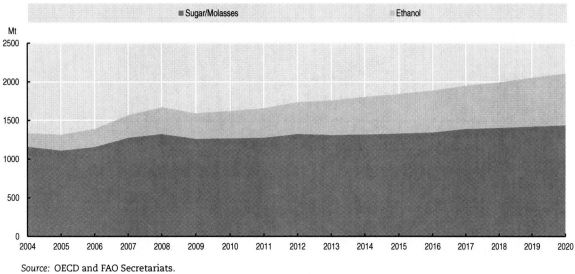

Source: OECD and FAO Secretariats.

StatLink ᘊᘖᓎ *http://dx.doi.org/10.1787/888932426201*

Commodity stocks are critical to market volatility

Global grain stocks for most cereals have decreased significantly since the 1990s as many governments moved away from holding public stocks, other than perhaps small emergency or strategic reserves. At the same time, private firms operating in food chains have also reduced their pipeline or operational stock requirements to minimum levels based on just in time inventory practices and other initiatives. The stocks that were available to the market in 2007-10 were clearly insufficient to off-set the production shortfalls that contributed to the price surges in that period.

The level of stocks that are accessible by the market has a strong inverse correlation with a commodity's price. The price crisis of 2007-08 was preceded by a large draw down in wheat and coarse grain stocks. The fall in stocks available to international trade was probably even larger as stock-to-use ratios in key exporting countries were drawn down to historical lows (Figure 1.16). Worldwide recession which slowed consumption and high supply response in producing countries rebuilt stocks quickly in 2009, but the production shortfall in the following season forced exporters to dig further into their reserves. This baseline projection anticipates difficulty in restoring stock levels over the medium term because of more slowly growing production and sustained high food, feed and non-food demand. Stocks of cereals are anticipated to recover very slowly from low levels in 2010, to the close of the projection period. Rebuilding of stocks is expected to help markets stabilise and reduce price volatility.

Figure 1.16. **Wheat and coarse grains stocks to remain relatively low**

Global stocks to use ratios of major exporters

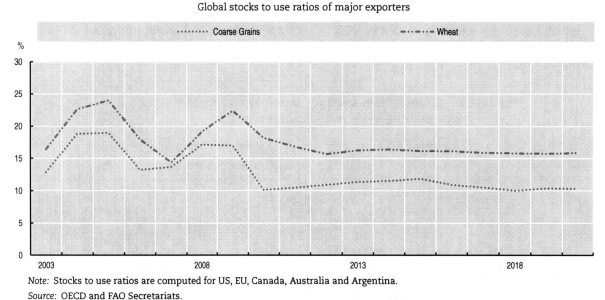

Note: Stocks to use ratios are computed for US, EU, Canada, Australia and Argentina.

Source: OECD and FAO Secretariats.

StatLink ⟹ http://dx.doi.org/10.1787/888932426220

Trade will grow more slowly with some new patterns emerging

Slower growth in export availabilities from traditional suppliers and greater domestic production by many importers to meet their domestic needs, along with trade policies will limit the growth in trade over the Outlook period. The volume of commodity trade is anticipated to grow by less than 2% annually, on average, roughly half the rate of the previous decade. Nevertheless, this will still amount to a substantial increase in trade in agricultural products to 2020.

While certain developed countries are projected to remain dominant exporters for a range of products, market shares are gradually shifting to developing and emerging countries. Exports, of mainly grains, from the Russian Federation, Ukraine and Kazakhstan and other countries in Eastern Europe and Central Asia are anticipated to grow very rapidly, albeit from a relatively low base. Higher exports from Brazil are anticipated for virtually all its main commodities, although a higher value of the Real constrains growth to below that of the previous decade. The growth in trade of high value livestock products from the United States is an important feature of this *Outlook*. In contrast, exports from Western Europe (EU) will be stagnant based on slow growth in production and a strong Euro (Figure 1.17). On the import side, rapid growth is anticipated from North Africa and the Middle East, given their oil-revenue based higher incomes. In Sub Saharan countries, the additional demand from population growth cannot be satisfied through domestic food

Figure 1.17. **Eastern Europe and Central Asia to gain greater share of trade**

Agricultural commodity and fish exports index by region

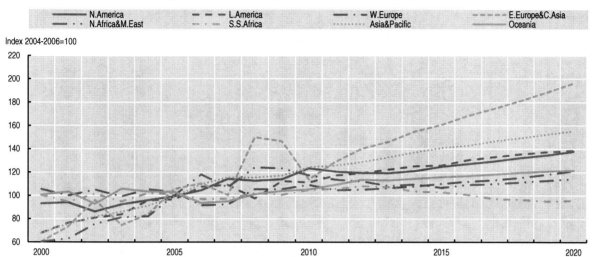

Index 2004-2006=100

Note: Indices are calculated to measure aggregate volume changes in food exports of commodities in this *Outlook*. The index weights commodities by international reference prices in the period 2004-06.

Source: OECD and FAO Secretariats.　　　　　　　　　　　　*StatLink* ☞ http://dx.doi.org/10.1787/888932426239

Figure 1.18. **Imports of North Africa and Middle East countries to grow most rapidly**

Agricultural commodity and fish imports index by region

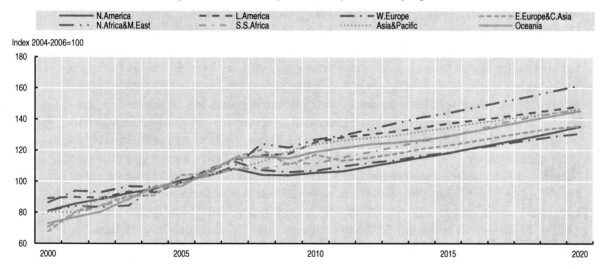

Index 2004-2006=100

Note: Indices are calculated to measure aggregate volume changes in food imports of commodities in this *Outlook*. The index weights commodities by international reference prices in the period 2004-06.

Source: OECD and FAO Secretariats.　　　　　　　　　　　　*StatLink* ☞ http://dx.doi.org/10.1787/888932426258

production. The *Outlook* thus projects growing food trade deficits for this region with food security implications that may result from increased dependence on global commodity markets (Figure 1.18).

Trade volumes of all agricultural commodities are projected to reach higher levels in 2020, when compared to the 2008-10 average (Figure 1.19). Trade of a number of commodities is expected to grow over 20% during the Outlook period for coarse grains, rice, sugar and oilseeds products, especially vegetable oil (mainly palm oil from Indonesia and Malaysia).

Figure 1.19. **Rice trade to show the largest growth over the Outlook period**
Growth in commodity trade in 2020 relative to the 2008-10 base period

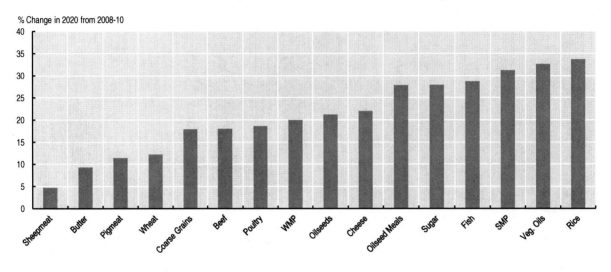

Source: OECD and FAO Secretariats.

StatLink http://dx.doi.org/10.1787/888932426277

Some new trade patterns are emerging for heavily traded products such as cereals. For wheat, world trade is relatively stable or growing only slowly. However, the share of exports held by the traditional top exporters (US, Canada, Australia, Argentina, EU) is trending down and may be less than 60% by the close of the Outlook period, while the share of the Russian Federation and countries in Eastern Europe and Central Asia is rising towards a 30% share. The focus of wheat imports is shifting to countries in Northern Africa and the Middle East which face a growing cereal deficit. With relatively higher returns, export supplies of coarse grains, and primarily maize, are anticipated to grow from the United States and Argentina. The main destinations are the EU, countries in Northern Africa, the Middle East, and increasingly China. Trade in rice is anticipated to grow more strongly than in the past, largely as a result of high export growth from Vietnam whose exports may exceed those of Thailand over the period. However, other countries of South East Asia, including several least developed countries, are also expected to increase exports considerably. Increased import demand by countries in the Middle East, certain countries in Africa such as Nigeria, and also large producing countries that face production limitations such as Bangladesh, are expected to boost rice imports in the next ten years.

Oilseeds and oilseed product exports continue to increase faster than most other products, with South America reinforcing its position as the global leader. However, Argentina is expected to relinquish market share in vegetable oil exports to Indonesia and Malaysia as it focuses more on the production and export of biodiesel. China's growing demand for oilseed and oilseed products has exploded in recent years, and will continue to pressure markets. The EU will remain the second largest importer, although with relatively stable volumes.

Sugar exports will remain dominated by Brazil with a market share in excess of 50% of global trade. The other traditional exporters, Thailand and Australia, will continue to focus their attention on the ballooning sugar deficit region of Asia. Imports remain more diversified over a larger group of countries. China has emerged as a larger importer, following a sharp surge in trade in 2010-11 and is anticipated to be the largest importer of sugar by the end of the Outlook period, reflecting a rapid rate of increase in demand and slower production growth. Other substantial importers are the EU and US. India is expected to continue to switch its trade balance periodically between substantial imports and exports, as a result of a production cycle, that will influence world sugar prices.

Growth in meat trade is expected to resume in the second half of the projection period, stimulated by better economic prospects and improved market access (such as the new KORUS agreement). Following the decline in meat trade from major suppliers after the financial crisis, the bulk of the projected 15% increase of world exports will originate from the American continents. One issue that inhibited meat trade in recent years is the numerous incidences of animal disease outbreaks and associated market risks that resulted in the immediate closing and delayed re-opening of national markets. Meat trade is expected to show only slow growth, as increased demand from major developing countries is met by increased domestic supply. On the export side, reflecting its rise in production, Brazil has become the dominant meat exporter, building a 20-25% market share in total meat exports. However, the US is also anticipated to increase its presence on world markets for beef, and will become the world's largest exporter of pigmeat. Exports of pigmeat from the EU are expected to decline considerably from their peak in 2010, while those of Canada should stabilise. Both these large exporters suffer from loss of competitiveness due to high domestic currency values. The Russian Federation, which in recent years has been the world's largest meat importer, is anticipated to decrease meat trade significantly under a concerted programme to stimulate domestic meat production, and curb imports using tariff quotas. Growth in meat imports will be most striking in the Middle East, particularly for poultry meat which rises dramatically to meet increased consumption requirements.

Exports of dairy products continue to grow from Oceania, but increasingly export supplies will emerge from other sources. The market presence of the EU, historically the key dairy exporter, is expected to decline further by 2020. Growing import demand by countries in Asia, especially China, and oil-rich countries in North Africa and the Middle East, will absorb additional exports. Butter imports by the Russian Federation, which were substantial in past years, are expected to stabilise at a lower level.

Fish and fishery products (e.g. fish for human consumption, fish meal and fish oil) will continue to be highly traded, with about 38% of world fishery production exported in 2020. World trade of fish for human consumption is expected to grow at a slower annual growth rate of 2.3% in the coming decade when compared to the 3.5% p.a. growth experienced in the previous ten years. Developed countries are expected to remain the main importers of fish for human consumption, while developing countries continue to be main exporters. However, the shares are gradually shifting. By contrast, developing countries will remain the main importers of global fish meal supplies, at 63% of the total, reflecting high demand for fish meal from expanding aquaculture production.

Risks and uncertainties

This *Outlook* has been prepared in a setting of high uncertainty. The outcomes described in the baseline projection are conditioned by a specific set of assumptions on the environment affecting the sector. These include a continuation of macroeconomic recovery in the developed countries and faster growth in the developing countries. Other assumptions are a continuation of existing agricultural and trade policy settings in each country, the absence of weather shocks and animal disease outbreaks and longer term productivity trends. Commodity prices are expected to ease back from the high levels at the beginning of the *Outlook* as markets respond to higher prices and increased profitability. However, harvests in 2011 will be critical to this outcome, as restoring market balances may take some time. Rebuilding stocks can help reduce the risks of further price surges and high volatility.

Uncertainties also present some downside price risks in the baseline. Much of the developed world is still recovering from the impacts of the economic and financial crisis in 2009, which created the deepest recession in almost a century. Major exporting countries continue to struggle with macroeconomic instabilities, including exchange rate fluctuations and changes in competitiveness (*e.g.* relative to a low US dollar) and high public debt rates. There are signs of rising inflation in some regions which may suggest a need to raise interest rates, which risks curbing growth. As witnessed in 2008-09, inflated oil prices can also fall precipitously. Furthermore, while extreme weather events in some regions appear to have become more frequent in recent years, bumper crops also happen, partly because of expectations of high commodity prices. Chapter 2 identifies the drivers of increased market volatility, including extreme weather events, new exporting zones, volatile energy prices, low stock levels, less responsive food demand, competing demand from energy sectors, and a faster transmission of macroeconomic factors onto commodity markets. A key question is, how sensitive the baseline projection is to its various assumptions?

Stochastic analysis illustrates the driving forces behind the price projections

A range of scenarios using the Aglink-Cosimo model has been undertaken to better understand how dependent the baseline projection is on its key assumptions. Stochastic analysis was undertaken to examine the range of possible price outcomes through random selection of conditioning variables such as cereal yields, oil prices, fertiliser prices and other macroeconomic variables. Results for coarse grain prices suggest that future prices could fluctuate widely around the deterministic projection presented in the baseline. The results, shown in Figure 1.20, suggest the band of possible outcomes is wide but not symmetric around the projection, with a median value above the projected level – indicating upside risk is more significant than downside risk. The methodology behind the stochastic analysis is described in the methodology annex of the report.

Price impact of different crude oil prices

One of the most important uncertainties in the projection of future commodity prices relates to crude oil prices. In order to assess the magnitude of the effect of changes in crude oil prices, simulations were conducted with crude oil prices set at 25% above and below the level assumed in the *Outlook*. The results show a strong relationship between oil and agricultural commodity prices on the supply and demand side. For example, on the supply side, crude oil prices are transmitted to agricultural commodity prices mainly through fertiliser and fuel costs. The simulations confirm the strong relationship between crude oil prices and agricultural production costs. A second impact channel exists from the demand for biofuels and agricultural feedstocks used in their production. The price of ethanol and biodiesel heavily depends on crude oil prices, with more than 60% and 40%, respectively, of their price changes reflecting adjustment to the crude oil price change. This is lower than one-to-one because biofuels are not perfectly

Figure 1.20. **Coarse grain prices show more upside potential**
Stochastic analysis of projected agricultural production – impact on world coarse grain prices

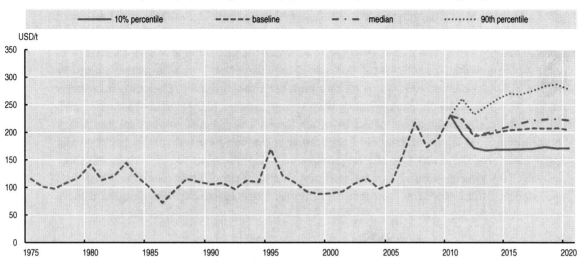

Source: OECD and FAO Secretariats.

StatLink ᐸᔛᐳ http://dx.doi.org/10.1787/888932426296

substitutable with gasoline or diesel for a number of reasons, including blending or marketing rigidities and limits at retail pumps. Other commodities, such as wheat, sugar and oilseeds, are also affected as feedstocks for biofuel production, which represents an additional demand for these commodities, through the use of energy inputs in production and transportation, and also through competition for scarce land. About 20% of the change in crude oil prices is estimated to be passed through to feedstock commodity prices (Figure 1.21). The price impacts obtained in these simulations are highly conditional on existing policy configurations, as interactions with mandates and subsidies for biofuels may have important implications for the results.

Figure 1.21. **Variable oil prices affect agricultural input and product prices**
Impact of a 25% increase/decrease of the crude oil price on world commodity prices (average over projection period)

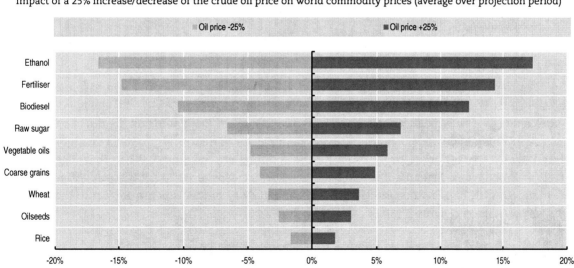

Source: OECD and FAO Secretariats.

StatLink ᐸᔛᐳ http://dx.doi.org/10.1787/888932426315

Price impact of yield growth – productivity is key to lowering commodity prices

The *Outlook* notes that growth in crop yields has been slowing in many key producing areas, lowering overall supply growth. An interesting question to address is what would happen if this *Outlook* has systematically over or underestimated the yield growth for cereals. To assess this question, the model was used to estimate the price effects of a +/- 5% change in annual yield growth across all cereals. The results show significant price impacts of up to 25% for the different commodities. There are two important conclusions to be drawn from these results. The first is that if average yields do respond more to higher prices than expected, agricultural commodity prices could be much lower. The second conclusion has policy implications. That is, sustained yield improvements through new technology could greatly lower price levels and increase the responsiveness of production to price changes, since potentially a greater supply can be attained during a production season. Continued productivity improvement is therefore an important strategy to counter rising and more volatile prices (Figure 1.22).

Figure 1.22. **Yield changes have strong impact on product prices**

Impact of 5% increase/decrease of annual yield of cereals on world commodity prices (average over projection period)

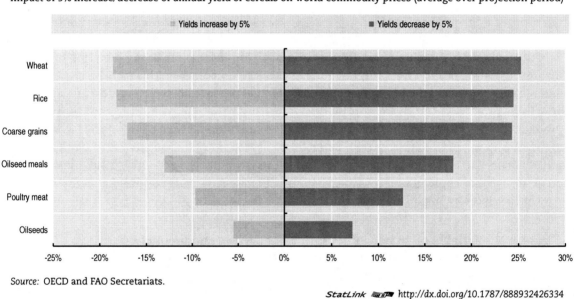

Source: OECD and FAO Secretariats.

StatLink http://dx.doi.org/10.1787/888932426334

Price impact of economic growth

Economic growth represents another factor that impacts on the projected baseline scenario. In order to assess the importance of this effect, a "shock" of +/- 1% change in expected GDP growth in all countries and regions was applied. Depending on the direction of the income shock, increasing/decreasing demand for agricultural products changes international market prices by up to 7% for the commodities examined. When this price change is applied to demand, it implies an increase/decrease of up to 2.2% in quantities demanded, with higher value foods such as beef and dairy products being subject to the strongest reactions (Figure 1.23).

Other important uncertainties include domestic and trade policies

The agricultural sector continues to be affected by distortive price support and subsidy schemes, as well as trade policies. Direct price support has diminished in recent years,

Figure 1.23. **Income changes have modest impact on commodity consumption**
Impact of a 1% increase/decrease of annual GDP growth on global commodity consumption
(average over projection period)

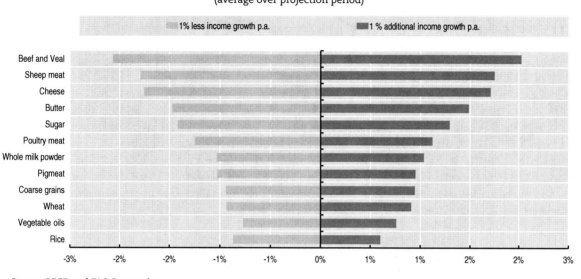

Source: OECD and FAO Secretariats.

StatLink http://dx.doi.org/10.1787/888932426353

with the shift to more market orientated policies in many developed countries and other, less distortive, policies have become more prominent in national policy frameworks. In the developing and emerging economies, many of which have also undergone significant reforms, there has been a tendency to resort to trade policy measures to combat the effects of high prices on their domestic economies. For example, one reaction to rising prices has been an increased propensity of some emerging exporting countries to apply export taxes and export bans.[3] This shows that as international prices vary, instability and lack of coordination of policy settings may exacerbate market reactions. On the other hand, another outcome of the food price crisis of 2006-08 is that many countries have adopted new strategies to invigorate their agricultural sectors and reduce their dependence on international markets.[4]

Box 1.3 provides a review of the main developments in food prices in the year ending January 2011.

Box 1.3. **Main developments in food prices**

Introduction

Food prices vary markedly across countries and over time, not only due to differing domestic agricultural supply conditions as well as processing and marketing systems but also due to the extent of domestic market integration with international commodity markets and food systems. The food price index of the CPI measures the cost of a fixed basket of foods at the retail level and reflects actual consumption patterns.* In some developing countries food expenditures still account for close to 50% of total household expenditures, though as incomes rise this share declines. In this respect differences in the share of expenditures devoted to food are notable between urban and rural areas in most middle and low income countries. Retail food prices also differ substantially from farm-gate and/or import prices of commodities and this applies for both developed and developing countries.

Box 1.3. **Main developments in food prices** (*cont.*)

Food prices are increasing

Rising commodity prices have been reflected in the evolution of food prices and inflation. Food prices have increased over the recent 12-month period ending January 2011 in most OECD and many non-OECD economies, with increases accelerating since mid-2010. This reverses the downward trend in food prices of 2009 and the first half of 2010. Three-quarters of the OECD countries experienced retail food price increases of 5% or less, while in six, price increases were over 5%. Two OECD countries, Korea and Estonia, experienced increases of over 10%. Brazil, China, Indonesia, and the Russian Federation all had double digit rates of food inflation during the past year, thus a significant acceleration over the previous year. Though food price increases remained moderate at 3.3% in South Africa, this rate represents a doubling from last year. Food price inflation was also found to have accelerated in the 2nd half of 2010 in a number of countries from Africa, Asia and Latin America. This was the case for Guatemala, Peru, Botswana, Niger, Burkina Faso, Senegal, Pakistan, Bangladesh and Sri Lanka. Nonetheless, a few countries continued to experience a slowing in food price increases, such as Ghana and Kenya, and in Rwanda prices actually decreased by about 2%.

Figure 1.24. **Food price inflation for selected OECD and developing countries: 2007-11**
Year on Year % change January to January

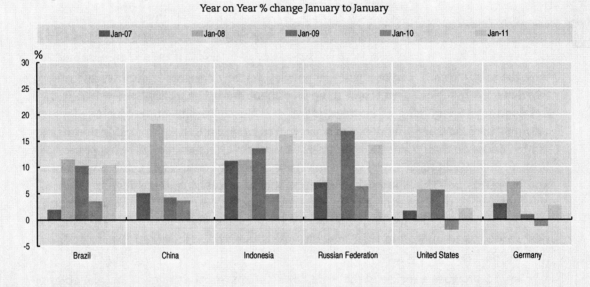

Source: *Main Economic Indicators*, OECD.

StatLink ⬛⬛⬛ http://dx.doi.org/10.1787/888932426372

In high income OECD countries the contribution of food price movements to inflation has been positive though small, generally around 0.5%. However, food price increases contributed over 1.5% points to inflation in countries such as Estonia, Turkey, Hungary and Korea. This contrasts with last year when food price movements decreased thus attenuating inflation. The contribution of food price movements to inflation this past year has been small both because food price increases were generally quite moderate and because the share of food expenditures in the overall consumer basket remains small.

* The CPI measures the change in cost of a fixed basket of goods over time thus its percentage change provides an estimate of inflation. Consumer expenditure surveys are used to determine expenditure share of products consumed used as weights in the calculation of CPI relative to a base period. Most countries use standard sampling and calculation procedures for the updating of the cost of the basket of goods. Prices are sampled usually at a fixed week during a month and employ specific statistical techniques to deal with quality, seasonality and other issues. The food component in the CPI varies widely across countries reflecting the structure of household expenditures.

Notes

1. The Aglink-Cosimo model is a partial equilibrium, dynamic multicommodity model of world agriculture developed initially by the OECD for its member countries and some large emerging economies and subsequently extended by FAO to encompass other developing, the least developed countries and regions of the world. The model is used to make 10-year projections for a number of crop and livestock products and for carrying out policy analyses.

2. A measure describing the level of carryover stock for a given commodity as a percentage of its total demand or use.

3. The Russian Federation has announced a lifting of the ban on foreign wheat sales on 1st July 2011.

4. See Dawe (2010) for a detailed assessment of policy responses during the rice price crisis in 2008.

References

FAO, "Rice Market Monitor", various issues, *www.fao.org/economic/est/publications/rice-publications/rice-market-monitor-rmm/en/*.

Dawe, D. (ed.) (2010), "The Rice Crisis: Markets, Policies and Food Security", FAO and Earthscan Publications Ltd.

ANNEX 1.A1

Statistical tables: Overview

1.A.1.	Economic assumptions	*http://dx.doi.org/10.1787/888932427569*
1.A.2.	World prices	*http://dx.doi.org/10.1787/888932427588*

Tables available online:

1.A.3.	Exchange rate	*http://dx.doi.org/10.1787/888932427607*
1.A.4.1.	World trade projections, imports	*http://dx.doi.org/10.1787/888932427626*
1.A.4.2.	World trade projections, exports	*http://dx.doi.org/10.1787/888932427645*

Table 1.A.1. Economic assumptions

Calendar year

		Avg 2008-10est.	2011	2012	2013	2014	2015	2016	2017	2018	2019	2020
REAL GDP[1]												
Australia	%	2.2	3.6	4.0	3.9	3.5	3.1	2.7	2.5	2.5	2.5	2.5
Canada	%	0.3	2.3	3.0	2.8	2.5	2.4	2.0	1.7	1.7	1.7	1.6
EU15	%	-0.7	1.7	2.0	2.1	2.3	2.4	1.9	1.7	1.6	1.7	1.6
Japan	%	-0.9	1.7	1.3	1.1	0.7	0.9	0.9	0.9	1.0	1.0	1.0
Korea	%	2.9	4.3	4.8	4.0	3.3	3.0	2.8	2.6	2.4	2.1	1.9
Mexico	%	0.0	3.5	4.2	3.9	3.6	3.4	3.1	2.9	2.8	2.7	2.6
New Zealand	%	0.4	2.7	2.5	2.6	2.8	2.9	2.5	2.3	2.4	2.4	2.4
Norway	%	-0.1	1.8	2.3	2.4	2.7	3.2	3.1	2.9	2.7	2.6	2.6
Switzerland	%	0.9	2.2	2.5	1.9	1.7	1.8	1.7	1.7	1.7	1.7	1.7
Turkey	%	1.1	4.2	4.4	6.0	5.3	4.5	3.8	3.2	2.8	2.4	2.1
United States	%	0.0	2.2	3.1	3.0	2.9	3.0	2.7	2.5	2.5	2.4	2.3
Argentina	%	5.4	5.1	4.8	2.8	2.7	2.7	2.5	2.5	2.5	2.5	2.5
Brazil	%	4.2	4.3	5.0	4.9	4.8	4.7	4.7	4.6	4.5	4.4	4.3
China	%	9.7	9.7	9.7	8.5	8.6	8.3	8.0	7.7	7.3	7.0	6.7
India	%	7.2	8.4	8.7	7.3	6.6	6.1	5.7	5.4	5.2	5.1	5.0
Russian Federation	%	0.4	4.2	4.5	5.8	5.1	5.0	5.0	5.0	4.9	4.9	4.9
South Africa	%	1.5	3.7	4.2	4.6	3.9	3.4	2.9	2.6	2.3	2.1	2.0
OECD[2,3]	%	-0.2	2.2	2.6	2.6	2.5	2.6	2.2	2.0	2.0	2.0	1.9
PCE DEFLATOR[1]												
Australia	%	3.1	2.7	2.9	2.7	2.5	2.5	2.5	2.5	2.5	2.5	2.5
Canada	%	1.1	1.5	1.3	1.8	2.1	2.1	2.1	2.1	2.1	2.1	2.1
EU15	%	1.4	1.3	1.2	1.7	2.0	2.0	2.0	2.0	2.0	2.0	2.0
Japan	%	-1.1	-0.7	-0.8	1.1	2.1	2.1	2.1	2.1	2.1	2.1	2.1
Korea	%	3.2	3.1	3.4	2.6	2.0	2.0	2.0	2.0	2.0	2.0	2.0
Mexico	%	5.7	4.0	3.5	3.5	3.2	3.2	3.2	3.2	3.2	3.2	3.2
New Zealand	%	2.7	3.9	1.8	1.9	2.1	2.1	2.1	2.1	2.1	2.1	2.1
Norway	%	2.7	1.9	2.5	2.2	2.1	2.1	2.1	2.1	2.1	2.1	2.1
Switzerland	%	0.9	0.7	0.8	1.6	2.1	2.1	2.1	2.1	2.1	2.1	2.1
Turkey	%	8.3	6.1	5.7	6.0	6.0	6.0	6.0	6.0	6.0	6.0	6.0
United States	%	1.7	0.9	0.9	1.5	2.0	2.0	2.0	2.0	2.0	2.0	2.0
Argentina	%	8.5	7.5	7.9	3.9	3.9	3.9	3.9	3.9	3.9	3.9	3.9
Brazil	%	5.2	8.3	7.1	4.3	4.3	4.3	4.3	4.3	4.3	4.3	4.3
China	%	2.9	3.7	3.0	3.9	3.6	3.6	3.6	3.7	3.7	3.7	3.7
India	%	8.4	7.0	6.5	6.0	6.0	6.0	6.0	6.0	6.0	6.0	6.0
Russian Federation	%	10.8	6.1	6.1	3.3	3.8	3.8	3.8	3.8	3.8	3.8	3.8
South Africa	%	7.0	4.6	5.3	6.0	6.0	6.0	6.0	6.0	6.0	6.0	6.0
OECD[2,3]	%	1.7	1.3	1.2	1.9	2.2	2.2	2.2	2.2	2.2	2.2	2.2

		2010est	2011	2012	2013	2014	2015	2016	2017	2018	2019	2020
POPULATION[1]												
Australia	%	1.0	1.0	1.0	1.0	1.0	1.0	1.0	0.9	0.9	0.9	0.9
Canada	%	0.9	0.9	0.9	0.9	0.9	0.9	0.9	0.9	0.9	0.9	0.9
EU(27)	%	0.4	0.4	0.4	0.3	0.3	0.3	0.3	0.3	0.2	0.2	0.2
Japan	%	-0.1	-0.1	-0.2	-0.2	-0.2	-0.2	-0.3	-0.3	-0.3	-0.4	-0.4
Korea	%	0.3	0.3	0.3	0.3	0.2	0.2	0.2	0.2	0.1	0.1	0.1
Mexico	%	0.9	0.9	0.9	0.9	0.8	0.8	0.8	0.7	0.7	0.7	0.7
New Zealand	%	0.9	0.9	0.9	0.9	0.9	0.8	0.8	0.8	0.8	0.8	0.7
Norway	%	0.9	0.8	0.8	0.7	0.7	0.7	0.7	0.7	0.6	0.6	0.6
Switzerland	%	0.4	0.4	0.4	0.4	0.4	0.4	0.4	0.4	0.4	0.4	0.4
Turkey	%	1.2	1.2	1.1	1.1	1.1	1.0	1.0	1.0	1.0	0.9	0.9
United States	%	0.9	0.9	0.9	0.9	0.9	0.9	0.9	0.8	0.8	0.8	0.8
Argentina	%	1.0	0.9	0.9	0.9	0.9	0.9	0.9	0.8	0.8	0.8	0.8
Brazil	%	0.9	0.8	0.8	0.7	0.7	0.7	0.7	0.6	0.6	0.6	0.5
China	%	0.6	0.6	0.6	0.6	0.6	0.6	0.6	0.5	0.5	0.5	0.4
India	%	1.4	1.3	1.3	1.3	1.2	1.2	1.2	1.1	1.1	1.1	1.0
Russian Federation	%	-0.4	-0.4	-0.3	-0.3	-0.3	-0.3	-0.4	-0.4	-0.4	-0.4	-0.4
South Africa	%	0.8	0.6	0.5	0.4	0.4	0.4	0.4	0.4	0.4	0.4	0.4
OECD[3]	%	0.6	0.6	0.6	0.6	0.5	0.5	0.5	0.5	0.5	0.4	0.4
World	%	1.2	1.2	1.1	1.1	1.1	1.1	1.1	1.0	1.0	1.0	1.0

Table 1.A.1. **Economic assumptions (cont.)**

Calendar year

		Avg 2008-10est.	2011	2012	2013	2014	2015	2016	2017	2018	2019	2020
GDP DEFLATOR[1]													
Australia	%	4.2	3.5	2.5	3.2	3.3	3.3	2.9	2.9	2.9	2.9	2.9
Canada	%	1.6	1.6	1.6	2.2	2.6	2.6	2.7	2.8	2.8	2.8	2.9
European Union	%	1.3	1.0	1.1	1.6	1.9	1.9	2.0	2.0	2.0	2.0	2.0
Japan	%	-1.2	-0.8	-0.8	0.8	1.7	1.6	1.6	1.6	1.6	1.6	1.5
Korea	%	3.2	1.8	2.6	2.3	2.0	2.0	1.9	1.9	1.9	1.8	1.8
Mexico	%	5.0	3.9	4.0	3.5	3.1	3.1	3.1	3.1	3.1	3.1	3.1
New Zealand	%	2.7	4.3	2.1	2.1	2.2	2.2	2.3	2.3	2.3	2.3	2.3
Norway	%	3.4	2.7	2.3	2.3	2.3	2.3	2.2	2.2	2.2	2.2	2.2
Switzerland	%	1.0	0.7	0.7	1.7	2.2	2.3	2.3	2.3	2.4	2.4	2.4
Turkey	%	8.3	6.1	5.7	6.0	6.0	6.0	6.0	6.0	6.0	6.0	6.0
United States	%	1.4	1.2	0.9	1.6	1.9	1.9	1.9	1.9	1.9	2.0	1.9
Argentina	%	14.2	7.5	7.9	3.9	3.9	3.9	3.9	3.9	3.9	3.9	3.9
Brazil	%	6.3	8.3	7.1	4.3	4.3	4.3	4.3	4.3	4.3	4.3	4.3
China	%	4.1	3.7	3.0	3.9	3.6	3.6	3.6	3.7	3.7	3.7	3.7
India	%	8.4	7.0	6.5	6.0	6.0	6.0	6.0	6.0	6.0	6.0	6.0
Russian Federation	%	10.6	6.1	6.1	3.3	3.8	3.8	3.8	3.8	3.8	3.8	3.8
South Africa	%	7.0	4.6	5.3	6.0	6.0	6.0	6.0	6.0	6.0	6.0	6.0
OECD[3]	%	1.5	1.3	1.2	1.8	2.1	2.2	2.2	2.2	2.2	2.2	2.2
WORLD OIL PRICE													
Brent crude oil price[4]	USD/barrel	78.8	91.4	92.3	93.7	95.5	97.4	99.2	101.2	103.1	105.1	107.2

Note: Calendar year: For OECD member countries (except Turkey, Chile and Israel), as well as Brazil, Argentina, China and Russia, historical data for population, real GDP, private consumption expenditure deflator and GDP deflator were obtained from the OECD Economic Outlook No. 88, December 2010. For other economies, historical macroeconomic data were obtained from the World Bank, November 2010. Assumptions for the projection period draw on the recent medium term macroeconomic projections of the OECD Economics Department, projections of the World Bank, and for population, projections from the United Nations World Population Prospects Database, 2008 Revision (medium variant). Data for the European Union are for the euro area aggregates.

1. Annual per cent change. The price index used is the private consumption expenditure deflator.
2. Annual weighted average real GDP and CPI growth rates in OECD countries are based on weights using purchasing power parities (PPPs).
3. Excludes Iceland but includes EU6 members that are not members of the OECD (Bulgaria, Cyprus, Latvia, Lithuania, Malta and Romania).
4. Short term update for crude oil price from the Energy Information Administration.

Source: OECD and FAO Secretariats.

StatLink http://dx.doi.org/10.1787/888932427569

Table 1.A.2. World prices

		Avg 08/09-10/11est	11/12	12/13	13/14	14/15	15/16	16/17	17/18	18/19	19/20	20/21
WHEAT												
Price[1]	USD/t	264.5	278.6	234.1	247.9	237.6	240.7	238.8	241.8	241.3	241.2	240.4
COARSE GRAINS												
Price[2]	USD/t	197.9	229.0	202.5	202.3	206.4	204.9	207.2	207.2	207.9	205.3	202.8
RICE												
Price[3]	USD/t	599.7	538.7	503.6	478.2	472.4	472.5	474.0	478.5	482.9	488.6	492.5
OILSEEDS												
Price[4]	USD/t	445.8	455.4	455.2	460.8	462.7	468.0	474.5	475.8	473.6	483.3	477.9
PROTEIN MEALS												
Price[5]	USD/t	362.0	356.8	345.9	337.2	337.6	327.3	327.2	328.5	328.3	330.6	327.8
VEGETABLE OILS												
Price[6]	USD/t	921.6	1 022.9	1 026.7	1 026.7	1 036.8	1 049.4	1 063.0	1 066.8	1 082.9	1 081.0	1 086.5
SUGAR												
Price, raw sugar[7]	USD/t rse	492.8	509.5	365.4	383.2	478.8	525.9	451.3	406.6	408.8	410.9	408.1
Price, refined sugar[8]	USD/t rse	550.2	614.2	464.1	472.4	550.1	608.7	543.5	503.3	506.7	509.6	507.8
BEEF AND VEAL												
Price, EU[9]	USD/t dw	4 416.6	4 328.5	4 414.5	4 442.1	4 743.7	4 800.3	4 901.0	4 864.0	4 872.9	4 813.5	4 788.1
Price, USA[10]	USD/t dw	3 210.9	3 655.5	3 579.4	3 553.8	3 593.2	3 530.5	3 631.3	3 709.8	3 726.6	3 688.5	3 779.0
Price, Brazil[11]	USD/t pw	2 715.9	2 914.1	2 756.6	2 750.8	2 708.7	2 808.0	2 819.0	2 845.1	2 827.5	2 882.6	2 857.4
PIG MEAT												
Price, EU[12]	USD/t dw	2 098.0	2 264.8	2 525.4	2 575.9	2 439.8	2 354.6	2 483.7	2 535.6	2 562.5	2 647.9	2 557.5
Price, USA[13]	USD/t dw	1 471.2	1 743.4	1 957.8	1 915.9	1 811.4	1 748.4	1 870.8	1 911.3	1 921.4	1 869.2	1 859.8
Price, Brazil[14]	USD/t dw	1 409.6	1 557.7	1 574.9	1 597.1	1 478.8	1 462.3	1 522.1	1 606.0	1 595.4	1 675.3	1 616.9
POULTRY MEAT												
Price, EU[15]	USD/t rtc	2 456.9	2 640.6	2 588.6	2 555.0	2 547.2	2 521.9	2 545.0	2 577.1	2 593.5	2 616.6	2 614.6
Price, USA[16]	USD/t rtc	1 062.4	1 152.7	1 221.1	1 250.5	1 240.5	1 200.7	1 222.2	1 220.5	1 254.3	1 231.0	1 250.1
Price, Brazil[17]	USD/t rtc	1 090.3	1 260.6	1 256.5	1 199.8	1 217.8	1 221.3	1 230.9	1 246.6	1 258.5	1 270.8	1 266.3
SHEEP MEAT												
Price, New Zealand[18]	USD/t dw	2 948.1	3 659.1	3 451.6	3 336.3	3 364.3	3 338.1	3 459.6	3 468.0	3 525.6	3 515.3	3 548.5
BUTTER												
Price[19]	USD/t	3 347.4	4 540.5	3 918.2	3 723.2	3 626.4	3 635.5	3 702.1	3 750.9	3 748.5	3 741.0	3 729.1
CHEESE												
Price[20]	USD/t	3 881.7	4 325.2	3 860.7	3 695.7	3 672.8	3 770.3	3 865.5	3 969.6	4 038.1	4 055.6	4 093.2
SKIM MILK POWDER												
Price[21]	USD/t	2 908.5	3 559.2	3 220.0	3 019.9	2 975.3	3 063.6	3 142.1	3 239.3	3 348.1	3 365.9	3 420.6
WHOLE MILK POWDER												
Price[22]	USD/t	3 263.9	4 067.8	3 452.5	3 263.2	3 215.0	3 277.1	3 354.6	3 436.7	3 514.4	3 534.2	3 589.4
WHEY POWDER												
Wholesale price, USA[23]	USD/t	672.5	993.7	906.1	827.4	822.0	833.6	869.8	900.6	931.8	948.8	980.5
CASEIN												
Price[24]	USD/t	8 038.3	8 395.0	7 604.0	7 829.6	7 862.7	7 850.2	7 888.2	7 963.0	8 219.1	8 274.2	8 420.5
ETHANOL												
Price[25]	USD/hl	49.6	64.4	63.8	63.5	64.0	64.8	66.2	67.4	67.6	67.4	66.4
BIODIESEL												
Price[26]	USD/hl	127.2	142.6	143.1	142.3	144.1	144.2	142.7	144.0	143.3	142.6	142.9

Note: This table is a compilation of price information presented in the detailed commodity tables further in this annex. Prices for crops are on marketing year basis and those for meat and dairy products on calendar year basis (e.g. 09/10 is calendar year 2009).

1. No. 2 hard red winter wheat, ordinary protein, USA f.o.b. Gulf Ports (June/May), less EEP payments where applicable.
2. No. 2 yellow corn, US f.o.b. Gulf Ports (September/August).
3. Milled, 100%, grade b, Nominal Price Quote, NPQ, f.o.b. Bangkok (January/December).
4. Weighted average oilseed price, European port.
5. Weighted average meal price, European port.
6. Weighted average price of oilseed oils and palm oil, European port.
7. Raw sugar world price, ICE Inc. No11 f.o.b, bulk price, October/September.
8. Refined sugar price, Euronext, Liffe, Contract No. 407 London, Europe, October/September.
9. EU average beef producer price.
10. Choice steers, 1100-1300 lb lw, Nebraska - lw to dw conversion factor 0.63.
11. Brazil average beef producer price.
12. EU average pig meat producer price.
13. Barrows and gilts, No. 1-3, 230-250 lb lw, Iowa/South Minnesota - lw to dw conversion factor 0.74.
14. Brazil average pig meat producer price.
15. EU average producer price.
16. Wholesale weighted average broiler price 12 cities.
17. Brazil average chicken producer price.
18. Lamb schedule price, all grade average.
19. F.o.b. export price, butter, 82% butterfat, Oceania.
20. F.o.b. export price, cheddar cheese, 39% moisture, Oceania.
21. F.o.b. export price, non-fat dry milk, 1.25% butterfat, Oceania.
22. F.o.b. export price, WMP 26% butterfat, Oceania.
23. Edible dry whey, Wisconsin, plant.
24. Export price, New Zealand.
25. Brazil, Sao Paulo (ex-distillery).
26. Producer price Germany net of biodiesel tariff.

Source: OECD and FAO Secretariats.

StatLink http://dx.doi.org/10.1787/888932427588

Chapter 2

Special feature:
What is driving price volatility?

Last year's *Outlook* featured an assessment of price volatility, price transmission and policy prescriptions which may help encourage more transparent and efficient markets, as well as address the impacts of volatility, especially on poor consumers. By August 2010, two months after the release of the *Outlook*, the anticipation of further bouts of high price volatility was realised as a shortfall in crop production (see the Cereals Chapter), and policy actions so impacted markets that prices rose precipitously toward 2007-08 levels by early 2011. International concern over volatility has been pronounced and in November 2010 the G20 at its Seoul Summit, requested that "...the FAO, IFAD, IMF, OECD, UNCTAD, WFP and the World Bank work with key stakeholders to develop options for G20 considerations on how to better mitigate and manage the risks associated with price volatility of food and other agricultural commodities without distorting market behaviour, ultimately to protect the most vulnerable."

With continued close attention being given to volatility, this special feature of the *Outlook* takes another look at the issue, with a specific focus on the key forces driving prices in the coming years and the uncertainties around these drivers. A key lesson from the *Outlook* is that high volatility may persist largely because of difficulties in building significant stocks to mitigate shocks, in a context of higher energy, related inputs and feed production costs, lower productivity growth and sustained high demand for agricultural commodities. Furthermore, market characteristics (*e.g.* higher incomes, more value added, increased biofuel use) mean that both demand and supply are becoming increasingly insensitive to commodity price fluctuations, at least in the short term.

Why price volatility is a problem

While there are many technical definitions of volatility, the interest here is in the variations from trend in agricultural prices over time. Volatility is not a major concern when price movements are gradual, exhibit seasonal patterns and are generally predictable in line with market fundamentals. However, problems arise when the amplitude of price swings is large, the frequency high or their occurrence sudden, predominantly in one direction. High and volatile prices attract the most attention but low prices and volatility is also problematic. Volatile prices create uncertainty and risk for producers, traders, consumers and governments and can have extensive negative impacts on the agriculture sector, food security and the wider economy in both developed and developing countries.

Measuring volatility is difficult and the results vary, depending on the commodities examined, the timeframe considered, and the type of data and frequency of observations. OECD/FAO analysis (OECD/FAO, 2010) suggests that while volatility of some commodity prices such as for wheat, maize, soybeans and sugar has been high in recent years, there is no indication of a trend increase in price volatility on international markets when viewed over the last fifty years. Recent price volatility is not unique to agricultural markets: many primary product markets, such as energy, metals, and industrial goods have also displayed higher volatility in recent years.

Commodity prices are volatile, notably because their supply is subject to variability while demand is relatively rigid. It is useful to distinguish between predictable and unpredictable variation in prices, the latter being characterised in terms of shocks or unexpected events. Shocks to both production and consumption can be transmitted into price volatility. In the case of production, yield variations can arise owing to disruptive weather patterns and diseases and these can also affect meat supplies. Consumption shifts due to changes in incomes, prices of substitutes, or preferences may be less abrupt, but may imply significant longer lasting changes which supplies must adapt to over time. Figure 2.1 shows that historical real price volatility has been a characteristic of agricultural markets, although periods of extreme volatility are much less common. Figure 2.2 provides more evidence that volatility for major crops implied from transactions in futures markets has increased in recent years.

Figure 2.1. **Annualised historical real price volatility (1957-2010)**

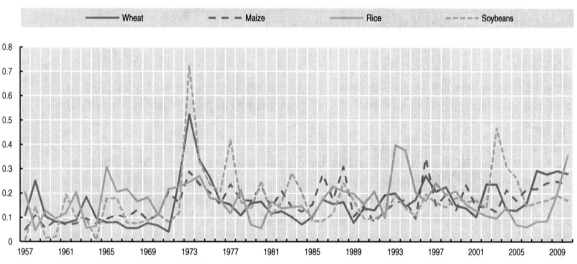

Notes: Annualised historical real price volatility was calculated using the definition found in the Glossary of Terms. Maize (US No. 2, yellow, US Gulf); rice (white rice, Thai 100% B second grade, f.o.b. Bangkok); soybeans (US No. 1, yellow, US Gulf).
Source: OECD and FAO Secretariats.

StatLink 🔗 http://dx.doi.org/10.1787/888932426391

The capacity of a country to grow or to buy food products at affordable prices constitutes a fundamental pre-condition for sustainable development and growth. High and volatile food commodity prices can jeopardise the often fragile economic and political stability of some developing countries. Behind concerns about volatile prices lie concerns about price levels. High food and commodity prices can have significant impacts on the macro economy through rising costs of living and inflation and in relation to balance of payment positions or government finance. Most affected will be the net food importing developing countries whose food imports are significant in balance of payment or government finance terms. These countries may face higher inflation, a deteriorating current account balance and possibly depreciation of the exchange rate as a result of high food prices. Policy responses in terms of budgetary or tax expenditures may result in increased government borrowing and reductions in other areas of economic development.

Figure 2.2. **Implied volatility of wheat, maize and soybeans (1990-2020)**

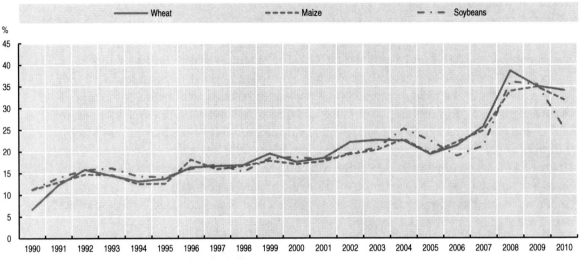

Note: Implied volatility is a measure used by future markets to indicate how much a commodity price may be expected to move in the future. See Glossary of Terms for definition. Refer to *Food Outlook*, FAO (2010a) for explanation.

Sources: Chicago Mercantile Exchange and calculations by FAO Secretariat.

StatLink  http://dx.doi.org/10.1787/888932436708

A further complication is that in developing countries, many households are both producers and consumers of food such that the net impacts of price volatility are difficult to assess.

On the supply side, food exporting countries and individual producers can benefit from high prices but low or volatile prices may pose significant problems. Of course, some producers can also be adversely affected by higher prices, for example, livestock farmers who face higher costs for animal feed and stock purchases for feedlots. Many producers may have little or no recourse to safeguard mechanisms to tide them over in periods of adversity, such as savings and insurance, to mitigate against large income fluctuations. Extreme volatility creates additional risks because of the delay between production decisions based on expected future prices and the prices actually received when production is realised at time of harvest or sale, some months into the future. Low and volatile prices can threaten the viability of agricultural producers (and other actors in the food chain) with impacts on production and investment decisions. Poor smallholders with limited access to credit may be unable to purchase the necessary inputs for the next season. These issues underscore an important point in the *Outlook* that supply response to periods of high prices is likely to be reduced when prices are volatile.

On the demand side, the most severe negative effects of high and volatile food prices are on the food security of the poor households in developing countries, especially the urban poor and landless and female-headed households, who may spend as much as three-quarters of their income on food. High food prices erode the living standards of households and worsen the prevalence of food insecurity and malnutrition by reducing the quantity and quality of food consumed. High and volatile food prices can lead to irreversible harm – a loss of physical and long-run human capital, which may reinforce poverty traps through diminished income, resulting in malnutrition, mortality, withdrawal of children from education and a consequent sustained high level of unemployment.

Irreversibility, in this regard is a critical concern, since it can result in a downward spiral of increasing vulnerability as fragile coping mechanisms are eroded. A lack of dietary diversification aggravates the problem as price increases in one staple cannot easily be compensated by switching to other foods.

Key drivers of agricultural markets and price volatility

Most agricultural commodity markets are characterised by price volatility, beyond that associated with traditional seasonal fluctuations, for three basic reasons. First, agricultural output varies from period to period because of natural factors such as weather, disease and pests. Second, price "elasticities" or the responsiveness of both supply and demand to price changes are relatively small, and on the supply side at least in the short run. In order to re-establish market equilibrium after a supply shock, prices therefore need to adjust rather strongly to reallocate an excess or shortfall of supply. Third, because production response may take considerable time in agriculture, supply cannot respond much to price changes in the short term, though it may do so much more once the production cycle is completed. The resulting lagged supply response to price changes may also cause cyclical adjustments (such as the so-called hog or beef cycles) that may add an extra degree of variability to the markets concerned.

Price volatility may be higher or lower in domestic markets depending on the policy environment. Some governments attempt to stabilise their domestic markets because they want to protect both producers and consumers against the inherent instability of agricultural prices. Other governments, particularly in developed countries, seek to stabilise producer income, rather than consumer prices, as agricultural commodities comprise a relatively small share in the cost of processed foods, as well as most household budgets. In both cases (with the exception of decoupled payments), the result is that instability is exported to world markets. This tendency of agricultural policies to stabilise domestic markets acts as a vicious circle: as world markets become more volatile, governments see even more reason to stabilise domestic markets, thereby adding further to instability in international trade.

Most of the key drivers of the agricultural markets are well known (FAO, 2009). Of concern here is the extent to which the drivers are, themselves, likely to exhibit greater variability and uncertainty in the future, or to condition market responses in ways that will exacerbate price volatility in the coming decade. The main drivers are discussed individually below. An empirical analysis of the contributions of these drivers to overall price volatility is described in the following section that illustrates the nature and size of the impacts on market prices.

Weather and climate change

One of the most frequent factors behind volatility on agricultural markets is weather, and adverse weather is indeed generally considered to have played a significant role in the 2006-08 price spike. In 2010, adverse weather also played a major role in the commodity price spike. For example, drought reduced the grain harvest in the Russian Federation and Ukraine by a third and flooding caused harvest problems in North-East Australia, affecting sugar and downgrading some wheat to feed quality. The growing importance of regions exhibiting high yield variability (like the Russian Federation and Ukraine) in global commodity supply has already shown its impact on world commodity price volatility.

Climate change is altering traditional weather patterns. The latest findings of the Intergovernmental Panel on Climate Change (IPCC) suggest that long-term changes in climate have already been observed, including changes in Arctic temperature and ice, widespread changes in precipitation, ocean salinity, wind patterns and aspects of extreme weather including droughts, heavy precipitation, heat waves and intensity of tropical cyclones (IPCC, 2007). Agricultural impacts are expected to be more adverse in tropical areas than in temperate areas. Developed countries will largely benefit as cereal productivity is projected to rise in Canada, northern Europe and parts of the Russian Federation. In contrast, many of today's poorest developing countries are likely to be negatively affected in the coming decades owing to a reduction in the area and potential productivity of their cropland. Sub-Saharan Africa is expected to be the most severely affected.

Other than foreseeing potentially higher prices, in part through higher costs associated with worsening conditions in arid and semi arid regions where agricultural production is already difficult, current global assessments of climate change have been unable to quantify the likely effects of climate change on price volatility. The main drivers of climate change induced price volatility would stem from impacts of extreme events such as drought and floods in major supply regions. However, existing assessments have not considered the possibility of significant shifts in the frequency of extreme events on regional production potential, nor have they considered scenarios of abrupt climate or socioeconomic change and the upheaval cause by shifting production and trade zones.

Stock levels

Stocks of storable commodities have long played a buffering role; mitigating discrepancies in short term demand and supply of commodities, helping to smooth prices and reduce their volatility. Expectations of future price developments affect purchases for and sales from stocks held primarily for transaction purposes. Stockholding by private and public agents may also have differing objectives. In some OECD countries for example, lower stocks of certain commodities have resulted from the partial dismantling of price support and intervention programmes following reforms aimed at increased market orientation.

Considering the relationship between stock levels and prices, the level of stocks may not be as important in affecting prices as the sensitivity of supply or demand from accessible stocks to prices and price expectations, which themselves are contingent on knowledge of current supplies, and expectations of future market developments. Typically this sensitivity is much larger than is either production or consumption, and hence changes in stocks will buffer price changes. However, if stocks are reduced to minimum levels, then clearly no buffering role is possible. But this may also occur if agents panic on future availability. If in such situations, agents increase their demand for stocks (or hoard), prices may spike upwards, as markets arbitrate a largely fixed production supply between stockholding and consumption. In other words, low stocks play an important role but this is not generally a sufficient condition for an extreme price spike. The price spikes of the early 1970s and of 2006-08 coincided with low stocks for wheat and coarse grains, but world rice stocks actually accumulated during this period. Market information plays an important role in affecting expectations on supply availability.

It is worth noting that a substantial share of world cereals output and use is not integrated into world trade and thus accessible to world markets for a number of reasons.

This may occur because the respective areas are (geographically or economically) distant, because in some countries stocks are held for domestic food security reasons and not available for trade or because trade barriers insulate domestic prices from international movements. The share of world exports in world production, of around 12% for coarse grain,18% for wheat and 7% for rice, provides some indication of the "thinness" or residual nature of trade for these markets. However, it does not reflect which part of overall output remains in areas that lack market integration.

For the market to function effectively, a minimum amount of the commodity must be held in the system to transport, market and process. Though stocks data are notoriously imprecise, general market sentiment suggests such minimum working stocks should be around 20% of use. When stocks are depleted (except for quantities absolutely needed to keep the pipeline operative), supply becomes very inelastic. Supply of an annual crop, such as wheat or maize, is nearly completely inelastic in the short term, although affected somewhat by the different harvest periods in northern and southern hemispheres. Even small additional gaps between demand and supply can result in rather large price increases. Price spikes in cereals markets have most often occurred at times when stocks-to-use ratios were extremely low.

Energy prices

The price spikes of the early 1970s and 2006-08 were both characterised by a simultaneous surge in prices for commodities and energy, and in particular, crude oil. Energy prices are an important cost factor in agricultural production, with two key elements being fertiliser and transportation costs. OECD/FAO analysis (OECD/FAO, 2008, 2009, 2010) has confirmed that a close relationship exists between rising energy prices and the costs of agricultural production. If oil prices had not increased so substantially in the period before 2008, it is likely that the prices of agricultural products would not have risen so significantly. The impact of potentially higher oil prices on selected commodity prices is discussed in the risks section of the Overview chapter.

Energy prices can have both short and long term impacts on agricultural commodity prices. Agriculture is becoming increasingly industrialised in many parts of the world, relying more heavily on petroleum-based products for fuels and fertilisers. Price increases of oil and petroleum impact the short-run costs of running farm machinery and irrigation systems, as well as the costs of processing, handling and transporting food along the value chain. Higher in-land and ocean freight costs can significantly affect both import and consumer prices. The longer term impact of energy prices is observed in a typical one year lagged response of agricultural production to price, reflecting producer decisions related to the costs of petroleum-based products, such as fertilisers and pesticides,

A second link between commodity prices and energy occurs through biofuels and the expanding use of agricultural commodities as feedstocks for biofuel production. Price transmission of oil price increases to crop prices may be more rapid. Global production of biofuels has grown substantially in the last ten years, primarily due to renewable energy mandates and other government policies. Between 2005 and 2007, when oil prices were rising and global food prices began to increase rapidly, the use of cereals (wheat and coarse grains) for biofuels production grew by 80%. The absolute increase (41 Mt) during that period accounted for about 50% of the overall increase of cereals use (81 Mt). Biofuels now account for a significant and growing part of global production of a number of crops. On average for the 2008-10 period, that share was 21% in the case of sugar cane, 11% for both vegetable oil and coarse grains, and 8% for sugar beets.

Biofuels can also have indirect effects on the prices of crops which are not widely used as biofuels feedstocks, as land begins to shift away from these commodities. Higher feed prices also may induce supply reductions in the livestock industries, although the full effect is somewhat mitigated with the incorporation of biofuels co-products into feed rations (distillers' grains, oilseed meal). Biofuel mandates and blending targets, which are satisfied regardless of price, introduce inflexibility into the demand for feedstocks, contributing to the extent of required price adjustments in the event of a shock and price volatility. In addition, depending on the relative prices of agricultural crops and oil, biofuel production in some countries may become economically profitable without government support. At sufficiently high crude oil prices, the result will be growing biofuel production and upward pressure on the prices of agricultural commodities, even in the absence of support policies.

Exchange rates

The interactions between macroeconomic factors and agricultural markets have come under increased focus in recent years, with currency movements in particular having the potential to impact food security and competitiveness around the world. Given that most commodity prices are expressed in US dollars, fluctuations in exchange rates affect domestic commodity prices (in local currency) in countries that are highly integrated into world markets.

An appreciating currency relative to the US dollar reduces an exporting country's price competitiveness. To compensate and maintain international market shares, domestic prices may fall. For net exporting countries, such a decrease in the domestic price would normally trigger a decline in production over time. For net importing countries, commodities become relatively less expensive and demand would normally rise. Higher demand combined with a reduction in supply can be expected to result in higher world prices, holding other factors constant.

Between 2002 and 2008, the US dollar depreciated significantly against other major currencies, including a 36% reduction in value against the euro. A 2010 study by Agriculture and Agri-Food Canada, using the AGLINK-COSIMO model for scenario analysis, examined the potential medium term impacts of such depreciation on world agricultural commodity prices. For each major currency, the average 2002-08 appreciation against the US dollar was calculated and held constant at this level in each projection year out to 2019. The scenario was compared against an updated version of the 2009-18 AGLINK-COSIMO baseline projection. Table 2.1 shows the increase in world prices for various agricultural commodities that result from the exchange rate shock, as implemented over the projection horizon. The contribution of the currency appreciations vis-à-vis the US dollar of various key market participants, to the commodity price changes are also noted.

The relative impacts are complex and depend on the market structure for specific commodities. For example, the Canadian dollar appreciation leads to a decline in domestic red meat and cereals prices, triggering reduced livestock production, feed demand and cereals exports. The reduction in feed demand mitigates the decline in exports, reducing the impact of the stronger Canadian dollar on world wheat markets. By contrast, meat prices in the EU are largely determined by local market conditions. Therefore, feed demand does not adjust to the extent that it does in Canada, resulting in a stronger euro

Table 2.1. **Estimated contributions to world agricultural commodity price increases (%) from simulated appreciation relative to the US dollar**

	Price increase	Australia	Brazil	Canada	China	E27	India	New Zealand	Thailand	Other	Total
Corn	10.7	1	27	0	13	29	1	1	2	26	100
Wheat	18.7	1	12	1	4	73	0	1	1	7	100
Rice	6.6	1	18	1	8	13	30	0	15	14	100
Soybeans	10.8	1	27	0	13	29	1	1	2	26	100
Vegetable Oils	13	0	33	0	33	20	4	1	0	9	100
Beef, Pacific	9.6	13	14	22	3	19	0	7	4	18	100
Pork, Pacific	14.1	0	16	24	4	25	0	2	2	27	100
Chicken	16.2	0	35	1	38	11	2	0	2	11	100
Butter	20.1	8	18	0	0	7	0	49	0	18	100
Cheese	19.8	10	46	0	3	18	0	13	0	10	100
SMP	14.3	10	32	1	6	35	0	8	2	6	100
Refined Sugar	24.5	3	78	1	1	6	1	0	3	7	100
Ethanol	14.3	0	72	0	2	21	1	0	1	3	100

Note: The currency appreciation used in simulation for each country is based on that experienced by each country over 2002-08. The effects on the world crude oil price were also estimated in the study but not reported here. See the study for details.
Source: Agriculture and Agri-Food Canada. *"The Consequences of a Strong Depreciation of the US Dollar on Agricultural Markets"*. Ottawa. August 2010. Available upon request by email: *econ.info@agr.gc.ca*.

StatLink http://dx.doi.org/10.1787/888932427493

contribution to the increase in world wheat prices. The impacts of each country on world prices depends on the degree of currency appreciation, the expected impacts on domestic production and their relative influence on specific international commodity markets.

Growing demand

Steady growth in demand does exert pressure on commodity prices. If the rate of growth in production does not keep pace with demand, upward pressure on prices will result. Net exports for coarse grains in China and India have gradually declined since 2000 (becoming negative in most recent years), parallel to an increase in the annual growth rate of consumption with respect to the previous decade and a considerable lowering of stocks. This excess of demand can play a role in raising international cereal prices over time. Also the rapid increase in imports of oilseeds by China in the 2001-10 decade has contributed to the increase in international oilseeds prices, which was transmitted through land substitution effects in exporting countries to the global cereal markets.

However, some commentators have related the 2007-08 price spike to the rapidly growing food demand in emerging economies, in particular China and India. This explanation is unconvincing for several reasons. First, food demand in this part of the world had already grown rapidly for some time, and not suddenly in 2007. Second, in the cereals sector, where the price spikes were particularly pronounced, India and China are almost self-sufficient. Moreover, the imports of meat during that period remained somewhat constant with the exception of China. The increase in meat imports by China in 2007 did coincide with a combination of animal disease and natural disaster which reduced the domestic animal inventory, particularly for pigmeat production. Therefore, this surge in imports should not be interpreted as a substitution of domestic feed grain demand through meat imports but rather as an effort to keep domestic prices at a reasonable level after the culling of millions of animals and their net exports (positive in most recent years) have not declined during the period in question. Third, the use of cereals in China and India has been relatively stable during the subsequent global financial crisis and continues to grow, which cannot explain why international food prices declined in 2008. Jones, D. and A. Kwiecinski (2010) provide an account of China's and India's wheat trade during the 2006-08 episode that also does not support the view that these two countries contributed in any significant way to the run-up in prices.

The latest UN estimates of population growth suggest that by the end of 2020 the planet will be populated by 7.7 bn persons. While the rate of population growth is slowing, this represents a rise of 1% annually over the next decade; while population in the least developing countries is still growing in excess of 2% per year. In terms of numbers, the increase in global population to 2020 is equivalent to the current population of Sub-Saharan Africa. What is striking is that the vast majority of this population growth (86%) is set to take place in large urban centres and mega cities in developing countries (Figure 2.3). Such a shift in location carries with it a change in the composition of the food basket to more processed, convenience and higher value-added products. Coupled with the demands of an increasing population is the additional demand induced by higher incomes. *Per capita* incomes in many poor countries may increase as much as 50% over the next decade; and such countries have a high propensity to buy food with additional income, including higher value-added commodities such as meats and dairy product

Figure 2.3. **Expected demographic change: 1961-2008**

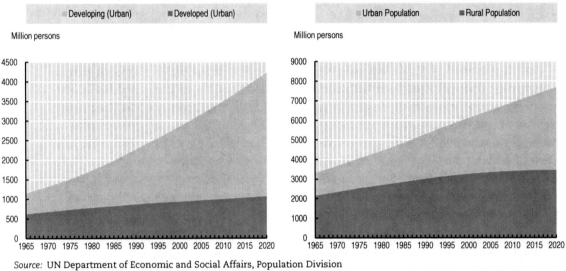

Source: UN Department of Economic and Social Affairs, Population Division

StatLink http://dx.doi.org/10.1787/888932426410

An important consequence of both higher incomes and population shifts toward urban locations is that aggregate food demand is becoming increasingly "inelastic" or insensitive to price developments. As expenditure shares for food fall, price changes have less impact on real incomes, and consumers adjust food purchases less in response to a rise in prices. In addition, as the component of primary agricultural products in food purchases declines (i.e., more value-added products), consumer prices for food do not fluctuate as much as primary producer prices. This lower elasticity effect induces larger changes in primary food prices, for a given change in supply or demand at the consumer level. A consequent effect on food insecurity is that higher income consumers maintain consumption as food prices increase, causing adjustments to be absorbed by the poor and food vulnerable sections of society. Urbanisation also implies greater dependence on purchased food without recourse to alternative household production. It has also raised political sensitivity to consumer food prices through a stronger consumer voice (public mobilisation and demonstration).

In addition to a more inelastic demand, countries with very large populations can shock international markets when demand rises sharply in response to domestic events. For example, imports to China soared in the aftermath of the melamine milk adulteration incidents as consumers lost confidence in domestic products. With the sugar production cycle in India, domestic demand in deficit years can account for a large share of world sugar exports (7% in 2009/10) with subsequent large additional supplies coming on to world markets in surplus years, contributing to the volatility in international sugar markets. Animal diseases, such as BSE and FMD, have also had major impacts on demand for meat and feed in some years following the imposition of trade bans.

Rising energy related production costs and resource pressures

The level and stability of commodity prices are highly dependent on maintaining gains in productivity growth. A main feature of the *Outlook* is that productivity growth is slowing due to a number of factors such as higher input costs, slower technology application, expansion into more marginal lands, and limits to double cropping, irrigation etc. Increases in production costs, due to higher energy costs, have been noted above. There are other cost pressures as well, particularly related to resource use and increasing scarcity. The level and productivity of variable inputs, such as energy, and resource inputs, such as land and water, affect the speed and ability of the agricultural sector to respond to shocks. In regions where resource inputs such as land and water are limited/expensive, variable input application is key to supply response. High input application also may limit output variability, such as to adverse weather or climate change.

This situation characterises the agricultural sectors of many developed countries which are regions of high productivity and traditional large suppliers to international markets. These countries are now displaying slower growth in crop production. There are decreasing returns to scale in input application, and good cropland is also lost each year to urban and industrial development, roads and reservoirs. For historic and strategic reasons, most urban areas are situated on flat coastal plains or river valleys with fertile soils. Given that much future urban expansion will be centred on such areas, the loss of good-quality cropland seems likely to continue, given the typically low economic returns to farm capital and labour compared with non-agricultural uses (Figure 2.4). The 2009 OECD-FAO *Outlook* report noted there was substantial additional land available for use in agriculture but that most of this land is in the lower productivity zones of Sub-Saharan Africa and South America, in some cases, bringing more land into production would generally incur higher costs. Therefore, as agricultural production moves into more marginal areas, the risks of production shortfalls will likely increase due to climatic conditions and less developed infrastructures, and result in more variable supply and consequently higher price volatility. The impact of using more marginal lands needs to be at least partially offset by the development of new production technologies. A good demonstration of this issue is provided in the *Outlook*'s projection that the Russia-Ukraine-Kazakhstan region will have the largest share of wheat exports. The high yield variability/export availability from this region has already demonstrated its impact on world commodity price volatility.

Figure 2.4. **Per capita arable land availability: 1963-2008**

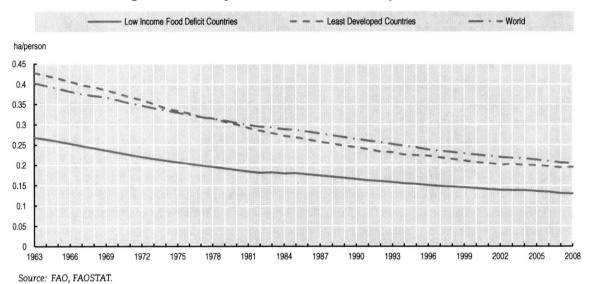

Source: FAO, FAOSTAT.

StatLink ⟐ *http://dx.doi.org/10.1787/888932426429*

There are mounting concerns about water availability. Agriculture consumes about 70% of the world's freshwater withdrawals (45% in OECD countries). Water use projections to 2050 suggest that the water supply to some 47% of the world's population, mostly in developing countries, will be under severe stress, largely because of developments outside of agriculture. In some instances, supporting agricultural production may not be regarded as the most socially or economically desirable use for scarce water supplies. This can already be seen in reductions of irrigated Saudi Arabian wheat production, and shifts in Australian dairy production due to water constraints. With demand for food and water rising, farmers will need to use water more efficiently and improve agricultural water management. Various farm management and technology approaches are being deployed to improve the efficiency of water management, for example, developing drought resistant cultivars and computerised linking of soil moisture monitors to drip irrigation systems. Moreover, water charges for farmers rarely reflect real scarcity or environmental costs and benefits, but raising water charges may also help encourage innovation in using water more efficiently. While increasing water charges has raised concerns that this may adversely affect farm output through higher production costs, evidence suggests that, where water prices have been increased to cover water supply costs, this has not led to reduced agricultural output (OECD, 2008a).

Trade restrictions

The 2010 *Outlook* report examined the question of the transmission of world prices to domestic markets, pointing out that price developments in domestic markets may be quite different from those at the global level. Over time, greater market integration through globalisation and trade liberalisation tends to enhance price transmission and mitigate the key drivers of volatility by increasing the global supply and demand elasticity. On the other hand, governments often respond to higher prices through interventions at the border and consumer subsidies, which by shielding the local population from volatility, diminishes price signals to producers and consumers. This is particularly true for rice in much of Asia and bread wheat in the Middle East.

Although differences in quality must be taken into account when comparing world and national prices, the degree to which prices on world markets are passed through to domestic markets varies considerably by commodity and country, with important differences between developing and developed countries. Price transmission is generally high in developed countries, and the raw material (*e.g.* wheat flour) often accounts for a small share of the total value of the product (*e.g.* bread); as a result, high global price volatility will have a marginal effect on retail price variability. In low-income countries what is consumed is often relatively unprocessed with little value-added to the raw material, so that primary product prices have a direct consequence on household budgets. Transmission, though, is often hindered by high transactions costs (including transport) that can result in local prices departing from those on world markets.

But trade policies such as import tariffs and quota regimes may also impede transmission, especially if they are changed in response to shocks. If international prices are not passed through, demand and supply responsiveness will be diminished. Export restraints, including export taxes and outright bans, can also amplify price volatility in international markets. This is particularly true when restraints are introduced by major exporters and when they are not notified in advance and uncertain in duration. The lack of rules or weak rules, and the lack of enforcement of current disciplines in the use of export restraints contribute to this uncertainty.

There is no doubt that government actions, and in particular export restrictions, contributed significantly to the food price spike during the 2006-08 period. Analysis of policy responses to the crisis in ten major emerging economies showed that export restrictions were not always effective in suppressing domestic price pressure (see Dawe, 2010 and Jones, D. and A. Kwiecinski, 2010). Where they were effective, such intervention was not without cost, with the need to increase support to producers in order to stimulate production, as price incentives were suppressed. The timing of these export constraints was important for the world market impact because it reduced or limited the export volumes at the moment when the price rise on world markets was already accelerating, creating greater uncertainty in markets. Thus, export restrictions imposed by major exporters contributed to the price spike.

Health risks can also affect price volatility by closing down trade literally overnight, and disrupting markets. Recent incidences of food contamination and animal disease outbreaks including Avian Influenza, Swine Flu, foot and mouth disease and BSE in cattle have had significant impacts on the food supply chain, All imports of the product in question from the source country may be banned unless the source of the problem can be quickly regionalised, and it takes time following a disease outbreak to re-open markets. Consumer reactions may also cause prices to collapse.

Sanitary and phyto-sanitary measures that address plant, animal and human health and safety issues can also affect trade. Creation of the WTO and Sanitary and Photo Sanitary (SPS) and Technical Barriers to Trade (TBT) Agreements established clear rules on the applications of standards by Member countries to minimise any negative trade effects. Governments now face increased scrutiny to ensure that standards are not introduced for the purpose of trade protection. The results in terms of disputes brought to the WTO would suggest that the WTO processes, particularly in relation to SPS matters, are having some degree of success in reducing trade protection resulting from the imposition of public standards (Anderson, K, *et al.* 2001).

Financialisation of agricultural markets

While speculation is needed for the efficient functioning of futures markets, financial speculation which involves trading in futures markets and commodity derivatives without any link to the underlying cash markets, has been suggested as one of the possible causes of volatile agricultural commodity price movements. A huge influx of funds and non-traditional participants into commodity markets, among them agricultural commodity markets, began in the mid-2000s. This shift has been attributed to several factors, among them the Commodities Futures Modernisation Act of 2000 in the United States, which exempted private over the counter derivatives (OTCs) from supervision by the US Commodity Futures Trading Commission (CFTC) and the US Securities and Exchange Commission (SEC). In addition, the arrival of large proprietary investment banks, as well as hedge fund, swap and other money managers in pursuit of portfolio diversification and profit, greatly increased trading activity as an investment strategy due to the realisation of the inverse correlation between yields on bonds and equities and those on commodities.

Many researchers and commentators have tried to investigate these links. Their findings diverge significantly. In work undertaken for the OECD, Irwin and Sanders (2010) investigate the impact of index and swap funds on commodity futures markets and conclude that there is no convincing evidence that positions held by index traders or swap dealers impact market returns. The Task Force on Commodity Futures Markets, established by the International Organization of Security Commissions to look into these matters, reviewed the available research and came to the conclusion that they "do not support the proposition that the activity of speculators has systematically driven commodity market cash or futures prices up or down on a sustained basis". In its October 2008 *World Economic Outlook*, the IMF concluded that there was no evidence of a long term systemic effect due to speculation on commodity prices, although it suggested that short term expectations can be influenced by sentiment and investor behaviour, which can amplify short-term price fluctuations, as in other asset markets. On the other hand, Tang and Xiong (2010) conclude that as a result of the bundling of commodities in index funds correlations among commodities have gone up and that shocks from oil and financial factors now spill-over more strongly to non-energy commodities. Masters (2008) asserts that speculative buying by index funds on such a wide scale created a "bubble" with the result that commodity futures prices far exceeded fundamental values during the 2007/08 period. Almost all researchers agree that non-commercial participation in futures markets may amplify price movements in the short term, even if they differ in their conclusions about other possible impacts (Baffes J. and T. Hanniotis, 2010; Robles, M. *et al.*, 2009; UNCTAD, 2009).

Most analysts remark on the inadequacy of the data itself, in part due to the regulatory framework. Because the Commodity Futures Trading Commission in the US has only recently begun to furnish a more disaggregated Commitment of Traders report on the position levels of commercials, swap dealers and managed money, analyses of the different behavioural dimensions of passive trading by swaps dealers *versus* active trading of money managers are lacking.

When discussing the possible role of speculation in agricultural (or other) commodity markets it is important to distinguish between financial speculation and speculation on physical markets. The latter was certainly a factor in the events of 2007/08. With prices rising and expectations of continuing increases, many market participants, ranging from households to governments, engaged in accumulation, and hoarding, either with a view to ensuring supplies amid real fears of scarcity, or with a view to gaining a premium in a rising market. This behaviour exacerbated the price rises in some markets.

Contributions of the key drivers to price variability

The relatively stable annual prices projected by this *Outlook* result from the assumption of "normal" conditions for the forces driving prices. However, uncertainties around yields and harvest outcomes, inventory levels in major exporting countries, macroeconomic developments, policy actions, and energy prices, suggest that future trends in agricultural commodities prices remain highly uncertain.[1]

One method of examining the importance of various drivers of volatility is to study the frequency distribution of variables which represent each driver (*e.g.* oil prices), and implement shocks to structural models that purport to represent the structures of agricultural markets. A series of stochastic simulations were implemented using the OECD-FAO AGLINK-COSIMO model to estimate the extent to which exogenous shocks can cause price variability of crops over the *Outlook* (OECD, 2011a). The AGLINK-COSIMO modelling framework provides both a well accepted partial equilibrium model and a projection database, which includes historical time series of supply, demand and prices for agricultural commodities. Agricultural commodity markets within this structure respond to changes in the macroeconomic environment and exogenous demand/supply shocks.

Three groups of exogenous sources of risk and variability were considered in the analysis: *a)* crude oil and fertiliser prices; *b)* macroeconomic variables including GDP growth and consumption deflators for selected leading economies;[2] and *c)* weather and technology related variables represented by yields for three types of crops (coarse grains, rice and wheat). Available historical information about the distribution of these variables was used to simulate the distribution of the stochastic variability over the *Outlook* projection. The first set of stochastic experiments let crude oil and fertiliser prices vary, the second set added some macroeconomic variables, and the third set included variable yields for coarse grains, rice and wheat (see OECD, 2011a for a discussion of methodology).

Table 2.2 presents the results of the three sets of experiments in terms of the median, the 10th percentile and 90th percentile of volatility estimated over the period 2015-19. As expected, volatility measures increase with the number of sources of exogenous risk taken into account. Variability of oil/fertiliser prices and yields has the greatest estimated impact on variability of annual commodity prices, well above the impact of macroeconomic variables. The distribution of the impacts seems to be skewed to the higher values of volatility, particularly for wheat and maize. In other words, there is potential for episodes of levels of volatility well above the median.

The partial stochastic analysis, incorporating all three exogenous sources of risk, presents a distribution of simulated results for maize which has a higher level of volatility stemming from the exogenous drivers studied in this analysis. Rice price volatility shows the weakest link to these drivers (Figure 2.5). This result may be explained by the fact that maize exports are highly concentrated with a high market share. Maize has the strongest link to both the biofuels sector, and income elasticities are also highest, given its links to the animal feed sector. Biofuel consumption mandates, when binding, make maize demand more inelastic under yield shocks. Wheat trade is less concentrated, and rice trade, while thin, is more highly managed and affected by trade policies. These policies are important sources of volatility – such as export restrictions, which are not simulated in this

Table 2.2. **Simulated volatility measures in 2019 for international crop prices**

		Maize	Rice	Wheat
Baseline		3.0%	0.4%	3.0%
1st set	10th percentile	2.1%	0.4%	2.1%
	Median	3.8%	1.1%	4.6%
	90th percentile	7.1%	2.3%	7.1%
2nd set	10th percentile	2%	0.4%	1.5%
	Median	4.3%	1.1%	3.7%
	90th percentile	8.1%	2.6%	8.6%
3rd set	10th percentile	5.1%	3.4%	4%
	Median	15.4%	5.5%	8.1%
	90th percentile	31.5%	8.7%	14.5%
Historical period: 1976-2009	Minimum	7%	7%	5%
	Median	19%	16%	21%
	Maximum	29%	54%	40%

Source: OECD (2011a).

StatLink ⟳ http://dx.doi.org/10.1787/888932427512

Figure 2.5. **Simulated median price variability in 2019**

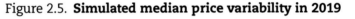

■ Median marginal increase linked to yields - 3rd set   ■ Median marginal increase linked to macroeconomic environment - 2nd set
■ Median marginal increase linked to input price assumptions - 1st set   ▰ Price volatility in baseline projections
◆ Average price volatility over 1976-2009

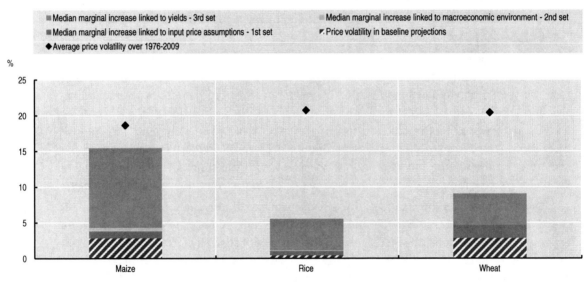

Source: OECD (2011a).

StatLink ⟳ http://dx.doi.org/10.1787/888932445372

experiment. (Timmer, 2009). If past historical levels of volatility are indicative of future volatility, then the driving forces assessed in this analysis may contribute significantly to maize volatility, but less so for wheat, and much less so for rice.

The results of this analysis show that while exogenous factors such as yields, crude oil and fertiliser prices as well as macroeconomic developments are not responsible for all potentially observed annual price variability, they do contribute to an important share of it. The stochastic simulations also indicate that a combination of exogenous shocks can increase the level of volatility if they occur in specific patterns, even if the likelihood of this happening is low. For example, low yields for a number of different commodities simultaneously combined with high oil prices can generate exceptionally high levels of commodity price volatility.

There are limitations to this type of analysis as only a few key uncertainties are covered and it uses annual price data where more frequent observations would provide a different picture of volatility. Moreover, the focus is on price volatility at the aggregate level. Prices at the farm level do not necessarily follow the same patterns as world prices, although market price variability is the main contributor to price risk at the farm level.

The policy challenge

Volatility is a characteristic feature of agricultural markets, caused by unexpected shocks, many of which are natural and not preventable. These shocks are compounded by low price elasticities of supply and demand. Isolation of domestic markets from international price fluctuation, through high transactions costs, or government policies that stabilise prices for producers and/or consumers, further aggravate volatility on international markets, and affect those who are most open to trade. Where appropriate institutions and infrastructures exist, private market participants can manage the moderate risks reasonably well. However, bouts of extreme price volatility may have negative consequences for sectoral development and especially for food insecurity which compel the attention of governments.

Downward deviations of prices from trend are typically limited in magnitude, but low price periods may prevail for some time and can threaten the viability of vulnerable producers. The most visible form of volatility on agricultural markets is occasional sharp price spikes that push prices up to record levels. With the experience of the 2006-08 and 2010 price hikes, and the trends in key drivers discussed in this Chapter, many observers have come to believe that extreme price spikes may become more rather than less frequent. Certainly, the potential for short run price spikes in the cereals market is relatively high with lower world production and stocks in 2010/11. Next year's crop is critical, especially for wheat and maize. A strong supply response to positive price signals may result, but unfavourable weather conditions could play a significant role. This continuing uncertain environment calls for coherent international approaches that will help restore confidence in the ability of agriculture and the food economy to meet the rising demands of the future.

The policy challenges in addressing the current environment are multidimensional. The basic ongoing challenge, which lies at the heart of agricultural development and the reduction of food insecurity, is to promote productivity growth, particularly for small producers, that improves their resilience to external shocks, and that assures increasing supplies to local markets, at affordable prices. However, recognising that volatility will remain a feature of agricultural markets, given weather variation and potential adverse consequences of climate change, coherent policies are required to reduce volatility on the one hand, but also to mitigate the impact of volatility on those who are most adversely affected.

Measures to increase productivity and resilience to shocks

One of the important indications from the *Outlook* is that agricultural supply is struggling to keep pace with the more steady growth in demand over the next decade. Supplies from traditional exporters are slowing, and demand in most developing countries is growing at a faster pace. In this environment, commodity stocks are not being rebuilt and sudden shocks in either supply or demand result in market volatility. For many years, productivity growth in the agricultural sector was strong, explaining in large part why real commodity prices have declined on average by over 1% per year in real terms (Timmer, 2010). Since the turn of this century, the decline in real prices has halted, and as projected in this *Outlook* real prices will remain higher on average over the next decade. Higher prices are signalling the need for expansion in supplies, and highly volatile prices signal the need for action to mitigate the associated negative impacts.

In this context, increasing the productivity and resilience of agriculture in developing countries, where demand growth is most significant, where large gaps in technology, inputs and management exist, and where agriculture income opportunities are significant, must be considered the primary strategic means of addressing the current environment of high prices and high price volatility. The yield scenarios presented in the Overview chapter indicate clearly that productivity growth has the strongest impact on the level of commodity prices, and in serving to restore stock levels, and also helps reduce volatility. Those results indicate, for example, that if world yields of crops were to be 5% higher, cereal prices would fall by up to 20%, on average, over the Outlook period.[3] The stochastic results presented above also demonstrate the significant role of yields in international price variations. In many cases, where a country is relatively closed to international markets, the impact of yield variation on local domestic prices may be much greater.

Measures to increase the productivity and resilience in developing country agriculture will require significant investments, and if higher commodity prices are transmitted to producers under the right conditions, underpinned with effective agricultural policies, private investments will lead growth. However, public sector investments are required, particularly in agricultural research and development, targeted to small-scale agriculture that will increase productivity and resilience towards weather/climate change and resource scarcity, and increase its integration into growing markets. Public non-agricultural investments are also required to improve the general institutional setting as well as infrastructure such as roads and communication, clean water supplies, health services, and education. Increasing women's access to productive assets would have a large impact on productivity of small scale agriculture (See FAO, (2011a)).

Action by the international community could strengthen productivity through existing programmes and institutions, such as the Global Agriculture and Food Security Program and official development assistance (ODA). Strengthening the CGIAR system to support innovation and transfer of technologies, specifically oriented to improving productivity and resilience of agriculture, would be a critical step to assure that technology gaps are reduced.

Increasing supply through higher productivity is not only about producing more output with a given set of inputs, but also about increasing product availability from a given output. Recent studies suggest that agricultural and food waste is high, as a result of post harvest losses, waste in processing, and waste in homes (See FAO, (2011b)). Estimates of waste range up to one-third in some countries. Investments to minimise waste to the extent possible by better management, storage facilities and education have immediate benefit in increasing supplies.

Measures to reduce price volatility

Market volatility is a feature of agricultural markets and will persist. However, volatility may be reduced by measures to increase market transparency and reduce uncertainty, and ensuring that volatility reflects underlying market fundamentals, and not misinformation, speculation, panic or incoherent policies.

Market information

Information is critical for markets to function efficiently. One of the lessons from the policy responses to extreme volatility on agricultural markets in recent years is that the extent that market upheaval came as a surprise. Governments and international organisations were not prepared for the turmoil on global food markets, neither institutionally or financially. The consequence was that policy responses were often *ad hoc*, uncoordinated and inconsistent. Decisions were made on the basis of both incomplete information of market situations, and the potential impact of their policy actions. In the view of some stakeholders, the situation may be deteriorating. The International Grains Council has expressed concerns about a declining availability and consistency of national data in some countries and possible cutbacks in funding for statistics and crop monitoring.

Greater efforts are required to improve both national and global surveillance systems on plantings and production prospects. At national levels, greater commitment is required to provide timely data on food production, consumption and stocks, as well as capacity to assess current situations and outlook, and its implications for food security. Where national capacity to provide information does not exist, it should be created through support by international assistance. This information needs to be widely and readily accessible to all market actors. Such systems would help temper uncertainty in organised markets that play a fundamental role in global price discovery while providing much earlier notice of potential market shocks. New developments in space technology (satellites, space communications, GPS systems) are also promising as a means of amassing more accurate and timelier information on markets. A brief overview on the current and potential use of space technology is provided in Box 2.1.

Global monitoring systems need to be enhanced. The FAO Global Information and Early Warning System (GIEWS) monitors the world food supply/demand and price situation and provides early warnings of impending food crises in individual countries. For countries facing a serious food emergency, FAO/GIEWS and the World Food Programme (WFP) also carry out joint Crop and Food Security Assessment Missions (CFSAMs) to provide timely and reliable information so that appropriate actions can be taken by the governments, the international community, and other parties.

Where information exists, it needs to be better coordinated and disseminated. International organisations and governments could co-operate more in developing timelier and more accurate market information, including national policy data, by sharing resources and data. Building on existing mechanisms and institutions, better information could be collected using up to date electronic means to improve market intelligence and outlook at the national and international level while strengthening global and national early warning systems. Co-operation with the private sector on gathering and dissemination of information on stocks and on improving crop forecasts would be important. An international body charged with identifying appropriate actions, co-ordinating responses and monitoring implementation of an information system would facilitate more transparent and consistent information, disseminated on a timely and coordinated basis.

The OECD-FAO *Outlook* programme and related market analysis attempts to provide better information, and to build global consensus on the medium term prospects for production, consumption, prices and trade and the importance of emerging issues. The *Outlook* process, which entails annual questionnaires/discussion with governments and producer organisations, expert judgement by analysts, and amassing of global databases, facilitates greater understanding of markets. Country requests to the two organisations for capacity building in the development of in-house outlook and market analysis capabilities using the AGLINK-COSIMO model have increased recently in response to the volatile market situation. Co-operation agreements are under development with Brazil and China, and India has expressed an interest in greater collaboration in the areas of agricultural outlook and food security.

Buffer stocks

Buffer stock schemes have been a policy instrument used by a number of countries and international commodity organisations to reduce domestic and international price volatility. However, they have been virtually abandoned in developed countries. These schemes aim to stabilise prices and, in some cases, to support them. However, lessons from past buffer stock schemes illustrate problems. While stockholding is a necessary component of a well functioning market, in particular to smooth out seasonal fluctuations and time lags in trade, year-to-year variations in domestic production can usually be buffered more effectively, and at less cost, by adjustments in the quantities imported and exported. Buffer stocks are costly to maintain and difficult to manage because of the need in practice to identify the appropriate price triggers. The costs in storage facilities, commodity purchases and administration can be prohibitively high. Moreover, buffer stocks are not targeted to those most in need. In effect, they provide subsidies to all consumers whether rich or poor.

Market based approaches may be more effective in limiting price volatility and improving food security in developing countries. Private storage in local villages and at the regional level can better match local supply and demand but are often discouraged by high material costs and a lack of credit. Policies to improve the investment climate, to strengthen farmer organisations and local co-operatives, as well as extension services should be encouraged.

Futures markets

It is clear that well functioning futures markets for agricultural commodities can play a significant role in reducing or smoothing price fluctuations. They provide instruments to transfer price risk, enabling commercial participants to hedge their products/purchases against the risk of fluctuating prices. They are also important mechanisms that facilitate price discovery, as new information becomes rapidly reflected and reported globally.

There is broad agreement that for futures markets to function well, appropriate regulations are required across all futures exchanges and markets, especially for over the counter trading which takes place off regulated commodity exchanges. Comprehensive and consistent data need to be collected and reported, including from off-exchange trading to facilitate greater market transparency and to enable market participants and regulators to understand what is driving prices. A number of initiatives have been taken in the EU, US and elsewhere to reduce systemic risk and improve transparency on agricultural derivatives markets. It is important that measures adopted are also coherent across markets.

Domestic and trade policies

Large parts of the world's population will only have access to food if food can be traded internationally. More open trade contributes to mitigating the key drivers of volatility by increasing the size and scope of markets and diluting the magnitude of shocks, effectively by facilitating wider supply and demand response. As such, trade is also an excellent buffer for fluctuations originating in the domestic market; and some spill over of international price volatility can provide an important signalling function for the allocation of resources. Yet, international trade has also been seen as a threat, both to the well-being of individuals suffering from the pressure of international competition and to price stability on domestic markets. Markets have long been highly distorted not only by trade policies but importantly by production-linked domestic support regimes which have encouraged excess supplies in international markets. A well functioning trading system, with transparent rules and disciplines is essential if all countries are to discover the benefits of trade, and if its potential benefits in reducing price volatility, both on domestic and international markets are to be realised. The evidence of the recent price spikes indicates that such a system remains elusive (Headey, 2011; Martin, W. and K. Anderson, 2011). In particular, at least for WTO members, the treatment of import measures which are bound is different from export measures which remain unbound.

Reform of the international trading system is required. WTO negotiations are still in progress, within this framework, governments should improve market access, while maintaining appropriate safeguards, especially for vulnerable developing countries, reduce trade distorting support, and eliminate export subsidy measures which provide unfair competition. At the same time, agreements should be sought to contain export restrictions, to assure these are time-limited measures of last resort to resolve legitimate domestic food security concerns that cannot be contained by other measures such as targeted safety-net measures. If export restrictions are deemed necessary, there should be vetting through international consultation and notification, and should take into consideration the food security needs of least developed net food importing countries.

Trade policies are not the only impediment to a more efficient global trading system. Poorly functioning markets, weak infrastructure, inability to meet sanitary and phyto-sanitary regulations and many other factors can limit the capacity to trade effectively. Initiatives should be encouraged such as the Aid-for-Trade programme of the WTO and OECD which help to overcome these domestic barriers to trade.

Biofuels policy

The rapid expansion of biofuels production and the related growing use of cereals as feedstocks may be one of several factors (including increased consumption from emerging markets such as China and India, stock policy changes, the devaluation of the US dollar and extreme weather events in some countries) that contributed to the decline in global cereal stocks in 2007-08. Biofuels still account for a significant share in the global use of some crops, which is also offset by some feed displacement of grains and provision of protein meals as co-products. The precise impact of biofuels on agricultural commodity prices is a matter of debate, and some quantitative analyses from Organisations around the world have concluded that biofuel support policies have a noticeable impact on international commodity prices. Analysis, including that undertaken in this *Outlook*, contends that most biofuel production is driven by policies aimed at energy security, rural development and climate change. Given the prospects of higher oil prices, the value of feedstock crops in the energy market may exceed their value in the food, feed or fibre markets, putting increased pressure on commodity prices as well as increasing the link with energy markets. Should recent volatility in world oil prices continue, this will contribute to further increases in food price volatility, especially if prices rise to levels where biofuel production becomes profitable without subsidies and more prevalent around the globe. Such developments may, in the long term, change the structure of the demand for agricultural production to one which is even more conditioned on energy markets.

Considering the link between the energy and agricultural markets and the food security issues, there is a need to reconsider the role of policies in biofuel production. Such policies, including mandates, subsidies or tax incentives, and tariffs not only encourage biofuel production, but also affect where it is produced. While few alternatives to biofuels exist in the transportation sector, given the global reliance on the internal cumbustion engine, policies should be assessed against other policy options for reduced carbon emissions, energy security, and those which promote energy efficiency. Appropriate such measures would seek a balanced approach for meeting key societal objectives, and not disadvantage international markets. One option worth examining may be the notion of flexible mandates or biofuel call options that could shift some agricultural feedstocks from non-food to food use in times of extreme food scarcity or prices spikes, although is is not clear how such measures might actually work in practice nor the implications for existing support measures.

Measures to mitigate the impact of price volatility
Emergency reserves at national and regional levels

Emergency food reserves are operated in a number of countries. They may be an effective approach to protect the most vulnerable as they can provide subsidised food to specific groups in the community without disrupting private markets. They should be combined with an effective early warning system, have transparent and well defined trigger systems, be independent of political processes and integrated with existing broader social safety nets.

Safety-nets

A range of safety-net measures exist at the international and domestic levels which may help both governments, producers and consumers cope with food price instability. International measures include programmes offered by the World Bank and IMF to provide assistance loans to avoid or reduce fiscal deficits, lower the costs of imported food, and maintain social assistance programmes. Programmes of IDA and IBRD, such as the Global Food Crisis Response Program provides lending and technical assistance to countries facing high food prices, and such assistance has been also supported through partnerships with both civil society organisations and UN organisations such as FAO, UNICEF and WFP. The IMF has overhauled its assistance to low income countries which suffer balance of payments difficulties from higher priced food imports. The commitment to such international measures needs to be strengthened and streamlined, to ensure that such assistance is effective and available rapidly.

Safety nets at the consumer level are critical to protecting the vulnerable poorer sections of populations from food price spikes as they may spend as much as 50 to 60% of their incomes on food purchases, and high prices cut deeply into real incomes, causing considerable hardship and potentially longer term humanitarian impacts. In some countries, consumer safety-net programmes already exist and may be scaled up in times of food price spikes. Certain programmes already exist in the form of targeted food safety and nutrition programmes, such as the Scaling Up Nutrition programme that is supported by civil society organisations, businesses and other international organisations. The definition of vulnerable groups is important for programmes to be effective.

Safety-nets may also be relevant for producers since higher input prices, such as for fertilisers, may limit their ability to respond with increased production to take advantage of higher commodity prices. Greater input use is particularly important for increasing productivity of small scale producers in developing countries. Programmes to assist producers in maintaining and expanding input use are needed, but may be very costly and difficult to manage. Temporary programmes targeted to those producers who can least afford to finance or pay for inputs may provide the most effective safety net assistance.

Market based risk management

Increasingly, market based instruments are available to assist producers and governments in managing production and price risk. However, for the most part such instruments, including the use of forward contracting and commodity futures exchanges are essentially only accessible to larger scale producers in developed countries. Smaller producers and particularly those in many developing countries do not have the knowledge, assets or access to institutions which may facilitate market based risk management. In this context, market based risk management is currently not an option for these producers, and greater efforts to establish knowledge and institutions are required.

For governments, however, which have greater access to expertise and have larger assets, market based mechanisms to help mitigate shocks that can affect the balance of payments and lessen their ability to implement social programmes, may be useful. For example, Malawi has implemented a subsidised weather-indexed insurance programme which helps to finance food imports when weather related domestic production shortfalls occur. Governments may also use option contracts to lock in future food import purchases, so that future import costs are known in advance. However, such risk management measures require technical capacity which many governments do not have. Increased international assistance is required to develop in-country financial risk management capacity.

International policy coordination

The 2007-08 price crisis provides ample evidence that coordination of policy responses at the international level is lacking. Incoherent and badly timed policy initiatives exacerbated international price volatility. Greater co-ordination and information flows are required at the international level if domestic policies are to appropriately take into consideration their broader impacts on price volatility which must be absorbed by international markets, and in particular by other vulnerable countries, consumers and producers. International organisations offer frameworks for such co-ordination. In the context of food security, the reformed Committee on World Food Security now has a structure that allows input from all stake-holders at global, regional and national levels.

Conclusion

Price volatility is certainly not new to agriculture. However, recent periods of high prices and increased price volatility are having significant impacts on food insecure populations. These events signal the need for responses by all stakeholders which address their concerns. For the most part, solutions addressing these issues are not new, but add greater clarity for appropriate policy responses. These include greater priority for productivity growth and improving resilience to shocks, implementing appropriate policies to address volatility and to mitigate its consequences. Finally, the international community needs responsible forums in which enhanced policy development and international co-ordination can work to address the policy challenge of securing the sustainable growth in the global food system which will be needed to feed the world in the years to come.

Box 2.1. **Better information through space technologies**

Satellites are increasingly important in reducing uncertainty surrounding projections of food production. Whether earth observation or meteorological satellites, space communications or global positioning systems, space systems are becoming an indispensable tool in the international effort to track and better understand our atmosphere, oceans, forests, fresh water resources and land use. In this context, space applications play a vital role in providing more accurate and timely information on agricultural production prospects.

Knowing what's planted where: satellite data can complement or even replace ground monitoring systems, which may be more difficult or more expensive to operate.

* *Near real time products* – governments, farmers and researchers can find today a range of near real time information on vegetation and land use, particularly on what types of crops are being planted around the world, and on soil moisture.

* *Improved land survey information* – in many countries, governments and farmers are mapping their arable land. In India, a dozen or so remote sensing satellites are used to award land titles and improve land-use planning nationally. The European Commission uses satellite navigation and remote sensing to verify eligibility for area-based payments.

Predicting agricultural production: many local and global ecological parameters are monitored using satellite-based data, contributing to predicting food production in many OECD and non-OECD countries as much as three to six months in advance.

* *A wide range of indicators* – over half the essential climate variables (atmospheric, oceanic, terrestrial) identified by the United Nations Framework Convention on Climate Change depend on satellite data. The Famine Early Warning Systems Network (FEWS NET) uses data from NASA's Aqua and Terra satellites to provide early warning and vulnerability information on emerging food security issues in Africa.

* *More archives for better monitoring and modeling* – several sensors have flown for decades on diverse families of satellites and provide useful archives on the evolution of land uses and possible environmental impacts of agricultural practices (*e.g.* the American AVHRR sensor with +30 years of data, the French SPOT VGT sensor +12 years of data).

Increasing agricultural productivity:

* *Increasing cost effectiveness* – farmers in several OECD countries (*e.g.* Canada, France, United States) have started using devices with GPS signals and satellite imagery for precision agriculture from planting to harvest, reducing inputs costs and increasing productivity.

* *Better irrigation practices* – adequate irrigation is essential to improve food productivity in many regions. In India, remote sensing technology has been used for preparing groundwater maps in ten states with a 90% success rate of bore wells, with plans to extend the practice nationally.

Challenges:

* Despite the significant capabilities from satellite sensors, raw data and seasonal forecasts are still missing for large parts of the world, due mainly to gaps in coverage and time lags in revisiting certain zones. Advances are being made through the development of new (optical and radar sensors) and more integrated systems around the world.

* The diversity of economic models providing remote sensing data and associated geospatial products to final users is causing inefficiencies and distorting access to information (*e.g.* free data policy in some countries; competition between commercial and institutional providers).

Further reading: OECD (2011), *Space technologies and food security*, Paris (upcoming), Website: *www.oecd.org/futures/space*.

Notes

1. It should be also noted that within year price volatility, not covered in this report, is equally important and receives considerable public attention.

2. Exchange rates are not included in group b) as their movements are very difficult to model at the global level.

3. Those results are baseline specific. The 20% decrease in cereals prices is influenced by the fact that biofuel mandates are binding in most counrties in the current baseline.

References

Abler, D. (2010), "Demand Growth in Developing Countries", *OECD Food, Agriculture and Fisheries Working Papers, No. 29.*

Agriculture and Agri-Food Canada (2010), "The Consequences of a Strong Depreciations of the US Dollar on Agricultural Markets", Ottawa, August 2010.

Anderson, K., C. McRae and D. Wilson (Eds), *The Economics of Quarantine and the SPS Agreement*, Centre for International Economic Studies and AFFA Biosecurity Australia, 2001.

Baffes J. and T. Haniotis, "Placing the 2006/08 Commodity Price Boom into Perspective", *World Bank Policy Research Working Paper 5371.*

Dawe, D., (2010), *The Rice Crisis: Markets, Policies and Food Security*, FAO, Rome.

FAO (2011a), *State of Food and Agriculture 2010-11: Women in Agriculture – Closing the Gender gap for Development*, Rome.

FAO (2011b), J. Gustavvson *et. al.*, *Global Food losses and Food Waste –Causes, Extent and Prevention*, Rome.

FAO (2010a), *Food Outlook*, November, Rome.

FAO (2010b), *Commodity Market Review 2009-2010*, Rome.

FAO (2009), *The State of Agricultural Commodity Markets: High Food Prices and the Food Crisis – Experiences and Lessons Learned*, Rome: Rome.

FAO (2006), *Agricultural Commodity Markets and Trade: New Approaches to Analyzing Market Structure and Instability*, Rome.

FAO (2003), *Consultation on Agricultural Commodity Price Problems*, Rome.

G20 Seoul Summit (2010), Leaders' Declaration, Seoul, Korea.

Headey, D. (2011), "Rethinking the global food crisis: The role of trade shocks", *Food Policy 36 (2011) 136-146.*

HighQuest Partners (2010), "Private Financial Sector Investment in Farmland and Agricultural Infrastructure", *Working Papers, No. 33.*

IMF (2008), *World Economic Outlook (WEO): Financial Stress, Downturns, and Recoveries*, Washington.

International Organization of Securities Commissions (2009), "Task Force on Commodity Futures Markets: Final Report", Madrid, Spain.

Irwin, S.H. and D.R. Saunders (2010), "The Impact of Index and Swap Funds on Commodity Futures Markets", *OECD Food, Agriculture and Fisheries Working Papers, No. 27.*

Jones, D. and A. Kwiecinski (2010), "Policy Responses in Emerging Economies to International Agricultural Commodity Price Surges", *OECD Food, Agriculture and Fisheries, Working Papers, No. 34.*

Martin, W. and K. Anderson, "Export Restrictions and Price Insulation during Commodity Price Booms", *World Bank Policy Research Working Paper 5645.*

Masters, M.W. (2008), Testimony before the Committee on Homeland Security and Government Affairs, US Senate, May 20, 2008.

OECD/FAO (2008), *OECD-FAO Agricultural Outlook, 2008-2017.*

OECD (2008a), *Sustainable Management of Water Resources in Agriculture.*

OECD/FAO (2009), *OECD-FAO Agricultural Outlook, 2009-2018.*

OECD/FAO (2010), *OECD-FAO Agricultural Outlook, 2010-2019.*

OECD (2010a), *Sustainable Management of Water Resources in Agriculture.*

OECD (2011a), "Aggregate Model Analysis of Exogenous Risk and Price Variability", Paris.

OECD (2011b), "An Assessment of International Commodity Agreements for Commodity Price Stabilisation", Paris.

Pachauri, R.K. and A. Reisinger (Eds), Contribution of Working Groups I, II and III to the Fourth Assessment Report of the Intergovernmental Panel on Climate Change, pp. 104, IPCC, Geneva, Switzerland.

Robles, M., Torrero, M. and J. von Braun, "When speculation Matters", IFPRI Issue Brief 57.

Tang K. and W. Xiong (2010), Index Investment and Financialization of Commodities.

Thompson, W. and G. Tallard (2010), "Potential Market Effects of Selected Policy Options in emerging Economics to Address Future Commodity Price Surges", OECD Food, Agriculture and Fisheries, Working Papers, No. 35.

Timmer, C. Peter (2010), The Rice Crisis: Markets, Policies and Food Security, FAO, Rome.

Timer, C. Peter (2009), "Rice Price Formation in the Short Run and the Long Run: The Role of Market Structure in Explaining Volatility, Centre for Global Development", Working Paper No. 172.

UNCTAD (2009), "The Financialization of Commodity Markets", UNCTAD Trade and Development Report 2009.

USDA (2010), "Commodity Costs and Returns", see www.ers.usda.gov/Data/CostsAndReturns/.

Wright, Brian, (2011), "Biofuels and Food Security: Time to Consider Safety Valves?", International Policy Council, Policy Focus, February 2011, www.agritrade.org.

Chapter 3

Biofuels

Market situation

World ethanol prices[1] increased by more than 30% in 2010 in the context of a new commodity price spike of ethanol feedstocks, mainly sugar and maize, and firm energy prices. This situation contrasts with 2007/08 where ethanol price movements did not follow the pace of the commodity price increases and ethanol profit margins were reduced. The US became for the first time a net exporter of ethanol in 2010, while exports from Brazil were reduced significantly in a context of sky-high raw sugar prices and relatively more competitive corn-based ethanol when compared to the previous years.

World biodiesel prices[2] have increased in 2010 in a context of rising rapeseed and other vegetable oil prices and high crude oil prices. This price increase is smaller in proportion than for ethanol due to the fact that biodiesel prices remained relatively firm in 2009 compared to crude oil and world vegetable oil prices.

Projection highlights

- World ethanol and biodiesel prices are expected to continue to rally in 2011. Over the Outlook period, ethanol and biodiesel prices are expected to remain firm as policies promoting biofuel use are being implemented and crude oil prices are expected to remain strong (Figure 3.1). Global ethanol (Figure 3.2) and biodiesel production (Figure 3.3) are projected to continue to expand rapidly over the next ten years.

- The US is expected to remain the largest ethanol producer and consumer. As raw sugar prices are projected to fall, sugar cane based ethanol should become more competitive than in 2010 and exports from Brazil should recover in the early years of the Outlook period. The European Union is expected to be by far the major producer and user of biodiesel. Some developing countries (Argentina, Malaysia and Thailand) could play a significant role in biodiesel exports.

- Biofuel production projections in many developing countries are quite uncertain following little or no production increases in recent years. The cultivation of new feedstocks, like jatropha or cassava, does not yet allow for large-scale biofuel production.

Figure 3.1. **Strong ethanol and biodiesel prices over the Outlook period**

Evolution of prices expressed in nominal terms (left) and in real terms (right)

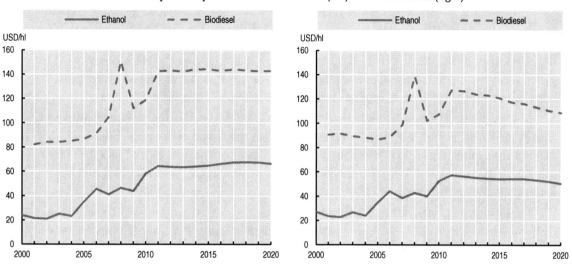

Notes: Ethanol: Brazil, Sao Paulo (ex-distillery), Biodiesel: Producer price Germany net of biodiesel tariff.

Source: OECD and FAO Secretariats.

StatLink http://dx.doi.org/10.1787/888932426448

Figure 3.2. **Development of the world ethanol market**

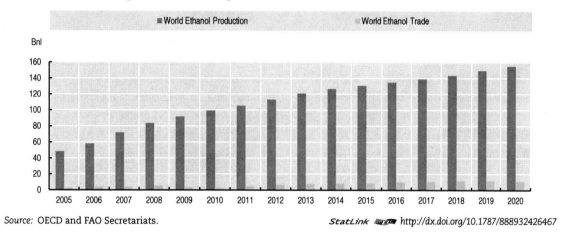

Source: OECD and FAO Secretariats.

StatLink http://dx.doi.org/10.1787/888932426467

Figure 3.3. **Development of the world biodiesel market**

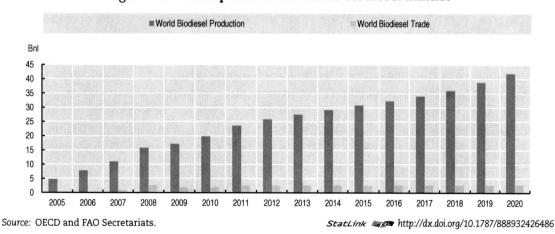

Source: OECD and FAO Secretariats.

StatLink http://dx.doi.org/10.1787/888932426486

Market trends and prospects

Prices

Crude oil prices are assumed to continue to rally in 2011 and to remain constant in real terms over the remainder of the Outlook period. Expressed in nominal terms, they are projected to reach USD 107/barrel by 2020. World ethanol and biodiesel prices are expected to increase further in 2011. This increase is expected to be stronger for biodiesel, which should bring price ratios of biodiesel to vegetable oil and crude oil closer to their pre-2007 levels.

The expansion of biofuel production and use over the projection period should be mainly driven as in the past years by policy support in the forms of use mandates or other targets that impact use, tax relief for producers and consumers of biofuels, broader protection measures and fuel quality specifications as well as by investment capacities in leading producing countries.

In this context, ethanol and biodiesel prices are expected to remain firm over the Outlook period (Figure 3.1). They are projected to be on average 80% higher than over the previous decade in the case of ethanol and 45% in the case of biodiesel. They will reach, respectively, USD 66.4 per hl and USD 142.9 per hl by 2020. Prices should decrease slightly when expressed in real terms over the Outlook period but the ratios of biofuel prices to major biofuel feedstock prices are expected to remain relatively stable.[3] Biofuels are expected to become somewhat more competitive over the course of the projection period as their prices should increase less rapidly than crude oil prices.

Production and use of biofuels

Driven by policy mandates and renewable energy goals around the world, global ethanol and biodiesel productions are projected to continue their rapid increases over the projection period and to reach respectively some 155 bnl and 42 bnl by 2020. These projections are subject to important uncertainties which are described below in the main uncertainties section.

IEA (2010) provides a clear definition of first generation biofuels and second generation biofuels. Typical first generation biofuels are sugarcane ethanol, starch-based or "corn" ethanol and biodiesel. The feedstock for producing first generation biofuels either consists of sugar, starch and oil crops or animal fats, which in most cases can also be used as food and feed or consists of food residues. Second generation biofuels are those biofuels produced from cellulose, hemicellulose or lignin. Examples of 2nd-generation biofuels are cellulosic ethanol and Fischer-Tropsch fuels.

Developed countries

With the implementation of the Renewable Fuels Standard (RFS2) Final Rule,[4] the United States will remain the major player on the ethanol market. Despite current policy uncertainty, this *Outlook* assumes that the tax credit to blenders of ethanol and biodiesel as well as the tariff on imported fuel ethanol will remain in effect. In the US, ethanol use for fuel is expected to increase continuously over the projection period and to reach almost 71 bnl by 2020 (Figure 3.4), below the 2020 standards of 110 bnl.[5] It should represent an average share of 8.4% in gasoline types for transport fuel by 2020.[6]

Research and development on cellulosic ethanol does not yet allow for large scale production. Second generation ethanol production is thus only projected to expand in the latter years of the projection period to reach 4.3 bnl in 2020 and to remain far from meeting

Figure 3.4. **Projected development of the US ethanol market**

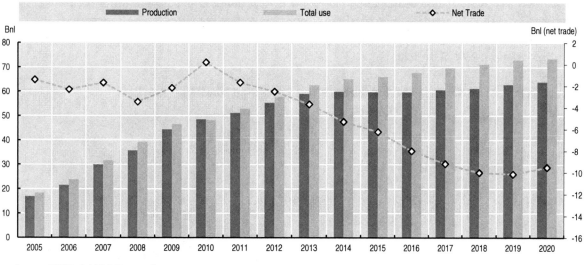

Source: OECD and FAO Secretariats.

StatLink ⟶ http://dx.doi.org/10.1787/888932426505

the RFS2 cellulosic biofuel requirement of 40 bnl. Domestic production, mainly derived from corn, should account for most of the US ethanol consumption. RFS2 allows 56.8 bnl of first generation corn based ethanol by 2015, which is capped thereafter.

The US Environmental Protection Agency provided a decision in January 2011 on the expansion of the ethanol blending permission into regular gasoline from 10% to 15%[7] for cars built in 2001 or later. In practice, the impact of this decision should be minimal in the short term as retailers are not likely to propose different types of gasoline to their consumers as different pumps would be needed and warranty as well as liability issues still need to be resolved. In the medium term, this decision should reduce the impact of the blending wall because of the price competitiveness of ethanol. Over the Outlook period, the blending wall of 10% of ethanol blended into regular gasoline is expected to be achieved by 2012.

The biomass-based diesel requirement mandate defined in the RFS2 calls for 3.8 bnl of biodiesel to be used by 2012. This mandate is not defined after 2012, it is assumed to remain unchanged over the rest of the Outlook period. It drives the initial growth in US biodiesel use, which should in the latter years of the projection period continue to increase to reach 4.8 bnl by 2020. Biodiesel use will contribute to filling the non-cellulosic advanced biofuels mandate of 57 bnl in 2020. Biodiesel production from tallow or other animal fat, waste oils as well as from corn oil by-product of ethanol plants is expected to represent more than 60% of US biodiesel production.

The Renewable Energy Directive (RED) implemented by the European Union states that the share of renewable energy sources (including non-liquids) should increase to 10% of total transport fuel use by 2020. The RED allows for substitution with other renewable sources such as electric cars. The contribution of second generation biofuels will be counted twice[8] toward EU RED mitigation targets. This Outlook does not make assumptions on the development of the fleet of electric cars or of alternative renewable energy sources.

Total biodiesel use in the European Union is projected to increase by almost 85% over the projection period and to reach around 20 bnl by 2020 representing an average share of biodiesel in diesel type fuels of 6.5%, 70% higher than over the 2008-2010 period.[9] Domestic biodiesel production should increase to keep pace with demand (Figure 3.5). Imports are expected to remain pretty stable at about 2 bnl on average over the projection period. From 2018, second generation biodiesel production is assumed to accelerate, with an output of about 2.2 bnl in 2020.

Figure 3.5. **Projected development of the European biodiesel market**

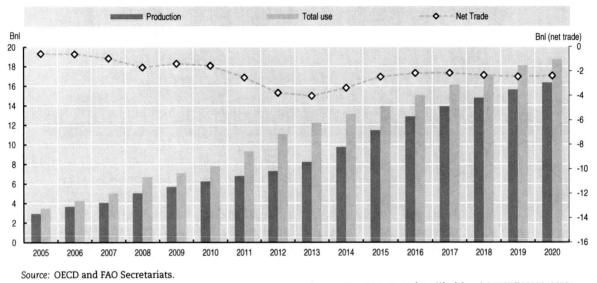

Source: OECD and FAO Secretariats.

StatLink 🔗 http://dx.doi.org/10.1787/888932426524

European ethanol production mainly wheat, coarse grains and sugar beet based is projected to increase to almost 16.5 bnl in 2020. The production of second generation ethanol is assumed to increase in the last years of the *Outlook* and to reach 1.6 bnl by 2020. Gasoline consumption is assumed to stagnate over the projection period when compared to the base period. This combined with the solid development of ethanol use for fuel should lead to an average ethanol share of 8.2% in gasoline types for transport fuels by 2020.

When the energy content of ethanol and biodiesel is added together and the contribution of second generation biofuels is counted twice as in the RED mitigation target calculations, this *Outlook* projects that the share of renewable energy sources coming from biofuels could reach almost 8.5% of transport fuel use of the gasoline and diesel vehicles fleet, up from 5% on average over the 2008-2010 period. Thus, this Outlook implies that the 2020 EU RED target would not be reached.

In Canada, the mandate calls for an ethanol share of 5% in gasoline type fuel use in volume terms. It is projected to be filled by 2011 and maintained throughout the projection period. Canadian ethanol consumption is thus projected to grow in line with fuel consumption. Domestic production is expected to rise over the projection period to reach almost 2.4 bnl in 2020. Biodiesel use is projected to comply with the biodiesel blending mandate of 1.6% (2% in volume terms) for all transport diesel as well as heating oil by 2012.

In Australia, the ethanol share in gasoline type fuel use is expected to remain almost unchanged over the projection period at about 1.6%. It is assumed to be driven by policies in place in New South Wales and Queensland where ethanol blending mandates have been introduced in 2010. The biodiesel share in diesel type fuel use should remain at around 2.7% all over the projection period. Most of biodiesel production should be based on animal tallow.

Developing countries

In 2010, biofuels production was significantly below expectations in most developing countries having implemented mandates or ambitious targets for the use of biofuels. Brazil and Argentina are the exceptions. This results primarily from the fact that commercial cultivation of alternative crops usable for biofuel production like jatropha or cassava is in most cases still on a project or small-scale level. This does not allow for large-scale biofuel production, except in a few countries like Nigeria or Ghana where cassava cultivation is well established. Over the projection period, due to slow growing domestic biofuel supply in the developing world, it is likely that biofuel consumption remains significantly below targets and/or mandates. Exceptions are countries which already have a high potential for sugar cane or vegetable oil, predominately palm oil, production.

Brazil, India and China, should account for 85% of the 71 bnl ethanol production in the developing world expected by 2020. In China, the majority of ethanol produced is used for non-fuel uses in the food and chemical industry. Asian and South-American regions should also become notable ethanol producers. In Thailand, production is expected to grow by 1.5 bnl to reach about 2.2 bnl by 2020.

Investments in ethanol producing capacities are expected to continue to occur and ethanol production derived from sugar cane is expected to rapidly expand, growing by almost 6% per year over the projection period to meet both domestic and international demand. Brazil is projected to be the second largest ethanol producer, with a 33% share of global production in 2020. The situation on Brazilian ethanol market should be different from the one that prevailed in 2010 as ethanol production is expected to regain competitiveness with respect to sugar production due to a combination of factors: raw sugar prices are projected to be lower in the early years of the Outlook period, sugar cane area is expected to expand, sugar cane yields are expected to recover from the bad 2010 harvest and investments in the ethanol markets are expected to continue such that production capacities should be further expanded. About half of the sugar cane output is expected to be channelled to ethanol production. Brazilian ethanol domestic use is expected to increase over the projection period to reach 41 bnl in 2020 (Figure 3.6). This growth is mainly driven by the growing fleet of flexi-fuel vehicles.

The greatest biodiesel producer in the developing world will still be Argentina which will account for about 25% (3.2 bnl) of total biodiesel produced in the developing countries and 8% of global biodiesel production by 2020. In Brazil, biodiesel production based on soybean oil or possibly palmoil is also expected to increase beyond 3 bnl by 2020 as a result of an increasing domestic demand driven by biodiesel mandates. By contrast, Argentina (after fulfilling her domestic consumption target) should continue to focus on export markets due to the incentives offered by the differential export tax system. The same is true for Malaysia, where production should further increase to about 1.3 bnl in 2020. Other East Asian countries like Thailand, Indonesia and India will also significantly increase their domestic biodiesel production, each to about 1-1.5 bnl. However, most of this would be for domestic consumption due to ambitious domestic biodiesel blending targets.

Figure 3.6. **Projected development of the Brazilian ethanol market**

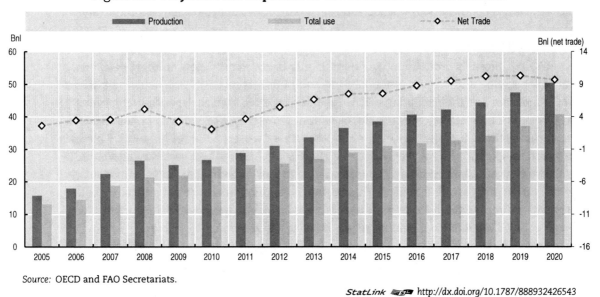

Source: OECD and FAO Secretariats.

StatLink http://dx.doi.org/10.1787/888932426543

Feedstocks used to produce biofuels

Figure 3.7 presents projected ethanol production growth by the various feedstocks used. Maize and sugar cane should remain the major ethanol feedstocks over the coming decade. By 2020, 44% of global ethanol is expected to be produced from coarse grains and 36% from sugar cane. Cellulosic ethanol production should represent only 5% of global production. In developed countries, the share of corn based ethanol over total ethanol produced should decrease from 89% on average over the 2008-10 period to 78% in 2020. Wheat based ethanol should account for 6% of ethanol production in developed countries compared to 3% over the base period, most of this development being in the EU. Sugar beet based ethanol should account for about 4% of ethanol production throughout the

Figure 3.7. **Evolution of global ethanol production by feedstocks used**

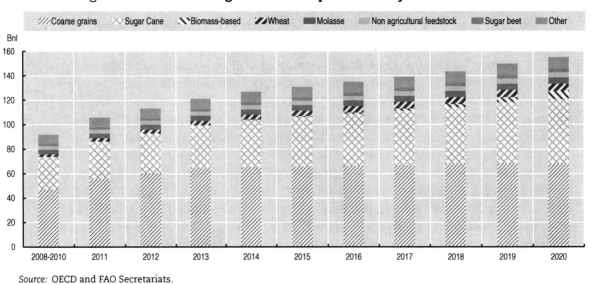

Source: OECD and FAO Secretariats.

StatLink http://dx.doi.org/10.1787/888932426562

projection period. Cellulosic ethanol production is expected to become increasingly important in developed countries from 2017, to represent about 8% of total ethanol production by 2020.

In developing countries, more than 80% of the ethanol produced in 2020 is expected to be based on sugar cane which results from the dominance of Brazilian ethanol production. Ethanol based on roots and tubers such as cassava is projected to account for only about 4%. The picture differs if the Brazilian ethanol market is excluded. In that case, in the developing world, if the share of molasses in ethanol production reaches 40% of ethanol production, the shares of sugar cane based ethanol as well as coarse grains based ethanol should be of 17%. The share of roots and tuber is also much higher (15%). In particular the cultivation of cassava for ethanol production might have a high potential in the developing world. However, high production costs and small-scale production structures, especially in comparison to sugar cane, currently hamper a noticeable market expansion.

Figure 3.8 presents the split of the projected biodiesel production growth between the various feedstocks used. More than 75% of global biodiesel production is expected to come from vegetable oil in 2020. Jatropha should account for 7% of global biodiesel production in 2020. In developed countries, the share of vegetable oil based biodiesel over total biodiesel produced should decrease from 85% on average over the 2008-10 period to 75% in 2020. Biodiesel produced from non agricultural sources such as fat and tallow, as well as from waste oils and by-products of ethanol production, should represent about 15% of total biodiesel produced in the developed world over the projection period. Second generation biodiesel production is expected to grow in developed countries from 2018 and to represent about 10% of global biodiesel in 2020.

Figure 3.8. **Evolution of global biodiesel production by feedstocks used**

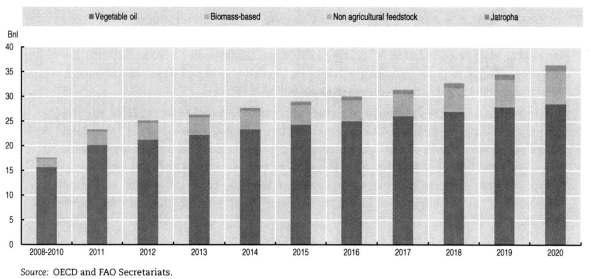

Source: OECD and FAO Secretariats.

StatLink ⟶ http://dx.doi.org/10.1787/888932426581

The most important biodiesel feedstock in the developing world should remain vegetable oils based on palm or soybean oil. This will be a result of the strong production increase in Argentina and Brazil, where biodiesel is produced predominately from soybean oil. The share of jatropha is expected to only account for 10% (19% when excluding Brazil and Argentina) of biodiesel produced in 2020 in the developing world due to the slow growth of cultivation capacities. Rapeseed oil is of minor importance for biodiesel production in developing countries with the exception of Chile where the climatic conditions allow for rapeseed cultivation. Biodiesel production from rapeseed oil is also expected to develop in transition countries like Ukraine and Kazakhstan. Less important from a global perspective but notable from a national perspective is the production of biodiesel based on tallow in Paraguay and Uruguay, as a result of the large livestock sector in these countries.

Biofuel use will continue to represent an important share of global cereal, sugar crops and vegetable oil production over the Outlook period. By 2020, 12% of the global production of coarse grains will be used to produce ethanol compared to 11% on average over the 2008-10 period 16% of the global production of vegetable oil will be used to produce biodiesel compared to 11% on average over the 2008-10 period and 33% of the global production of sugar compared to 21% on average over the 2008-10 period. Over the projection period, 21% of the global coarse grains production's increase, 29% of the global vegetable oil production's increase and 68% of the global sugar cane production's increase are expected to go to biofuels.

Trade in ethanol and biodiesel

Trade in ethanol[10] is expected to represent about 7% of global production on average over the projection period. It is expected to recover from the 2010 situation where Brazilian ethanol exports were very low. To keep pace with demand and given the expected slow growth in second generation ethanol production, net imports from the US should reach 9.5 bnl in 2020. Imports of sugarcane based ethanol can be counted in the RFS2 mandate towards the "advanced" category. Part of the US ethanol imports are expected to be Brazilian ethanol dehydrated in the Caribbean, imported with duty-free access under the Caribbean Basin Initiative. At the global level, growth in trade comes almost entirely by expanding exports from Brazil and Thailand. Brazilian ethanol exports are expected to reach 9.7 bnl by 2020. For Thailand, ethanol exports are expected to increase to about 0.5 bnl in 2020. In the EU, ethanol imports should initially grow to meet increasing ethanol demand to reach about 4 bnl in 2013. Due to the sustainability criteria of the RED and the expected development of cellulosic ethanol in the latter years of the Outlook period, ethanol imports are expected to decrease to 2.3 bnl by 2020.

Argentina is expected to remain the most important biodiesel exporter. Here, exports should reach about 2.5 bnl by 2020. Malaysian exports will also increase by 0.4 bnl to total 0.8 bnl and Colombia will export 0.25 bnl in 2020. Biodiesel trade will remain low as most countries with binding mandates tend to produce biodiesel domestically. Import needs from the EU are expected to remain fairly constant over the projection period at around 2 bnl per year as European production is expected to increase in line with European demand.

Main issues and uncertainties

The development of biofuel markets is subject to many uncertainties which are discussed in this section. Box 3.1 draws on OECD (2010, 2012) to describe possible implications of the projected expansion of agricultural bioenergy feedstocks on water systems.

Evolution of policies

The last few years have shown how biofuel markets can be strongly affected by changes in policy packages, macroeconomic events and changes in crude oil prices. The interplay of those different factors impacts on the profitability of the industry and thus modifies investors' decisions and spending on R&D. At the moment, there is considerable uncertainty concerning the renewal of the US blender tax credit and ethanol tariff. If those policy elements were to be removed, the full integration of the US in the world ethanol market would change the prospects of this *Outlook*. For example, US biodiesel production could decline substantially as was the case when the renewal of the blenders credit was delayed in 2010. Brazilian ethanol exports could be channelled directly to the US with sugar cane based ethanol being relatively more competitive than corn based ethanol. With the maturity of the biofuel industry and the growing concerns on the competition between food and fuel and its impact on food prices, it is possible that government subsidies and other budget-sensitive measures in support of biofuel production or consumption could be subject to gradual cuts.

From first generation biofuels to other sources of renewable energy

Biofuels produced from agricultural feedstock were, and still are, envisaged as a first step towards the development of renewable energy sources for liquid transportation fuels. The future transition to second generation biofuels produced from lignocellulosic biomass, waste material or other non-food feedstocks depends on the advancement of R&D over the next few years and on investments that are currently being made, as well as on the continuation of biofuel policy packages that have set up ambitious mandates for the production of second-generation biofuels. In this context, commercial production does not depend solely on full economic viability. This *Outlook* remains very cautious on the medium-term potential of second generation biofuels which is only expected to be realised towards the very end of the projection period. Continued slow development of second generation biofuels could lead to additional import demand for the countries with strong biofuel use mandates. Other sources of renewable energy could play a larger role in future years. The RED explicitly allows for renewable electricity used in the transport sector to count towards the 10% renewable energy share in transport fuels. The pace of development of electrical or hybrid vehicles remains uncertain for the time being but could potentially reduce the need for biofuels derived from agricultural products to meet the mandates set up by European member states.

Sustainability criteria

The sustainability criteria that are embedded in the policies of major countries consuming biofuels are expected to continue to affect biofuel markets. Biofuel producers in the United States and in the EU have to comply with more drastic GHG emission targets. The RFS2 Final Rule requires specific GHG emission reductions for the various biofuels. Conventional renewable fuels must reduce GHG by 20% when compared to gasoline, advanced biomass-based diesel and non-cellulosic advanced biofuels by 50% and cellulosic biofuels by 60%. Existing conventional ethanol production facilities are exempt from this requirement, but new plants will have to comply. The RED specifies that a given biofuel has to achieve a saving of at least 35% in GHG. This 35% threshold will rise to 50% in 2017 for existing plants and 60% for new production facilities.

On the trade side, the impacts of the sustainability criteria may also be considerable as they could limit the availability of imported biofuels or biofuel feedstock if countries do not comply with the policies in place in importing countries. Disputes are likely to develop on the GHG emission savings of different biofuels. For example, for the US RFS2, the default

GHG emission saving of soybean oil based biodiesel is defined as 57%, above the 50% threshold fixed by the policy. For the RED, this default saving is only 31%, below the 35% threshold fixed by the policy. This difference could affect trade of soybean, soybean oil (for biodiesel production) or soybean oil based biodiesel once the RED is implemented. Meanwhile, trade in palm oil based biodiesel may be affected by requirements to certify environmentally and socially sustainable production.

Development of biofuel industries in developing countries

Availability of reported data concerning biofuel production and use is not good in many developing countries. The stated intention in some of these countries is to substantially increase production capacities as well as domestic use in the coming years. If the countries have low domestic production capacities for biofuel feedstocks, it is uncertain that they will be able to meet domestic demand without using imports. In countries where traditional biofuel feedstocks are not produced in large quantities, plans are in place or being developed to increase the production capacities of alternative, non-edible feedstocks, first and foremost jatropha. These crops might be a very effective option for biofuel production. However, competitive large-scale jatropha production does not currently exist and the current production quantities from small-scale plantations are far below the initial expectations. Rapid improvement of planting materials adapted to different growing conditions using biotechnology and advanced breeding methods could dramatically change jatropha's potential. Thus, it is still possible that a notable increase in these alternative feedstocks may occur but as to when and to what extent is very uncertain.

Another aspect concerning developing countries is where high biofuel production capacities have already been installed. Some of these countries could become important exporters in the future, such as Malaysia and Indonesia in the case of biodiesel. Current production in Malaysia accounts for approximately 45% of the available production capacity, estimated at 1.75 bnl in 2010. Even less of available capacity is currently used in Indonesia, where only about 10% of the installed capacity (estimated to about 4 bnl) was used in 2010. It is not clear if these capacities might be more fully utilised or might even continue to grow over the next years. The EU RED sustainability and certification scheme is likely to affect palm oil based biodiesel imports and thus might negatively impact Malaysian and Indonesian biodiesel production and exports.

Box 3.1. **The implications of the projected expansion of agricultural bioenergy feedstocks on water systems**

World agriculture faces an enormous challenge in the coming decades, to produce more food, feed and fibre due to rising populations and incomes and changing dietary habits. With additional pressures from growing urbanisation, industrialisation and climate change, sustainable management of water systems will be vital.

The projected growth in agricultural bioenergy feedstock production (e.g. from grains, oilseeds, etc) has raised concerns about the pressure this may have on water systems. In practice, as the cultivation of feedstocks for agricultural bioenergy is no different than the same crops destined for food, fibre or feed purposes, their environmental consequences should be similar. Nevertheless, the rapid expansion of bioenergy feedstock production has raised concerns related to the competition for water resources in regions where scarce water resources are an issue and the impacts on water quality where water pollution is a concern.

Box 3.1. **The implications of the projected expansion of agricultural bioenergy feedstocks on water systems** (cont.)

Overall impacts on **water resources** from cultivation of agricultural feedstocks to produce bioenergy (biofuels, power and heat) can be difficult to trace. The extent to which feedstock production draws on the need for irrigation varies by feedstock type and region. Rain-fed rapeseed in Europe, for example, requires no irrigation, while maize in the United States is largely rain-fed, with only about 3% of national irrigation water withdrawals devoted to biofuel crops. Globally some 1% of water withdrawn for irrigation is estimated to be applied for biofuel crops. The amount of water needed to produce each unit of energy from second generation biofuel feedstocks (*e.g.* harvest cellulosic residues) is three to seven times lower than the water required to produce ethanol from maize, rapeseed, etc.[*]

Second generation feedstocks, such as from trees, can capture a greater share of annual rainfall, compared to annually sown crops, in areas where much of the rainfall occurs outside the normal crop growing season, and also help reduce soil erosion and bring flood control benefits. While second generation feedstocks offer the potential for reducing irrigation water demand, it is not necessarily a clear outcome, as this may depend on the feedstocks grown, location of production and the reference first generation feedstocks. Moreover, some second generation feedstocks may require irrigation during establishment and to achieve high yields, hence, the final impact on water balances are uncertain.

The **water quality** impacts from bioenergy feedstock production derive from the management practices used in their cultivation, including the use of agro-chemicals, while the processing plants to convert raw materials to bioenergy can also have impacts on water quality. Much of the projected production of biofuels are expected to be derived from maize, which could result in increased levels of soil sediment and nutrient water pollution, particularly where maize is cultivated on marginal agricultural land which contributes to the highest soil sediment and nutrient run-off loads. This may have significant consequences for water quality, especially rivers and coastal areas. For wood plantations used as bioenergy feedstocks, the clearance of streamside vegetation in wood management systems may change physical properties of water systems, such as the turbidity, stream temperature and light infiltration of water bodies. If nutrient inputs are required for wood plantations, infiltration of nutrients may also pose a risk to groundwater.

A key **conclusion** from most studies on the links between bioenergy production from agricultural feedstocks on water is that in general feedstocks from annual crops, such as maize and oilseeds, can have a more damaging impact on water systems than second generation feedstocks, such as reed canary grass and short rotation woodlands. Another important conclusion is that the location of production and the type of tillage practice, crop rotation system and other farm management practices used in producing feedstocks for bioenergy production will also greatly influence water systems. Moreover, the increasing use of bioenergy from agricultural and food wastes and residues (*e.g.* straw, manure, food waste, animals fats) may help to lower the demand for production of feedstocks from cultivated crops and hence, reduce environmental impacts.

But a note of caution is important here, as the potential impacts on water resource and quality from growing agricultural feedstocks for bioenergy production have not been fully evaluated.

[*] See Hoogeveen, J; J-M Faurès; N. Van de Giessen (2009), "Increased Biofuel Production in the Coming Decade; To What Extent will it Affect Global Freshwater Resources?", *Irrigation and Drainage*, Vol. 58, pp. S148-S160.

Sources: For the full bibliography from which this Box is drawn see OECD (2010), *Sustainable Management of Water Resources in Agriculture*, Publishing Service, Paris, *www.oecd.org/agriculture/water*; and OECD (2012 forthcoming), *Sustainable Management of Water Quality in Agriculture*, Publishing Service, Paris.

Notes

1. Brazil, Sao Paolo (ex-distillery).

2. Producer price Germany net of biodiesel tariff.

3. Cycles in raw sugar production imply fluctuations in the world raw sugar price. The ratio between the world ethanol price and the world raw sugar price is not expected to remain stable over the Outlook period. However, the strong expected decrease in world raw sugar price in the early years of the Outlook period is expected to lower the pressure on world ethanol markets.

4. More information can be found on the RFS2 Final Rule on the following website: *www.epa.gov/otaq/renewablefuels/420f10007.htm*

5. The 110 bnl figure represents the sum of the Conventional Renewable fuels mandate in 2020 (15 bn gallons, *i.e* 57 bnl) and of the mandate for total advanced biofuels except biomass-based diesel (14 bn gallons, *i.e.* 53 bnl).

6. All biofuel use shares are expressed on the basis of energy contained unless otherwise specified.

7. Expressed in volume share. See *www.epa.gov/otaq/regs/fuels/additive/e15.index.htm*

8. "For the purposes of demonstrating compliance with national renewable energy obligations placed on operators and the target for the use of energy from renewable sources in all forms of transport referred to in Article 3(4), the contribution made by biofuels produced from wastes, residues, non-food cellulosic material, and ligno-cellulosic material shall be considered to be twice that made by other biofuels". Directive 2009/28/EC of the European Parliament and Council (Renewable Energy Directive), 2009.

9. Diesel consumption is assumed to increase by 9% in the EU over the Outlook period when compared to the 2008-10 period.

10. Note that trade projections for ethanol, in addition to pure fuel alcohol, also include ethanol for other purposes as well as the ethanol share in gasoline blends.

Reference

IEA (2010), Sustainable Production of Second-General Biofuels: Potential and Perspectives in Major Economics and Developing Countries.

ANNEX 3.A

Statistical tables: Biofuels

Table 3.A.1. Biofuel projections: Ethanol

	PRODUCTION (MN L)		Growth (%)[1]	DOMESTIC USE (MN L)		Growth (%)[1]	FUEL USE (MN L)		Growth (%)[1]	SHARE IN GAZOLINE TYPE FUEL USE(%)				NET TRADE (MN L)[2]	
										Energy Shares		Volume Shares			
	Average 2008-10est.	2020	2011-20	Average 2008-10est.	2020	2011-20	Average 2008-10est.	2020	2011-20	Average 2008-10est.	2020	Average 2008-10est.	2020	Average 2008-10est.	2020
NORTH AMERICA															
Canada	1 483	2 359	3.08	1 530	2 408	0.57	1 324	2 202	0.66	2.2	3.4	3.3	5.0	-48	-49
United States	42 857	63 961	1.89	44 663	73 474	3.32	42 338	70 484	4.13	5.3	8.4	7.7	12.1	-1 806	-9 514
of which second generation	3	4 368	..	..	..	..	..	..	..	..	..	..	..	..	..
WESTERN EUROPE															
EU(27)	5 651	16 316	10.50	7 186	18 690	7.31	4 687	16 173	8.09	2.3	8.2	3.4	11.8	-1 536	-2 374
of which second generation	0	1 626	..	..	..	..	..	..	..	..	..	..	..	..	..
OCEANIA DEVELOPED															
Australia	299	492	0.75	299	492	0.75	299	492	0.75	1.0	1.6	1.5	2.3	0	0
OTHER DEVELOPED															
Japan	307	946	13.28	704	1 715	5.81	90	1 687	18.26	0.0	0.0	0.0	0.0	-398	-769
of which second generation	0	593	..	..	..	..	..	..	..	..	..	..	..	..	..
South Africa	384	421	0.44	93	47	0.07	0	0	4.62	0.0	0.0	0.0	0.0	291	374
SUB-SAHARIAN AFRICA															
Mozambique	25	59	6.17	21	29	0.56	0	9	1.48	0.0	3.3	0.0	4.8	4	29
Tanzania	29	55	7.14	33	52	5.97	1	19	37.15	0.1	2.7	0.2	4.0	-4	3
LATIN AMERICA AND CARRIBBEAN															
Argentina	303	470	2.20	240	402	0.97	110	272	1.47	1.6	3.4	2.3	5.0	63	68
Brazil	26 091	50 393	5.98	22 589	40 695	5.15	21 061	38 383	7.28	47.3	67.1	57.2	75.3	3 502	9 698
Columbia	310	587	5.63	353	385	-1.20	315	347	-1.33	4.5	5.6	6.6	8.1	-44	202
Mexico	64	90	2.29	168	275	2.29	0	0	..	0.0	0.0	0.0	0.0	-104	-184
Peru	71	217	2.55	25	175	1.47	20	174	1.48	1.1	8.2	1.7	11.7	46	41
ASIA AND PACIFIC															
China	7 189	7 930	0.71	7 041	6 685	0.18	2 024	2 975	4.34	1.8	1.5	2.6	2.3	148	1 246
India	1 892	2 204	1.78	2 109	2 818	1.48	183	800	1.48	0.9	3.0	1.4	4.5	-217	-614
Indonesia	210	248	0.99	169	168	0.15	0	0	6.77	0.0	0.0	0.0	0.0	41	80
Malaysia	66	74	0.80	87	85	0.09	0	0	5.38	0.0	0.0	0.0	0.0	-21	-11
Philippines	118	603	12.74	263	450	3.49	193	350	-0.30	2.1	3.0	3.1	4.4	-144	153
Thailand	672	2 111	9.32	599	1 602	8.72	424	1 389	4.54	3.8	11.2	5.6	15.9	73	509
Turkey	64	88	0.98	108	142	3.43	50	87	5.23	0.6	0.9	0.9	1.3	-44	-54
Viet Nam	150	423	4.75	95	334	14.84	8	255	25.87	0.1	3.5	0.2	5.1	55	90
TOTAL	**91 657**	**154 962**	**3.98**	**91 821**	**155 983**	**3.95**	**73 742**	**136 123**	**4.45**	**5.3**	**8.8**	**7.7**	**12.6**	**3 792**	**11 012**

1. Least-squares growth rate (see glossary).
2. For total net trade exports are shown.
.. Data not available.
Source: OECD and FAO Secretariats.

StatLink http://dx.doi.org/10.1787/888932427664

Table 3.A.2. Biofuel projections: Biodiesel

	PRODUCTION (MN L)		Growth (%)[1]	DOMESTIC USE (MN L)		Growth (%)[1]	SHARE IN DIESEL TYPE FUEL USE(%)				NET TRADE (MN L)[2]	
							Energy Shares		Volume Shares			
	Average 2008-10est.	2020	2011-20	Average 2008-10est.	2020	2011-20	Average 2008-10est.	2020	Average 2008-10est.	2020	Average 2008-10est.	2020
NORTH AMERICA												
Canada	236	594	6.57	202	672	3.65	0.4	1.6	0.5	2.0	34	-78
United States	1 658	4 002	2.24	909	4 757	5.39	0.3	1.3	0.4	1.6	748	-755
WESTERN EUROPE												
European Union	9 184	17 610	5.17	10 802	19 794	4.75	3.9	6.6	4.9	8.1	-1 619	-2 184
of which second generation	0	2 190	..	..	..	..					..	..
OCEANIA DEVELOPED												
Australia	627	719	1.14	627	719	1.14	2.7	2.7	3.4	3.3	0	0
OTHER DEVELOPED												
South Africa	57	100	3.65	57	100	3.66	0.0	0.0	0.0	0.0	0	0
Sub-Saharian Africa												
Mozambique	51	80	1.85	0	32	1.47	0.0	0.0	0.0	0.0	51	48
Tanzania	50	61	-0.13	0	58	159.22	0.0	0.0	0.0	0.0	50	3
LATIN AMERICA AND CARIBBEAN												
Argentina	1 576	3 231	3.36	247	656	2.13	1.9	4.0	2.3	5.0	1 329	2 576
Brazil	1 550	3 139	2.66	1 550	3 139	2.66	2.7	4.0	3.4	5.0	0	0
Columbia	302	768	4.88	228	430	4.77	1.6	4.0	2.0	5.0	75	338
Peru	174	130	3.74	174	315	4.35	1.6	4.0	2.0	5.0	0	-185
ASIA AND PACIFIC												
India	179	3 293	26.87	241	3 291	26.87	0.0	0.1	0.0	0.1	-61	2
Indonesia	369	811	6.65	272	1 100	14.37	1.3	5.7	1.7	7.0	98	-289
Malaysia	765	1 331	3.96	206	500	8.35	1.6	4.0	2.0	5.0	559	831
Philippines	158	271	3.97	158	200	1.70	0.0	0.0	0.0	0.0	0	71
Thailand	584	1 697	8.15	561	1 200	5.67	1.9	4.0	2.3	5.0	24	497
Turkey	62	52	5.54	62	187	3.39	0.0	0.0	0.0	0.0	0	-135
Viet Nam	8	100	17.76	0	100	17.93	0.0	0.0	0.0	0.0	8	0
TOTAL	**17 608**	**41 917**	**5.99**	**16 314**	**40 938**	**6.44**	**2.0**	**3.8**	**2.5**	**4.7**	**2 111**	**2 737**

1. Least-squares growth rate (see glossary).
2. For total net trade exports are shown.
.. Data not available.
Source: OECD and FAO Secretariats.

StatLink http://dx.doi.org/10.1787/888932427683

Chapter 4

Cereals

Market situation

As 2010 progressed, the global supply outlook worsened after a severe drought in the Russian Federation – prompting the country to impose a ban on grain exports – and unexpected weather events adversely affected other major grain producing countries. Within a few months, the forecast for 2010 world cereal production, initially expected to be the second highest on record, had to be revised downward by roughly 31 Mt. Actual 2010 production fell 1.4% below 2009 levels.

Not all cereals were affected negatively by adverse climatic conditions. Rice production reached record levels in 2010 which, combined with high opening stocks, helped rice markets withstand the upward price pressure other cereals experienced. Both wheat and coarse grain production were hampered by unfavourable weather, pushing up international prices during the first half of the season. Initially, wheat and barley markets reacted vigorously; however, good inventory levels, relatively large export supplies and reduced import demand (because of good production in many importing countries) helped mitigate surging world prices. On the other hand, the maize supply situation deteriorated considerably when yields in the US were poorer than initially expected. With inventories already low and overall demand not showing signs of easing, international maize prices surged, surpassing 2008 records. High maize (and soybean) prices helped sustain the international prices of other grains, wheat in particular, throughout most of the season.

Projection highlights

- By 2020, wheat prices in nominal terms are projected well above the historical average. Maize prices are expected to be up sharply from the historical average, narrowing the wheat to maize price ratio. Nominal rice prices are projected at around USD 490/t by 2020. In real terms, cereal prices are expected to decline, yet remain above levels in previous decades.

- World cereal production is expected to rebound in 2011 and 2012 as a response to higher returns, increasing gradually during the rest of the projection period. Cereal stocks are projected to moderately expand but stocks-to-use ratios remain below historical averages.

- Trade of wheat and coarse grain increases at a slightly slower pace than in the past. Whereas the US keeps its leading position as maize exporter, the Commonwealth of Independent States (CIS) becomes the major source of wheat exports in 2020. Trade of rice is expected to increase faster than in the past, which may turn Vietnam into the world's largest exporter.

Figure 4.1. **Cereal prices in nominal and real terms**[1]

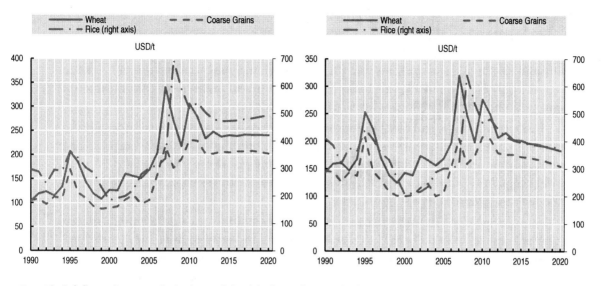

Note: The left figure shows nominal prices and the right figure shows real prices.

1. The world reference price for wheat is the No. 2 Hard Red Winter, USA f.o.b. Gulf Ports. For coarse grains, it is the US maize price No. 2 Yellow, f.o.b. Gulf Ports and for rice, it is the Thai white 100% B, milled, f.o.b.

Source: OECD and FAO Secretariats.

StatLink ⟊⟊ http://dx.doi.org/10.1787/888932426600

Figure 4.2. **Cereal production, demand and closing stocks**

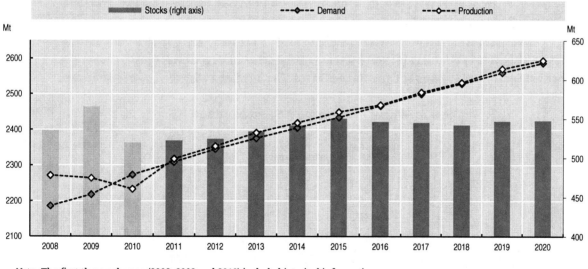

Note: The first three columns (2008, 2009 and 2010) include historical information.

Source: OECD and FAO Secretariats.

StatLink ⟊⟊ http://dx.doi.org/10.1787/888932426619

Market trends and prospects

Prices

US wheat prices could average slightly lower in 2011, in anticipation of rebounding world production (Figure 4.1). By 2012, the 2010 price spike is assumed to have been mitigated by the higher supply response. By 2020, nominal wheat prices are projected to approach USD 240/t, well above the historical average. In real terms, prices are expected to slightly decline, albeit from higher levels than in past decades.

While increasing in nominal prices over the projection period, maize prices could reach USD 203/t in 2020, which would be up sharply from the historical average; in real terms, they are still heading for a decline. Nominal rice prices are projected at USD 493/t by 2020. Similar to wheat and coarse grains, real prices of rice are expected to decline, yet remain above historical levels.

An expected trend in world markets is a narrowing of the price differential between wheat and maize, with the wheat to maize price ratio expected to approach 1.2 by 2020, compared to 1.4 in the previous decade. The primary driver is an anticipated tighter supply and demand balance for maize relative to wheat, related to the overall demand for wheat (mostly food) tending to be less elastic than the derived maize demand for feed and biofuel.

Production of cereals

World wheat production is projected to reach 746 Mt by 2020, about 11% higher than in the base period 2008-2010, but with slower annual growth relative to the previous decade (Figure 4.3). Area expansion is projected to be modest, 2% higher than the base period by 2020. The largest area expansions are projected for the Russian Federation, Ukraine and Kazakhstan. Average global yield growth for wheat is projected at only 0.8% p.a., reflecting strong historical yield growth in major producing countries.

World coarse grain production is expected to reach 1 321 Mt by 2020, up 18% from the base period (Figure 4.4), with significant increases projected for Argentina, Brazil, China, the Russian Federation, Ukraine and the United States. The increase in the total coarse grain area

Figure 4.3. **Wheat production and stock ratios**

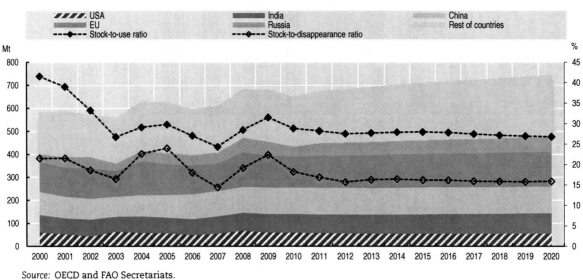

Source: OECD and FAO Secretariats.

StatLink ⌨ http://dx.doi.org/10.1787/888932426638

Figure 4.4. **Coarse grain production and stock ratios**

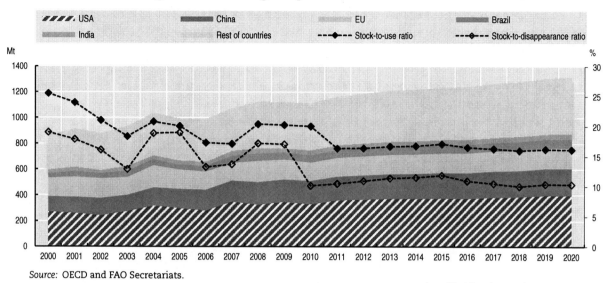

Source: OECD and FAO Secretariats.

StatLink http://dx.doi.org/10.1787/888932426657

is projected to be more significant by 2020, up 6.6% from the base period, with notable increases in Brazil, Argentina and Canada, as well as several Sub-Saharan African countries. Coarse grain yields are projected to increase by 0.8% p.a., below historical trends.

In 2020, world rice production is projected at 528 Mt, roughly 67 Mt higher than the base period (Figure 4.5). The annual growth rate is forecast at 1.3%, significantly slower than 2.2% p.a. in the previous decade. Yield growth (1.1% p.a.) is the main driver behind the global production increase, as little change in total rice area is expected. Developing countries are expected to account for virtually all of the projected production increase, particularly India, Cambodia, Myanmar and African countries. Among large producers, China is expected to cut output by 7 Mt, as the sector responds to declining domestic consumption and strong competition for land.

Figure 4.5. **World rice production and stock ratios**

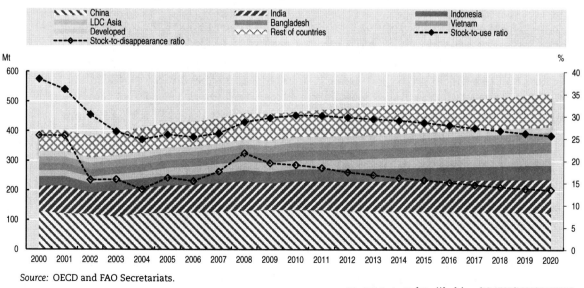

Source: OECD and FAO Secretariats.

StatLink http://dx.doi.org/10.1787/888932426676

Use of cereals

Total wheat utilisation is projected to reach nearly 746 Mt by 2020. Wheat is expected to remain a commodity predominantly consumed for food, roughly 68% of total use by 2020, slightly below its current share (Figure 4.6). *Per capita* food consumption is projected to remain around 66 kg per person p.a. World wheat feed utilisation is expected to reach 145 Mt by 2020, growing at a slightly slower pace than in the historical period, though still representing around 19.5% of total use. Wheat use for biofuels will reach 2% of world wheat utilisation by 2020 compared to 0.9% in the base period. The projected increase of 9% p.a. will be driven largely by growth in EU wheat-based ethanol production which, by 2020, may account for almost 75% of global wheat use for biofuel production (compared to 63% in the base period).

Figure 4.6. **Wheat consumption in developed and developing countries**

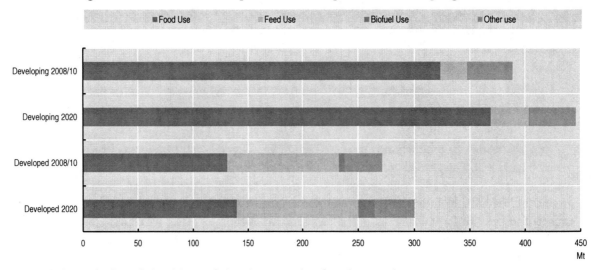

Note: "Other use" refers to industrial uses of wheat (*e.g.* processing of starch or straw).
Source: OECD and FAO Secretariats.

StatLink ⊞⊞ http://dx.doi.org/10.1787/888932426695

World coarse grain utilisation is projected to increase to 1 313 Mt by 2020 (18% compared to the base period), driven largely by expansion in feed and biofuel demand (Figure 4.7). Projected annual growth (1.4%) is less than in the previous decade (2.6%) because reduced coarse grain food demand is expected to exceed increased feed and industrial use. Food use is projected to reach 235 Mt, up 19% from the base period, with per capita consumption around 30.6 kg p.a. Total feed use is projected at 729 Mt, up 16% from the base period, mostly driven by strong growth in the CIS and United States. Maize-based ethanol production in the US is projected to expand until 2015 before slowing down in the years after, due to the introduction of ethanol from cellulosic material within the US mandate. World use of coarse grain for biofuels is projected to reach 166 Mt, nearly 34% more than in the base period, although its share of total production in 2020 is expected to remain at 12.6%.

Rice is consumed mainly as food, with about 14% accounting for feed or post-harvest losses. World overall rice utilisation is set to reach 529 Mt in 2020, up from a 2008-2010 average of 453 Mt. The projected annual utilisation growth rate is 1.3%, slightly below the

Figure 4.7. **Coarse grain consumption in developed and developing countries**

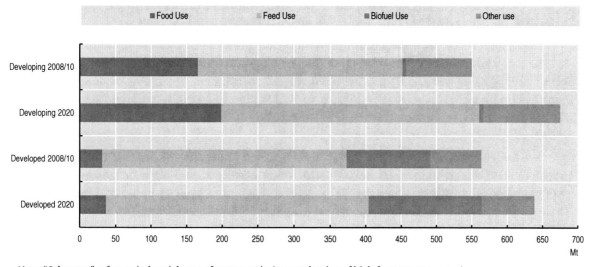

Note: "Other use" refers to industrial uses of coarse grain (e.g. production of high fructose corn syrup).
Source: OECD and FAO Secretariats.

StatLink ⬛ http://dx.doi.org/10.1787/888932426714

past decade (1.5%). *Per capita* food consumption of rice is set to increase at a rate of 0.5% p.a., reaching 60 kg per person in 2020. Rice consumption in Africa is anticipated to rise particularly fast, amid relatively strong population expansion and a continued shift in diets towards rice. The opposite is expected in China, where slow population growth, steady income growth and urbanisation may depress total rice consumption by 0.3% p.a.

Cereal stocks[1]

Wheat stocks are set to recover from the low levels in 2010 and slightly increase over the projection period under normal weather conditions (200 Mt in 2020). Most of the build-up is expected in CIS and in the Near East, offsetting declines in the US and EU. Inventories in China are projected to remain below 60 Mt. At this level, the ratio of world wheat stocks-to-use will approach 27% in 2020, slightly below the base period, but three percentage points above 2007, when the world faced the last major food crisis (Figure 4.3). Similarly, the ratio of major exporters' wheat stocks-to-disappearance[2] is projected at 16% in 2020.

World coarse grain stocks are projected to remain steady at base period levels (211 Mt). Chinese stock accumulation (66 Mt in 2020) is expected to offset declines in the EU and US. The world stocks-to-use ratio for coarse grain is projected at 16%, slightly below the average of the last decade (Figure 4.4). More importantly, the stock-to-disappearance ratio is projected to remain at 10-12% through the projection period.

World rice inventories have been increasing strongly since 2008, boosted by strong production and by a few governments moving to increase public rice reserves. Stock accumulation is expected to slow, reaching 136 Mt by 2020. This downward trend is mainly driven by China and India. The rice stocks-to-use and stocks-to-disappearance ratios are projected to decrease to 26% and 13% respectively in 2020.

Trade of cereals

World cereal trade is projected to reach 328 Mt, up 17% from the base period. United States, the Russian Federation, Canada, EU, Australia, Ukraine, Kazakhstan and Argentina will account for a 90% share of the world total (Box 4.1). For coarse grains, shipments from the major exporters will account for 84% of the world total. Projections of Russian wheat exports include the announced lifting of the export ban which is to come into effect July 1st.

Wheat imports by developing countries are projected to increase by 2.1% p.a. to 120 Mt in 2020, representing 83% of global wheat trade. The biggest volume increases are projected for Brazil, Egypt, Nigeria and Saudi Arabia. Aggregate coarse grain imports by developing countries are projected to increase by 2.3% p.a. to 102 Mt, representing 71% of the global total. The largest increases in import volumes are expected from China, EU, Egypt, Saudi Arabia and several countries in Latin America.

Rice trade is expected to grow at 2.2% p.a., faster than in the past decade. By 2020, it is projected at 41 Mt, up from 31 Mt in 2008-2010. Trade expansion will likely be fuelled by rising demand from African countries. Because of its high price policies and rising costs, Thailand is foreseen to cut exports and reduce its export market share from 30% in 2010 to 23% in 2020, losing its leadership in rice trade. Sustained export growth however, may turn Vietnam into the world's largest exporter. Rice shipments from Egypt are projected to disappear, due to stringent policies on water use. Other Asian countries, in particular Myanmar and Cambodia, are expected to make major inroads in the international rice market, with exports growing by 10% p.a. to 2020. US exports are expected to grow steadily at 1.1% p.a., while EU imports are projected to grow vigorously.

Main issues and uncertainties

The 2010 production year has been severely affected by adverse weather conditions, including drought in the Russian Federation and Ukraine and floods in Australia. This makes the next harvest for cereals in the Northern hemisphere critical with already some problems observed in Europe due to drought and in North America due to flooding during spring. In the medium term, it becomes increasingly important to consider the adaptation of agriculture to climate change: how average yields might be affected and where these effects are likely to take place. Moreover, the introduction of market protective measures by major grain exporters to sustain domestic prices becomes also increasingly uncertain in the medium term (see Russian case in Box 4.1). In this respect, the outcome of the World Trade Organization negotiations could play a key role.

An additional source of uncertainty is the level of world cereal stocks, given their importance as an indicator of market tightness. In the current baseline, world cereal stocks increase in the early years of the projection period under the assumption of normal weather conditions and average yields. Biofuel markets continue being an important source of demand for cereals. The evolution of crude oil prices, affecting the economic incentives to use biofuels, is a key assumption in the baseline. Moreover, political uncertainty about the renewal of US ethanol policies could also have an impact on projections. Maize use for ethanol is already significant in the base period and is expected to moderately expand until 2015, driven by the structure of the US mandate.

Another source of uncertainty is the level of production at any given year. In view of the fact that prices of most crops are projected to remain strong, competition for land is likely to intensify with planting decisions very much shaped by the inherent inter-seasonal price volatility (e.g. maize and soya in the US), which in turn, will contribute to unexpected changes in production levels.

Box 4.1. **Russian Federation, Ukraine, Kazakhstan: a larger role in world wheat markets**

Russian Federation, Ukraine and Kazakhstan (RUK) are expected to surpass the US as the world's largest wheat exporter over the next decade. Analysis conducted by the USDA's Economic Research Service (USDA, 2010) has been updated using the current OECD-FAO projections to 2020, to illustrate the changing dynamics in global wheat markets observed in this outlook.

By 2020, wheat exports from the Russian Federation are projected to be just below US exports, with total RUK exports expected to be nearly double the US level. Figure 4.8 compares historical and projected world market shares of major wheat exporters. Whereas US exports are projected to decline by 2.7 Mt (a decrease in export share of 7.4 percentage points relative to 2001-10 average), the RUK export share is projected to expand by 11.8 percentage points, with exports increasing by about 22.3 Mt. The market shares of other major wheat exporters like Argentina, Australia, Canada and the EU are also projected to fall over this period.

Figure 4.8. **Share of world wheat exports by major exporters: 2001-10 and 2020**

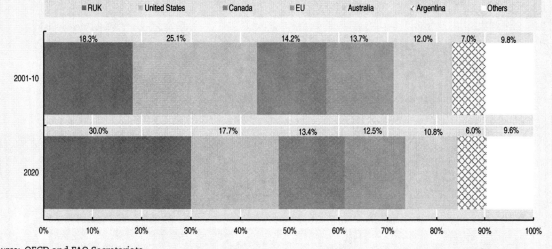

Source: OECD and FAO Secretariats.

StatLink http://dx.doi.org/10.1787/888932426733

The USDA report noted that declining US wheat production began after the elimination of commodity-specific Federal farm program payments in the 1996 Farm Act. Producers began switching acreage from wheat to more profitable crops, such as maize or soybeans, both of which were gaining a competitive advantage due to varietal and genetic improvements. Growth in demand for maize-based ethanol was also a contributing factor. In the case of RUK, export growth has been driven by improved production, generated with the rise of large, vertically-integrated farming operations (big farm co-operatives) actively pursuing better agronomic and management practices. In 2008, a Russian state-owned grain company was created to promote exports of wheat and other grains, to improve infrastructure, and to facilitate state grain purchases in domestic markets.

Growth in RUK production and exports is a feature of the current OECD-FAO agricultural outlook and should serve to improve exportable supplies of wheat, thereby helping to mitigate global food security concerns in the medium term. Low quality food wheat is not currently perceived as a problem, due to the developed practice by importers of using food additives which enables bread to be baked from low-quality grain. However, the growing importance of RUK as a major world wheat exporter may be hampered by unexpected supply disruptions. Historically, production in the region has suffered from erratic yields driven by sudden changes in climatic conditions. Such uncertainties are often exacerbated by the imposition of export restrictions and other policy measures designed to protect domestic markets, as is currently the case in the Russian Federation, or was the case in 2007-08 in both the Russian Federation and Ukraine.

Notes

1. Cereals stocks include public (strategic + intervention) and private storage (also on-farm).

2. The stock-to-disappearance ratio for wheat and coarse grains is defined as the ratio of stocks held by the traditional exporters (Argentina, Australia, Canada, EU and the United States) to their disappearance (i.e. domestic utilisation plus exports). For rice the major exporters considered in the calculation are India, the US, Pakistan, Thailand and Vietnam.

Reference

USDA (2010), Former Soviet Union Region To Play Larger Role in Meeting World Wheat Needs, Economic Research Service, US Department of Agriculture. Amber Waves, June 2010.

ANNEX 4.A

Statistical tables: Cereals

Table 4.A.1. World cereal projections

Crop year

		Avg 08/09-10/11est	11/12	12/13	13/14	14/15	15/16	16/17	17/18	18/19	19/20	20/21
WHEAT												
OECD[1]												
Production	mt	280.7	275.3	274.6	277.9	282.0	281.7	284.8	285.3	288.4	290.3	292.1
Consumption	mt	215.4	219.9	220.9	221.3	225.7	226.8	230.1	232.2	233.7	234.6	235.6
Closing stocks	mt	57.5	50.5	47.2	48.4	49.6	49.3	49.6	49.2	49.3	49.5	50.0
Non-OECD												
Production	mt	393.3	402.2	410.2	416.3	424.3	430.2	434.6	439.1	443.6	448.9	453.8
Consumption	mt	444.6	459.1	466.6	470.6	476.6	482.9	488.3	493.5	498.8	504.5	510.0
Closing stocks	mt	137.8	141.0	142.0	143.3	146.4	149.1	150.2	150.I	149.8	149.9	149.9
World[2]												
Production	mt	674.0	677.4	684.9	694.2	706.3	711.9	719.4	724.9	732.1	739.3	745.9
Area	mha	223.2	223.6	223.2	223.8	225.3	225.1	226.0	226.3	226.7	227.3	227.6
Yield	t/ha	3.0	3.0	3.1	3.1	3.1	3.2	3.2	3.2	3.2	3.3	3.3
Consumption	mt	660.0	679.0	687.4	691.9	702.3	709.7	718.4	725.7	732.5	739.2	745.7
Feed use	mt	126.2	132.3	134.2	133.7	137.1	137.0	138.9	140.6	142.2	143.3	145.1
Food use	mt	454.2	463.4	468.8	472.4	477.7	483.5	489.1	494.0	499.0	503.9	508.5
Biofuel use	mt	5.7	7.2	7.8	9.2	10.8	12.2	13.4	14.3	14.9	15.2	14.9
Other use	mt	74.2	76.1	76.7	76.6	76.7	77.0	76.9	76.8	76.4	76.7	77.2
Exports	mt	129.0	125.4	127.3	127.6	132.1	133.8	136.0	137.8	140.1	142.9	144.7
Closing stocks	mt	195.3	191.5	189.2	191.7	196.0	198.5	199.8	199.3	199.1	199.4	199.9
Price[3]	USD/t	264.5	278.6	234.1	247.9	237.6	240.7	238.8	241.8	241.3	241.2	240.4
COARSE GRAINS												
OECD[1]												
Production	mt	570.4	595.1	604.4	614.0	615.3	623.7	621.5	634.9	640.3	654.1	655.8
Consumption	mt	559.4	576.5	586.4	594.4	596.7	600.0	606.2	614.4	620.0	625.9	629.9
Closing stocks	mt	99.9	78.2	81.8	85.0	86.2	89.1	83.9	82.1	79.9	83.0	83.2
Non-OECD												
Production	mt	551.1	572.8	587.2	599.4	606.9	617.4	625.1	635.9	644.9	656.2	664.9
Consumption	mt	553.7	583.6	595.0	606.3	616.2	628.1	638.8	649.8	660.4	672.5	683.3
Closing stocks	mt	111.2	111.3	111.9	115.1	117.1	121.0	121.8	124.0	124.9	127.6	128.7
World[2]												
Production	mt	1 121.6	1 167.9	1 191.7	1 213.4	1 222.1	1 241.1	1 246.7	1 270.7	1 285.2	1 310.3	1 320.7
Area	mha	325.9	331.7	334.6	337.1	337.3	340.0	340.1	342.6	343.9	346.4	347.3
Yield	t/ha	3.4	3.5	3.6	3.6	3.6	3.7	3.7	3.7	3.7	3.8	3.8
Consumption	mt	1 113.0	1 160.1	1 181.4	1 200.8	1 212.8	1 228.1	1 245.0	1 264.2	1 280.3	1 298.4	1 313.2
Feed use	mt	627.2	640.9	651.1	660.0	666.5	677.2	689.0	699.6	709.3	719.8	728.7
Food use	mt	197.2	206.9	209.3	212.7	215.6	219.3	222.5	225.8	228.9	232.3	235.5
Biofuel use	mt	123.7	147.0	157.0	165.5	167.5	167.5	166.9	167.8	167.2	168.2	166.2
Other use	mt	126.9	127.0	125.7	123.7	123.9	124.5	126.4	130.6	134.2	136.9	141.3
Exports	mt	121.0	123.8	124.8	126.3	128.4	131.3	132.8	135.4	137.2	140.2	142.6
Closing stocks	mt	211.1	189.5	193.7	200.1	203.3	210.1	205.6	206.1	204.8	210.5	211.9
Price[4]	USD/t	197.9	229.0	202.5	202.3	206.4	204.9	207.2	207.2	207.9	205.3	202.8
RICE												
OECD[1]												
Production	mt	23.1	23.8	23.7	23.7	23.9	24.0	24.0	24.0	24.0	24.1	24.1
Consumption	mt	24.4	24.5	24.7	24.8	24.8	24.9	25.0	25.1	25.1	25.2	25.3
Closing stocks	mt	6.0	6.0	5.8	5.6	5.6	5.7	5.9	6.0	6.2	6.3	6.5
Non-OECD												
Production	mt	437.6	448.7	453.4	459.9	466.6	472.2	478.8	485.1	491.2	497.7	504.0
Consumption	mt	428.5	445.3	451.8	458.3	465.0	471.5	478.5	485.0	491.3	497.6	503.6
Closing stocks	mt	127.5	135.4	135.9	136.4	136.7	136.2	135.1	133.7	132.1	130.6	129.4
World[2]												
Production	mt	460.8	472.5	477.1	483.6	490.4	496.2	502.9	509.1	515.2	521.7	528.1
Area	mha	159.5	160.8	160.8	161.0	161.4	161.7	162.0	162.2	162.3	162.5	162.7
Yield	t/ha	2.9	2.9	3.0	3.0	3.0	3.1	3.1	3.1	3.2	3.2	3.2
Consumption	mt	452.9	469.7	476.5	483.0	489.8	496.4	503.5	510.1	516.4	522.8	528.9
Feed use	mt	13.5	13.8	14.0	14.1	14.3	14.3	14.6	14.6	14.9	15.0	15.2
Food use	mt	387.5	400.3	406.9	413.3	419.9	426.4	433.2	440.0	446.6	453.4	460.0
Exports	mt	30.8	33.5	34.8	35.9	36.8	37.3	38.1	38.8	39.6	40.4	41.2
Closing stocks	mt	133.5	141.4	141.6	142.0	142.3	141.9	141.0	139.7	138.3	137.0	135.9
Price[5]	USD/t	599.7	538.7	503.6	478.2	472.4	472.5	474.0	478.5	482.9	488.6	492.5

Note: Crop year: Beginning crop marketing year - see Glossary of Terms for definitions.
1. Excludes Iceland but includes EU6 members that are not members of the OECD (Bulgaria, Cyprus, Latvia, Lithuania, Malta and Romania).
2. Source of historic data is USDA.
3. No. 2 hard red winter wheat, ordinary protein, USA f.o.b. Gulf Ports (June/May), less EEP payments where applicable.
4. No. 2 yellow corn, US f.o.b. Gulf Ports (September/August).
5. Milled, 100%, grade b, Nominal Price Quote, NPQ, f.o.b. Bangkok (January/December).
Source: OECD and FAO Secretariats.

StatLink http://dx.doi.org/10.1787/888932427721

Chapter 5

Oilseeds and oilseed products

Market situation

The oilseeds complex has gone through a turbulent period characterised by considerable price swings and by prices trending upward compared to previous years. After the dramatic rise and subsequent drop seen in 2008, during 2009, prices embarked on a steady upward trend, reflecting a progressive tightening in global supplies, the resumption in demand growth (following the global economic crisis), and robust buying interest by main importing countries. Growing supply tightness relative to demand caused global stock-to-use ratios to fall below historic levels.

From mid 2010 onward, prospects of prolonged market tightness propelled prices up further, eventually resulting in levels close to the 2008 peak. Concurrence of several factors led to the tightening: adverse weather conditions causing low output of rapeseed and sunflower on one side and marked downward corrections in soybean and palm oil production estimates on the other; continued strong import demand for oil crops and derived products; resuming demand growth for vegetable oil by the biodiesel industry; and the prospective competition for land among arable crops (in particular oilseeds and coarse grains) in certain regions. External drivers also contributed to the strengthening in prices, notably price spill-over effects from tight grain markets; prolonged firmness in mineral oil prices; and the continued weakness of the US dollar.

Projection highlights

- Prices in the oilseed complex are expected to remain firm and above historical levels, with the exception of meal prices, which, after an initial fall, are projected to level off (Figure 5.1). Growth in global production and consumption of oilseeds and derived products slows with price firmness and reduced income growth.

- Two-thirds of global expansion in oilseeds plantings is earmarked to occur in the developing world. Developing countries will also lead the increase in global vegetable oil output. The market share of Malaysia and Indonesia increases further, but growing environmental constraints could alter projections.

- Developing countries, in particular China and other Asian countries, should continue to dominate the rise in vegetable oil consumption (Figure 5.2). Biodiesel production is projected to contribute significantly to global consumption growth.

Figure 5.1. **Oilseeds and oilseed products prices to remain above historical levels**

Evolution of prices expressed in nominal terms (left) and in real terms (right)

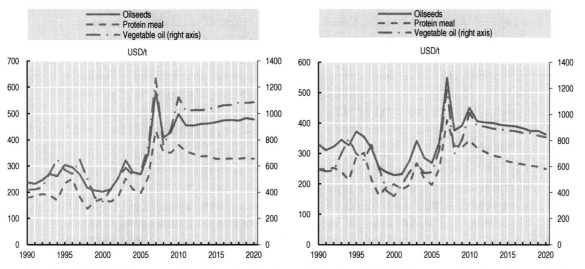

Note: Oilseeds: Weighted average oilseed import price, Europe. Oilseed meal: Weighted average oilseed meal import Price, Europe. Vegetable oil: Weighted average export price of oilseed oils and palm oil, Europe.

Source: OECD and FAO Secretariats.

StatLink 🔗 http://dx.doi.org/10.1787/888932426752

Figure 5.2. **Developing countries to dominate the rise in vegetable oil consumption**

Comparison of average annual growth rates of vegetable oil consumption

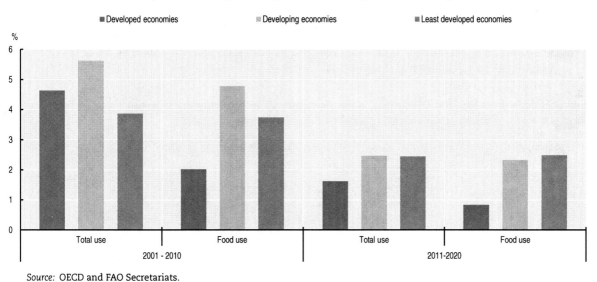

Source: OECD and FAO Secretariats.

StatLink 🔗 http://dx.doi.org/10.1787/888932426771

Market trends and prospects

Prices

World prices for oilseeds and oilseed products expressed in nominal terms are projected to remain well above levels recorded prior to the 2007-08 food crisis. After a short initial dip, oilseed and vegetable oil prices should rise throughout the Outlook period (Figure 5.1). In line with other feed commodities, meal prices are expected to weaken during the first half of the *Outlook* and stabilise or strengthen slightly thereafter. Expressed in real terms, prices are projected to fall gradually in all three product groups, though remaining strong compared the level prevailing before 2007-08, in particular in the case of seeds and oils.

The general downward correction in prices expected in 2011 reflects the prompt response of oilseed supplies to the 2010 surge in prices. Thereafter, historically weak production growth and successive reductions in stock-to-use ratios are expected to lead to a gradual increase in nominal prices for both, oilseeds and vegetable oils. In case of the latter, sustained demand for food uses in developing countries, further rising demand from biodiesel producers and the anticipated strength in mineral oil prices should contribute to gradual price appreciation. Oilseed meal values, by contrast, are less prone to increase given the lingering effects of the recent economic crisis on livestock industries, which contribute to weakened meal demand.

Oilseed output and crush

World oilseeds production is expected to expand by 23% over the Outlook period, marking a strong slowdown in growth relative to the past. The anticipated production increase is based equally on higher plantings and yield improvements. The US remains the world's top oilseed producer, followed by Brazil, China, Argentina, India and the EU (Figure 5.3). The share held by Latin American and Eastern European producers is likely to increase at the expense of China and the US.

Figure 5.3. **Oilseed production to be dominated by few market players**

Evolution of global oilseed production over the projection period

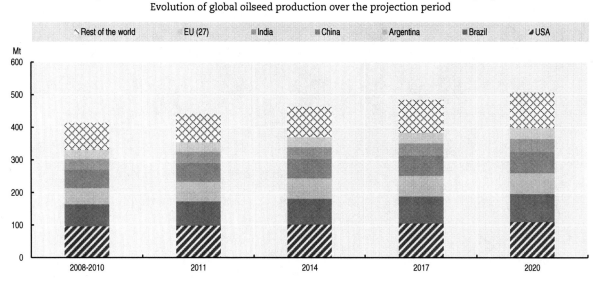

Source: OECD and FAO Secretariats.

StatLink 🔗 http://dx.doi.org/10.1787/888932426790

Annual yield improvement is expected to slow down, compared to the last decade, and the productivity gap between developing and developed countries will diminish only marginally. The growth in oilseed plantings is also projected to slow down markedly in both developed and developing countries due to high marginal costs of area expansion, environmental constraints and sustained profitability of competing crops. Two-thirds of global area expansion should take place in the developing world: growth is expected to be concentrated in Brazil, India and China. Relatively strong area expansion is projected for small, emerging producers in South America. Among developed countries, some further area expansion is expected in Canada, Australia and among Eastern European producers, whereas in the US and the EU plantings should only grow marginally.

Annual growth in global crushing is also projected to slow down, with deceleration more pronounced in the developing world. When comparing individual countries, Canada, the Russian Federation, the Ukraine, Argentina and Brazil stand out for projected above-average expansion in crush volumes.

The global stock-to-use ratio for oilseeds should remain below the levels recorded prior to the recent market turbulence, supporting the projection of firm world oilseed prices.

Vegetable oil production and consumption

Led by developing countries, global vegetable oil production is expected to increase by over 30% by 2020. However, in terms of annual growth rate, production slows down compared to the last decade. In Malaysia and Indonesia, where land restrictions and environmental regulations should become more binding, combined palm oil output will, nonetheless, expand by almost 45%, raising their share in global output to 36%. Other major expected sources of vegetable oil production growth are China, Argentina, the EU and Brazil. Also noteworthy is the expansion projected for Canada, the Russian Federation and the Ukraine. Only modest growth is expected in the US and India.

Average annual increase in global vegetable oil consumption slows down to 2.2% compared to 5.3% in the last decade due partly to the projected price firmness. Based on *per capita* income and population growth, three-quarters of global demand expansion is expected to occur in developing countries, with Asian countries weighing most and food use dominating consumption (Figure 5.2). China should remain the world's leading vegetable oil consumer, followed by the EU, India and the US. While in China and India, growth occurs primarily in food use, in the EU and the US, the biodiesel industry is projected to represent a significant source of demand. In *per capita* terms, the discrepancy between edible oil intake in developed and developing countries is expected to narrow; however, looking at overall consumption (i.e. food and non-food uses), the lead developed countries have over developing ones should increase slightly. Among least developed countries, positive income prospects should allow a reversal of the recent negative trend in *per capita* consumption. However, consumption levels are expected to take the full decade to return to levels recorded before the 2008-crisis (Box 5.1.).

Demand for non-food uses of vegetable oil (in particular for biodiesel) should account for about one-third of global consumption growth. By 2020, biodiesel production accounts for 15% of total consumption, compared to 10% in the 2008-10 base period (Figure 5.4). Higher mandatory use in developed countries but also rising biodiesel production in a number of developing nations drives this increase. In the EU, demand from the biodiesel industry is projected to nearly double over the Outlook period. By 2020, vegetable oil use for biodiesel production is expected to account for more than half of the EU's total domestic consumption. Although biodiesel driven demand is also projected to grow in the US and Canada, its role remains much smaller in those markets. As Argentina continues to develop its export-oriented biodiesel industry, by 2020 the latter should account for 72% of domestic consumption supported by the system of differential export taxes in place. Demand from biodiesel producers for a range of oil-based feedstock is also projected to increase in several other developing countries in South America (Brazil, Colombia and Peru) and Asia (India, Indonesia, Malaysia and Thailand), where expansion is mainly earmarked for domestic consumption.

Figure 5.4. **Biodiesel production to account for 16% of total vegetable oil consumption**

Share of vegetable oil consumption used for biodiesel production in selected countries

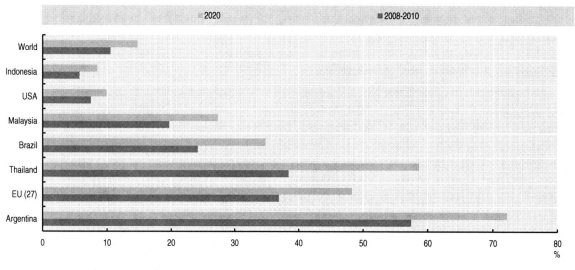

Source: OECD and FAO Secretariats.

StatLink ᴀᴵˢᴾ http://dx.doi.org/10.1787/888932426809

Oilseed meal production and consumption

In developing countries, oilseed meal consumption is expected to grow at about 2% per year, about a third of the previous decade's rate. Demand for livestock products, and thus meals, is taking time to recover after income growth slowed down in the wake of economic crisis. In developed countries, where livestock industries are more mature and demand is more stable, meal consumption is expected to grow at a similar rate as in the past (Figure 5.5).

In China, demand growth should slow down compared to the previous decade as its livestock industry is expected to expand at a slower pace. Additional meal demand will be met primarily by domestic production (which continues to rely strongly on the crushing of imported oilseeds). The country is expected to remain the world's leading oilseed meal consumer, with the share in global consumption rising to 24%. In the rest of (developing) Asia, meal use expands by about one-third during the Outlook period. In South America, consumption expands by a similar rate, with growth concentrated in Brazil and Argentina.

Figure 5.5. **Oilseed meal consumption to slow down compared to the previous decade**

Comparison of average annual growth rates of oilseed meal consumption

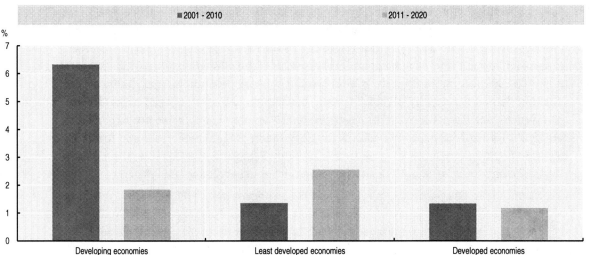

Source: OECD and FAO Secretariats.

StatLink 🔗 http://dx.doi.org/10.1787/888932426828

Among least developed countries, the growth of relatively young meat industries is expected to continue, and oilseed meal consumption should expand faster in the coming ten years than during the last decade (Figure 5.6).

In the EU, the world's second largest meal consumer, demand grows slowly over the decade, with about 50% of consumption continuing to come from imported meals. US oilseed meal use will resume growing, following a period of decline that was caused by rising availability of lower priced dried distillers grains (DDG).

Figure 5.6. **Vegetable oil exports to remain concentrated**

Evolution of vegetable oil trade over the projection period

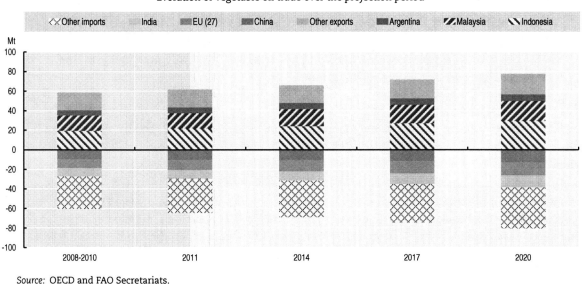

Source: OECD and FAO Secretariats.

StatLink 🔗 http://dx.doi.org/10.1787/888932426847

Trade in oilseeds and products

Growth in world oilseeds trade is projected to slow down significantly. On the import side, developing countries will account for most of the slowdown. In particular China's imports should expand at a much slower pace than before. But the country will continue to dominate world trade, with purchases accounting for half of total global imports in 2020. Imported material continues to represent close to half of the oilseeds crushed in the country. In the EU, the volume of imports should remain more or less unchanged, as increased crushing demand is met by higher domestic production. All main oilseed exporters will experience poor export growth. In Argentina and Canada oilseed sales are expected to remain flat as crushing capacity and thus the exportation of higher-value oils and meals are expanded. Only some emerging exporters, notably Paraguay, the Ukraine, the Russian Federation and Uruguay should experience a significant expansion in seed exports.

Also trade in oilseed products is expected to slow down markedly. Regarding vegetable oil exports, the combined share of Indonesia and Malaysia in total exports should climb to 68% by 2020 (Figure 5.6). Argentina is the third largest exporter with a world share of 9%. About 65% of the country's output is exported, in part due to the differential export tax system that favours sales of oilseed products. The US and Brazil, by contrast, are expected to remain the world's key suppliers of oilseeds. The Ukraine and the Russian Federation will continue to expand sales of both vegetable oils and oilseeds.

Developing countries in Asia led by India and China should account for almost 50% of global vegetable oil imports in 2020. On average, in developing Asia, 45% of consumption will come from imports. In India, where foreign purchases are estimated to expand nearly 50%, the rate of import dependence rises to 62%. China, in addition to covering a considerable part of its vegetable oil needs *via* the crushing of imported oilseeds, is set to expand edible oil imports by almost 35%, which brings the share of imports in total consumption to 36%.

In the EU, to meet both industrial and traditional vegetable oil demand, imports should rise by 42%. This maintains the EU as the world's leading importer, which alone should account for almost 18% of the market. The same holds for China, where, in addition to oils, oilseed imports (and subsequent crushing) will also be used to meet domestic consumption requirements.

As for oilseed meals, about 70% of the anticipated expansion in trade is projected to occur in the developing world, with countries in Asia accounting for half of the increase. In the EU, the world's largest importer, meal purchases should grow only marginally, in line with the livestock sector's stable consumption.

Box 5.1. **Impact of high prices, global economic crisis and biofuel policies on vegetable oil food consumption in low-income countries**

Background

In many developing countries *per-capita* vegetable oil consumption followed a strongly increasing trend until 2006 and then slowed down considerably for the years 2007 to 2010. This was triggered by the 2007/08 price peak and the subsequently persisting higher price level for all commodities. Additionally, the global economic crisis reduced incomes severely which in poor countries impacted food expenditures in general and income-sensitive items like vegetable oil in particular. Various policy instruments mitigated or heightened the effects of these global developments in the individual domestic markets.

Box 5.1. **Impact of high prices, global economic crisis and biofuel policies on vegetable oil food consumption in low-income countries** (*cont.*)

Effect on food consumption pattern in 2007-10

The stagnation in consumption was most pronounced in least developed countries. Simulating the continuation of their *per-capita* vegetable oil food consumption trend of the pre-crisis decade (1997-2006) until the year 2010 shows that without the crisis these countries could have consumed about 1.3 Mt, or 21% more vegetable oil for food in that year. For other developing countries the impact was less severe: *per capita* consumption fell only about 4% (or 3.2 Mt) short of trend in 2010. Interestingly, at the same time, the emerging biodiesel industry in some developing countries utilised in total about 7 Mt of vegetable oil in 2010. There were only small trade-offs between food and fuel within countries. Most food consumption reduction happened in least developed countries in Africa and Asia while biofuel industries developed in emerging economies like Argentina, Brazil, Colombia or Malaysia. Developed countries converted another 10 Mt of edible oil into biodiesel. The policy driven expansion of biodiesel was one of several factors that mitigated the price impact of the reduced food demand.

Outlook period: slow consumption recovery

Over the Outlook period, the growth of vegetable oil food consumption in developing countries is not expected to reach pre-crisis levels. Prices are projected to remain firm and above the levels seen before 2006. Also, the lingering effects of the economic crisis depress consumption growth and high crude oil prices depress economic growth in energy-importing countries. Compared to a continued on-trend (historic) growth of *per capita* food consumption, least developed countries as a whole are projected to consume about 4 Mt (53%) less in 2020; for other developing countries, the trend simulations suggest a 16 Mt (or 15%) deficit in consumption. At the same time, vegetable oil use for biodiesel production in developing and developed countries is projected to reach, respectively 11 Mt and 18 Mt by the end of the Outlook period. Although this simple trend analysis does not allow any conclusions about causalities, it does illustrate continued expectations of rather subdued vegetable oils food consumption – in particular among poor developing countries – in contrast to sustained strong world-wide growth in biofuels.

Figure 5.7. *Per capita* **food consumption and real price of vegetable oils**

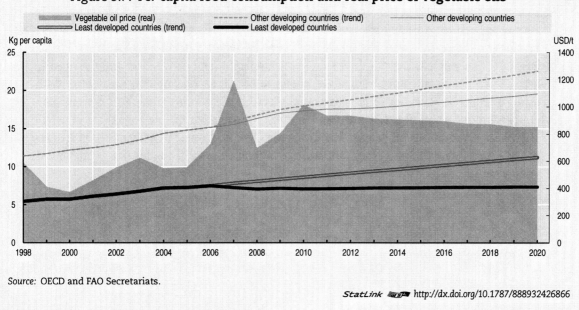

Source: OECD and FAO Secretariats.

StatLink http://dx.doi.org/10.1787/888932426866

Main issues and uncertainties

National policies and repercussions on markets

The recent trend towards a gradual tightening of supply and demand for oilseeds and the resulting price firmness has started affecting consumers of oilseed products, in particular poor households in developing countries. Governments in affected countries are showing increased concern and have started resorting to a variety of measures to protect consumers from higher prices. Initiatives taken include: measures to facilitate imports, creation of state reserves for public distribution, production incentives, domestic marketing restrictions and control of export flows. All these interventions affect the behaviour of domestic consumers, producers, other market participants and international traders, eventually leading to adjustments in production, consumption and trade in oilseeds and oilseed products. With world prices projected to remain firm and above historic levels, more policy interventions can be expected in the future. What type of effects and how big an impact the interplay between various national policy measures is going to generate in domestic and world markets remains difficult to predict and requires continued monitoring and analysis of concerned markets and relevant policies.

Uncertain supply responses

The country projections seem to suggest that some relatively new, emerging players are able to respond more dynamically to market incentives than some of the more traditional suppliers to the world market. Countries in Eastern Europe and central Asia, Paraguay, Uruguay and Colombia are seen to belong to this group. As net exporters of oilseeds and derived products, some of these countries could play an increasingly important role in the global market. However, the real production and export potential of these countries is difficult to assess with accuracy, as reliable information about productivity levels, infrastructural constraints and national policy priorities is limited.

A second source of uncertainty in export markets concerns the two leading suppliers of palm oil, Indonesia and Malaysia. Both countries face low productivity growth in oil palm cultivation. Future advances in this area depend on scientific and economic factors as well as national policy measures. Depending on the assumptions made, diverse production paths emerge for the future. Furthermore, environmental and social challenges in production (such as the CO_2 emission associated with land conversion and the need to actively involve local communities) are bound to be felt increasingly in the sector. With awareness about such issues growing rapidly across the commodity chain, pressure on concerned governments, investors and traders to take appropriate measures is set to augment. Assumptions made as to the future direction and speed of adjustment processes in palm oil production and trade will strongly influence projections for the world's most widely consumed and traded vegetable oil.

ANNEX 5.A

Statistical tables: Oilseeds and oilseed products

Table 5.A.1. World oilseed projections

		Avg 08/09-10/11est	11/12	12/13	13/14	14/15	15/16	16/17	17/18	18/19	19/20	20/21
OILSEED (crop year)[1]												
OECD[2]												
Production	mt	146.3	150.8	153.1	153.6	155.8	157.3	160.7	163.3	166.7	167.5	170.5
Consumption	mt	129.6	132.5	134.3	135.2	136.4	137.6	139.6	140.9	142.8	143.8	145.5
Crush	mt	115.2	118.3	120.1	120.7	121.8	122.9	124.9	126.1	128.0	129.0	130.6
Closing stocks	mt	15.4	15.6	15.1	15.1	15.6	15.5	15.3	15.4	15.5	15.5	15.6
Non-OECD												
Production	mt	267.4	290.3	295.8	301.6	307.2	312.2	316.7	321.2	326.2	331.2	336.6
Consumption	mt	281.2	302.6	309.5	314.3	320.3	326.2	332.4	337.9	344.2	349.3	355.7
Crush	mt	226.6	245.8	251.8	255.5	260.5	265.2	270.3	274.5	279.7	283.7	288.8
Closing stocks	mt	24.5	29.3	29.0	29.1	29.3	29.5	29.4	29.5	29.6	29.6	29.9
WORLD												
Production	mt	413.7	441.1	448.8	455.1	463.0	469.5	477.5	484.5	492.9	498.8	507.2
Area	mha	203.3	217.9	220.0	221.5	223.4	225.2	227.4	229.4	231.8	233.1	235.1
Yield	t/ha	1.9	2.0	2.0	2.1	2.1	2.1	2.1	2.1	2.1	2.1	2.2
Consumption	mt	410.8	435.0	443.9	449.5	456.7	463.8	472.1	478.8	487.0	493.2	501.2
Crush	mt	341.8	364.1	371.9	376.1	382.3	388.1	395.2	400.7	407.7	412.7	419.5
Other use	mt	18.2	18.1	18.1	18.5	18.5	18.7	18.7	18.9	19.0	19.0	19.1
Exports	mt	94.8	115.2	116.3	116.6	118.8	120.5	122.2	123.2	124.9	125.3	127.0
Closing stocks	mt	39.9	44.9	44.2	44.2	44.9	45.0	44.8	44.9	45.1	45.1	45.5
Price[3]	USD/t	445.8	455.4	455.2	460.8	462.7	468.0	474.5	475.8	473.6	483.3	477.9
OILSEED MEALS (marketing year)												
OECD[2]												
Production	mt	79.6	81.5	82.9	83.2	84.0	84.7	86.1	86.9	88.1	88.7	89.8
Consumption	mt	109.1	112.8	115.0	115.9	116.8	117.4	119.4	120.1	121.7	122.4	124.0
Closing stocks	mt	1.3	1.3	1.3	1.3	1.3	1.3	1.3	1.3	1.3	1.3	1.3
Non-OECD												
Production	mt	162.0	175.9	180.2	182.9	186.5	189.9	193.6	196.7	200.4	203.3	207.0
Consumption	mt	129.6	141.7	144.7	146.5	149.9	153.4	156.6	159.8	163.1	166.0	169.1
Closing stocks	mt	12.2	11.5	11.4	11.6	11.8	12.1	12.2	12.4	12.6	12.8	13.0
WORLD												
Production	mt	241.6	257.5	263.1	266.2	270.5	274.6	279.7	283.6	288.5	292.1	296.8
Consumption	mt	238.7	254.5	259.7	262.4	266.8	270.8	276.0	279.9	284.8	288.4	293.0
Closing stocks	mt	13.5	12.8	12.7	12.9	13.1	13.4	13.5	13.7	13.9	14.1	14.3
Price[4]	USD/t	362.0	356.8	345.9	337.2	337.6	327.3	327.2	328.5	328.3	330.6	327.8
VEGETABLE OILS (marketing year)												
OECD[2]												
Production	mt	31.1	32.2	32.8	32.9	33.3	33.7	34.3	34.7	35.3	35.7	36.3
Consumption	mt	44.0	45.7	47.3	48.2	49.1	50.0	50.7	51.6	52.4	53.3	53.9
Closing stocks	mt	3.2	2.9	2.8	2.8	2.8	2.8	2.9	2.9	2.9	2.9	2.8
Non-OECD												
Production	mt	106.6	114.0	117.5	120.5	123.7	126.9	130.2	133.4	136.7	139.9	143.2
Consumption	mt	95.7	103.7	105.8	108.0	110.8	113.6	116.5	119.3	122.3	125.1	128.2
Closing stocks	mt	11.3	11.1	11.4	11.6	11.6	11.6	11.8	11.9	12.2	12.3	12.6
WORLD												
Production	mt	137.7	146.3	150.2	153.4	157.0	160.6	164.5	168.1	172.0	175.5	179.5
Of which palm oil	mt	45.7	49.3	51.1	52.9	54.7	56.5	58.3	60.2	62.1	64.0	65.8
Consumption	mt	139.7	149.4	153.0	156.2	159.9	163.6	167.2	170.9	174.7	178.4	182.1
Food	mt	112.6	123.6	126.0	128.1	130.6	133.2	136.0	138.6	141.4	144.0	147.0
Biofuel	mt	18.4	18.8	19.8	20.7	21.8	22.7	23.4	24.4	25.2	26.2	26.8
Exports	mt	54.3	61.6	62.6	64.4	66.1	67.9	69.6	71.7	73.7	75.8	77.7
Closing stocks	mt	14.4	14.0	14.2	14.4	14.5	14.5	14.7	14.8	15.1	15.2	15.5
Price[5]	USD/t	921.6	1 022.9	1 026.7	1 026.7	1 036.8	1 049.4	1 063.0	1 066.8	1 082.9	1 081.0	1 086.5

1. Beginning crop marketing year - see Glossary of Terms for definitions.
2. Excludes Iceland but includes EU6 members that are not members of the OECD (Bulgaria, Cyprus, Latvia, Lithuania, Malta and Romania).
3. Weighted average oilseed price, European port.
4. Weighted average oilseed meal price, European port.
5. Weighted average price of oilseed oils and palm oil, European port.
Source: OECD and FAO Secretariats.

StatLink ═══ http://dx.doi.org/10.1787/888932427835

Chapter 6

Sugar

Market situation

The world sugar market continues to experience considerable price volatility. The world indicator price for raw sugar witnessed a succession of peaks and downward corrections in 2010 before soaring to a 30-year high of USD 36.08 cts/lb (USD 795.4/t) in February 2011. Market fundamentals driving volatile prices were large global sugar deficits in the previous two seasons and adverse weather in a number of countries that reduced the size of the expected rebound in production to higher prices (Figure 6.1). World sugar stocks, which had already been drawn down, fell to their lowest level in 20 years in 2010-11, supporting higher as well as more volatile market prices.

International sugar prices are expected to ease back over the remainder of 2011 and into 2011/12, as production responds around the world to recent high prices and the global balance moves into a larger surplus that allows the start of stock rebuilding.

Projection highlights

- The raw sugar price (Intercontinental Exchange No. 11 spot, fob, Caribbean ports) in nominal terms is projected at nearly USD 408/t (USD 18.5 c/lb.) in 2020-21. This is lower than the historical peak at the start of the *Outlook*, but prices are expected to remain on a higher plateau and to average higher in real terms (when adjusted for inflation) over the projection period, when compared with the last decade. White sugar prices (Euronet, Liffe, Contract No, 407, London) follow a similar pattern and are projected to reach USD 508/t (USD 23cts/lb.) in 2020-21, with the white sugar premium narrowing with higher export volumes to average above USD 90/t over the coming decade (Figure 6.2).

- Brazil's sugar production, as one of the lowest cost sugar producers with considerable capacity to expand sugar cane area on a large scale, along with the projected growth in ethanol production, will be key determinants of global sugar production, which is projected to reach over 209 Mt in 2020-21. Government policies that intervene in sugar markets, and production cycles in some major cane producing countries of Asia, will continue to influence world sugar production and price volatility over the longer term. World sugar consumption is expected to grow at a lower average rate over the longer term in response to higher prices to reach 207 Mt in 2020-21.

- Stocks should rebuild in the near term, but the stocks-to-use ratio is expected to average lower over the coming decade than in the previous ten years, providing support for higher prices (Figure 6.3).

Figure 6.1. **World sugar balance moves into surplus**

World sugar production less consumption

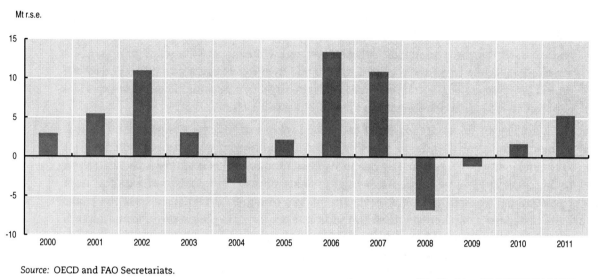

Mt r.s.e.

Source: OECD and FAO Secretariats.

StatLink http://dx.doi.org/10.1787/888932426885

Figure 6.2. **World prices to decline but to remain on a higher plateau**

Evolution of world sugar prices in nominal (left figure) and real terms (right figure) to 2020[1]

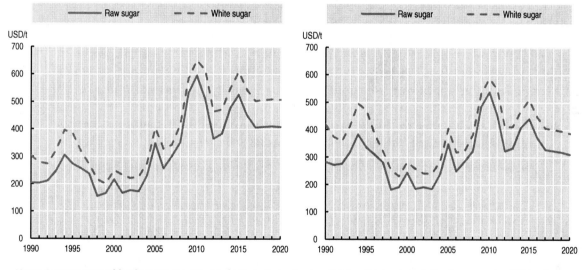

Notes: Raw sugar world price: ICE Inc. No. 11, f.o.b., bulk spot price, October/September. Refined sugar price: White Sugar Futures Contracts, No. 407, Euronext market, Liffe, London, October/September.

1. Real sugar prices are nominal world prices deflated by the US GDP deflator (2005 = 1).

Source: OECD and FAO Secretariats.

StatLink http://dx.doi.org/10.1787/888932426904

Market trends and prospects

Prices

World sugar prices are projected to decline from historical highs at the start of the *Outlook*, but to remain on an elevated plateau and to average higher in real terms to 2020-21, compared with the past decade. The margin between raw and white sugar – the white premium – is expected to decline from the high level in 2010 and then to average above USD 90/t over the projection period, reflecting increased sales of white sugar by some traditional sugar exporters and from new destination refineries in the Middle East and Africa.

World sugar prices are expected to follow a wave pattern over the projection period, similar to the past decade, as a result of a continuation of government policies that intervene in sugar markets in many countries and production cycles in Asia, particularly in India, that cause large, periodic swings in trade between imports and exports. As a consequence, world prices are projected to fall to a trough in 2012-13 as production peaks in India and rises in other countries and additional exports are placed on (or lower imports are drawn from) the world market. Subsequently, the cycle in India enters the down phase leading to a shortfall in production and the need for large imports to meet consumption needs that boost the world price in 2015-16. The upturn in the cycle then recommences leading to a further drop in world prices in 2017-18 and so on.

Brazil, as the leading sugar producer and dominant global trading nation, has attained the status of a "price setter" on the world market with international sugar prices usually correlated with its relatively low production costs. Sugar production costs in Brazil, along with those of other major exporters of Australia and Thailand, have increased in recent times with the appreciation of their currencies against the US dollar. The size of the annual sugar cane crop in Brazil, together with its allocation between ethanol and sugar production are key factors underlying the projection of international sugar prices to 2020-21. Sugar production in Brazil is expected to continue to account for less than 50% of its enormous sugarcane harvest which should approach 1 bt by the close of the decade.

Figure 6.3. **Global stocks-to-use to rise in near term and then decline**

Evolution of world sugar production, consumption and stock-to-use ratio to 2020

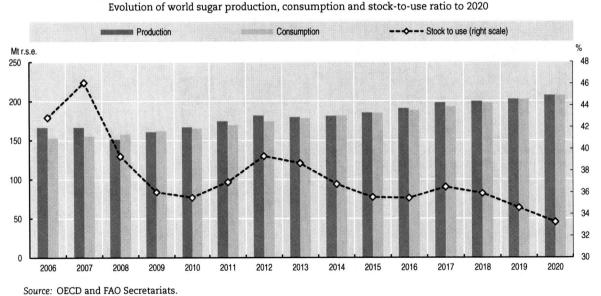

Source: OECD and FAO Secretariats.

StatLink ⟪⟫ http://dx.doi.org/10.1787/888932426923

Production and use of sugar

Sugar crops in many parts of the world are projected to expand in response to rising demand for sugar and other uses and relatively high market prices. World sugar production is expected to increase by 50 Mt to reach over 209 Mt in 2020-21. The bulk of the additional sugar production will come from the developing countries and the main burden of growth will continue to fall on Brazil. Brazil has expanded production rapidly in the past two decades, but a slowdown in investment in new mills occurred after the financial crisis of 2008, slowing overall growth in following years. The recent surge in sugar prices has improved profitability and should trigger additional investment to come on stream within the decade, with output rising by around 11 Mt to nearly 50 Mt by 2020-21.

India, the second largest global producer and the world's leading consumer, is expected to boost production substantially to 32 Mt of sugar per year, on average, in the coming decade, or some 50% higher than in 2008-10, when production fell sharply. Annual sugar output will continue to be subject to periodic large swings in response to the longstanding production cycle (Figure 6.4). Some other countries of Asia, such as China and Pakistan, are also expected to continue to experience milder forms of production cycles, which contribute to fluctuations in production and their import volumes. Outside this group, an expansion drive underway in Thailand is expected to continue as investment projects currently in the pipeline come on stream, lifting production to around 8.7 Mt by 2020-21, and maintaining its position as the world's third largest producer.

Figure 6.4. **India's production cycle to influence world prices**
Evolution of India's sugar production, consumption and imports to 2020

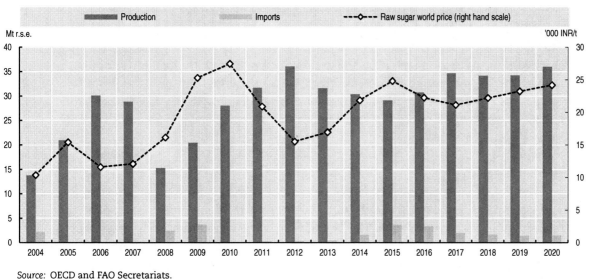

Source: OECD and FAO Secretariats.

StatLink 🔗 http://dx.doi.org/10.1787/888932426942

In contrast, to the expansion trends in the developing world, the traditional sugar industries in a number of developed countries are expected to witness static or lower production over the coming decade. For instance, in the European Union quota based sugar production has declined with policy reform and is expected to stabilise around 13.4 Mt wse (14.4 Mt rse), with a continuation of existing production quotas, to equilibrate the domestic market in a context of stable consumption, a fixed volume of subsidised exports and projected higher imports. Some additional out-of-quota sugar beet production is expected to arise over the projection period for use in ethanol production and the chemical industry. Production of sugar in the United States is expected to show little growth and to remain well below the 85% minimum allotment level of the 2008 FCE Act. US producers are expected to focus on improving their sugar margins by cutting costs and essentially leaving Mexico to fill the expanding gap between stable production and higher US consumption requirements.

Assured access to higher prices in the slowly growing US market is expected to encourage some further investment and growth in Mexico's sugar production to 2020-21. The sugar industry in Australia, although devastated by flooding and a cyclone in 2010, is expected to recover in coming years. However, with continuing pressure on land available for sugarcane production, sugar producers will likely focus on higher productivity, based on farm consolidation and improved cane varieties and higher sugar yields, rather than cane area expansion, in lifting output to around 5 Mt in 2020-21. The sugar industry in the Russian Federation has undergone a transformation in recent years and is projected to continue to expand production, under the stimulus of high domestic support measures, to reach nearly 5 Mt by 2020-21.

Global sugar consumption has continued to increase despite the continuing economic difficulties in many developed countries, compounded by the period of high sugar prices and increased volatility. This has slowed sugar use at the start of the Outlook period and slower consumption growth is expected to continue over the longer term as world sugar prices average higher in real terms. Global consumption is projected to grow at 2.2% p.a. to 2020-21, and down from 2.6% p.a. in the previous ten years. The developing countries will continue to experience the strongest growth in sugar consumption, fuelled by rising incomes and populations, although with considerable variation between countries. The sugar deficit regions of Asia and the Far East as well as Africa, will be responsible for most of the expansion in use. In contrast, sugar consumption in many developed countries, with their mature sugar markets, are expected to show little or no growth. Total consumption in these countries is expected to increase from 48Mt to nearly 52 Mt over the projection period. This reflects, among other things, slowing population growth and dietary shifts that are underway as a result of increasing health awareness and concerns with obesity and related health issues.

Trade

Over the last decade, there have been a number of structural changes affecting the evolution of trade patterns which will continue to influence international sugar transactions in the coming period. These include increased concentration in sugar export trade, with a smaller number of global exporters, and a decline in the volume of white sugar traded internationally (Figure 6.5). The reform of the sugar regime in the European Union led to an abrupt decline in white sugar exports, of the order of 6-7 Mt, as production quotas were progressively reduced below consumption requirements. As a consequence, the EU has switched from a large net exporter of white sugar to a large importer of mainly raw sugar for further refining and sale in the domestic market.

The white sugar trade is expected to recover over the coming years. This will occur as more refined sugar is exported by traditional exporters in response to the high white sugar premium at the start of the Outlook and as new destination refineries in a number of countries in Africa and the Middle East progressively come on stream and begin to export increasing quantities of white sugar to neighbouring countries and regional markets.

Figure 6.5. **Sugar exports remain highly concentrated and dominated by Brazil**

Comparison of export volumes of leading exporters between 2008-10 and 2020

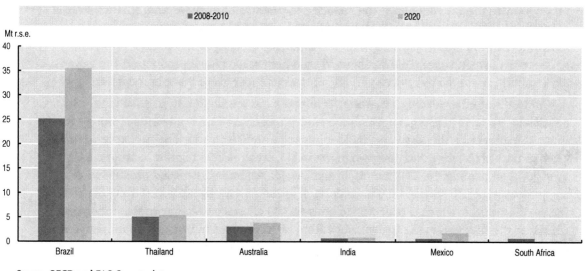

Source: OECD and FAO Secretariats.

StatLink ⬛ http://dx.doi.org/10.1787/888932426961

Brazil is expected to consolidate its position as the leading global exporter and will account for over 55% of global trade and over 63% of all additional sugar exports by the close of the projection period. While the bulk of Brazil's exports will continue to comprise high quality raw sugar (VHP), which increase to 21 Mt in 2020-21, the composition of trade will also start to favour white sugar shipments which grow by 50% and amount to over 12 Mt, in the same period (Figure 6.6). The growing concentration of global sugar exports is not without risks for sugar users as world export supplies depend increasingly on the growing conditions of a single country. This may be another factor, in addition to

Figure 6.6. **Sugar production and exports to grow in Brazil as ethanol output expands**

Evolution of sugar production, exports and ethanol output from sugarcane in Brazil

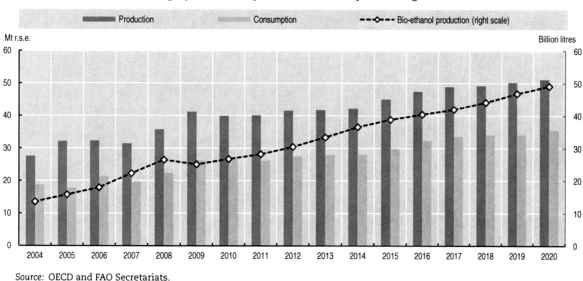

Source: OECD and FAO Secretariats.

StatLink ⬛ http://dx.doi.org/10.1787/888932426980

production cycles in Asia, which contributes to future market volatility. A possible counterweight is that a majority of Brazil's sugar cane will continue to be used for ethanol production and many mills have the capacity to produce both sugar and ethanol. Brazil also remains the only exporter that can switch 5-10% of milling capacity between sugar and ethanol production within a year in response to changes in relative profitability between the two end uses. This flexibility should help assure sugar production and export availabilities, when relative prices periodically favour sugar over ethanol production.

In terms of other leading exporters, Thailand plays a unique role in Asia as the only consistent producer of a large sugar surplus and with a natural trade advantage, along with Australia, to service the large and ballooning sugar deficit in that region. Exports from Thailand, which is ranked number two in the world, are projected to grow to around 5.8 Mt by 2020-21, exceeding the 2003 record. In the case of Australia, increased production over the projection period should support exports of around 3.8 Mt by 2020-21. Strong demand for HFCS in Mexico, which is expected to grow to 75% of total sweetener consumption and similar to the situation in the US, will substitute for sugar used in beverage manufactures, releasing surplus sugar for export to the US market. Mexican exports to the preferred US market are projected to exceed 1.8 Mt by 2020-21.

Sugar importers make up a broader, more diversified group of countries (Figure 6.7). A significant development in 2010-11 was that China exceeded for the first time the TRQ of 1.95 Mt established on sugar imports at the time of its entry to the WTO in 1998. Rapid economic growth and urbanisation trends are promoting the industrial use of sugar in food manufacture and preparations. Along with low *per capita* sugar consumption levels of only 11 kg per person in the population at large and tightening government controls on the production and use of artificial sweeteners, these are expected to lead collectively to strong growth in sugar use in China in coming years. Sugar disappearance is projected to grow by over 3% p.a., exceeding the growth of production which is increasingly limited by tightening water availability, and boosting sugar imports to over 5 Mt by 2020-21. This will make China the largest importer exceeding that of the EU, US and the Russian Federation (Figure 6.8).

Figure 6.7. **Sugar importers are more diversified**

Comparison of import volumes between 2008-10 and 2020

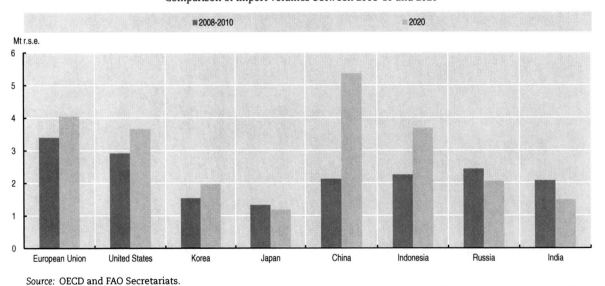

Source: OECD and FAO Secretariats.

StatLink http://dx.doi.org/10.1787/888932426999

Figure 6.8. **China's imports to rise strongly**

Evolution of China's sugar production, consumption and imports to 2020

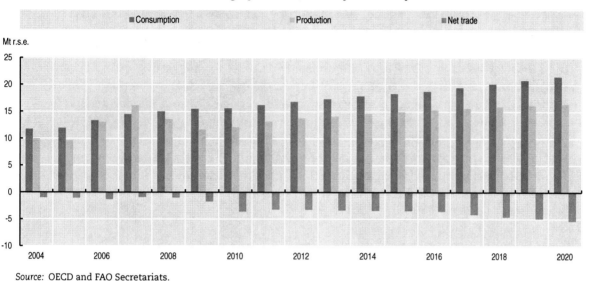

Source: OECD and FAO Secretariats.

StatLink ⌗ http://dx.doi.org/10.1787/888932427018

Figure 6.9. **Higher US consumption fed by rising Mexican imports**

Evolution of US sugar production, consumption and imports to 2020

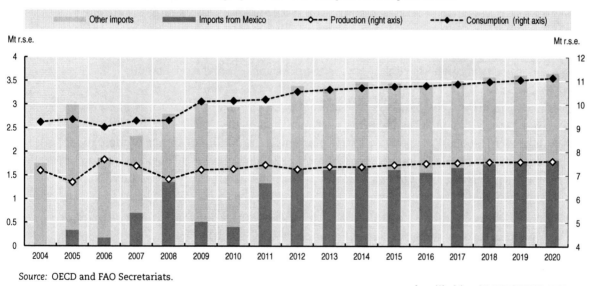

Source: OECD and FAO Secretariats.

StatLink ⌗ http://dx.doi.org/10.1787/888932427037

High world sugar prices at the onset of the Outlook period and declining internal prices with sugar policy reform have made the European Union a less attractive destination for preferential exports from LDC countries under the EBA initiative and Economic Partnership Agreements. As world prices recede, the EU as an assured market will likely become an attractive destination once more for many of these countries, although ongoing problems with infrastructure and technology adoption could constrain some LDC countries from exploiting fully their export opportunities. The United States sugar market remains heavily insulated from the world market with prohibitive tariffs and safeguard measures on imports in excess of minimum TRQ volumes. With duty-free and unrestricted imports expected to grow from Mexico under NAFTA over the coming decade, US imports under its WTO TRQ and other trade agreements are projected to be maintained at minimum levels. Total US imports are projected to reach 3.6 Mt in 2020-21, and are not assumed to trigger the Feedstock Flexibility Program (FFP) under the FCE Act for converting excess sugar supplies to ethanol in order to maintain domestic sugar prices above support levels (Figure 6.9). For its part, Mexico is expected to backfill periodically from the world market to assure its domestic consumption requirements and exports in periods of lower production. Finally, imports of the Russian Federation, which historically had been a leading destination for white sugar, before switching in the early 1990s to raw sugar imports for domestic processing, are projected to decline to around 1 Mt in 2020-21, as expanding domestic production and stable consumption lead to further import substitution.

Main issues and uncertainties

The medium term sugar projections discussed in this chapter are a conditional scenario of likely market developments based on economic, policy and normal weather assumptions. Should any of these assumptions change, the resulting set of sugar projections would also be different. For the international sugar market a number of major uncertainties remain. In the light of the relatively tight world market situation at the beginning of the Outlook period with stocks at 20 year lows, any major production disruptions in the main producing countries of Brazil and India, could radically change the market outlook in the near term, igniting further bouts of high volatility and prolonging the period of high world sugar prices.

Another issue is whether the recent high prices and improved profitability could lead to a repetition of over investment in sugar production capacity in major sugarcane producing countries. This has been a feature of past periods of high prices in countries where sugar production is based on the perennial sugarcane crop. Sugarcane with multi-year harvests (ratoons) associated with one planting is the dominant source of sugar today. This characteristic can go a long way to explaining the history of world sugar prices – short price spikes, followed by longer periods of low and depressed prices until steady consumption growth eventually erodes the production surplus.

The world sugar market has undergone a number of reforms and structural changes over the past decade. Nonetheless, it remains heavily distorted by government policy interventions that contribute to high price volatility. Changes in domestic support policies and border measures, such as the imposition of export restrictions, have a major bearing on trade volumes and international prices. Other uncertainties are future policy choices for sugar in the European Union and the sugar provisions of forthcoming US Farm Bills. Changes in oil and energy prices and their implications for the share of sugarcane dedicated as a feedstock for ethanol production, particularly in Brazil, will also influence the market.

Box 6.1. **India: The role of policies in the sugar production cycle**

The international sugar market remains one of the most volatile of all commodity markets. One of the contributory factors to this volatility is policy-induced production swings among some Asian countries, particularly India. A longstanding feature of the sugar market in India is the cyclical nature of production, where 2-3 years of surplus are followed by 2-3 years of deficit. In recent years, the cycle has been more pronounced, with larger swings in production and trade. After an increase in 2006/07 to 30.1 Mt, 33% over the record 2002/03 crop, sugar output declined to 15.2 Mt in 2008/09 and is currently estimated at 28 Mt for 2010/11. Trade generally follows a similar trend, with imports exceeding 2 Mt during the deficit phase of the cycle, replaced by large exports during the surplus phase. Weather patterns of course are a key factor as sugarcane yields are greatly affected by the level of rainfall, notably during the critical monsoon season. But, domestic sugar polices amplify the cycle through their effect on incentives along the sugar value chain, including for farmers and sugar factories.

There are four broad areas of public intervention that regulate the sugar market in India. First, both the Central and the State Governments set a price support for sugarcane. In general, the Central Government announces a price level, referred to as the statuary minimum price for sugar (SMP),* at which sugar factories are legally required to pay farmers for their sugarcane. The SMP is then raised by State Governments to account for differences notably in productivity and transportation cost. The second area of intervention is through restrictions on sugar quantities to be sold on the market, as well as imposing on the sugar factories a so-called sugar levy, by which they are required to sell at below market price to the public distribution centres. In addition, the government regulates sugar trade via export limitations and marketing restrictions, such as limits on private stockholdings.

Initially, the government introduced these polices to sustain the income of sugarcane farmers while at the same time protecting consumers from sugar price inflation. Reconciling these objectives is a challenge as fixed sugarcane prices are disconnected from the relatively market-based sugar prices. In the years of surplus production, sugar factories are caught in a price-cost squeeze with low sugar prices and relatively elevated fixed sugarcane costs. As sugar mills struggle to pay farmers at the obligatory price, growers eventually substitute alternative crops for sugarcane. As cane area is reduced and input use on standing cane is reduced, cane production falls significantly – this corresponds to the trough of the cycle. The downfall in production shifts the sugar balance into the deficit phase and provides an upward support to sugar prices. Eventually, sugar factories become solvent and begin to repay arrears to growers. As the incidence of default declines, sugarcane cultivation becomes attractive once more, shifting the domestic sugar balance into the upside phase of the cycle. Hence, the accumulation of arrears, brought about by a lack of instantaneous alignment between sugarcane and sugar prices, is causing, to a great extent, the cyclical nature of sugar production in India. Further, inelastic supply in the short-run, because of the perennial nature of sugarcane, means that farmers cannot adjust quickly to the realities of the market, hence prolonging the upside and downside phases of the cycle.

Against a backdrop of recurrent large swings in production, sugar demand in India has been growing steadily at about 4% per year over the past 10 years. Therefore, the domestic production and consumption balance moves from periods of surpluses and deficits, leading to often significant changes in the trade position. For instance, in 2007/08, exports reached 4.7 Mt (9.7% of world exports), but in 2009/10, these were replaced by imports of about 4 Mt (7% of world imports). These changes in trade channel the swings in domestic production to the international sugar markets, contributing to its volatility, especially during periods of global market tightness.

Box 6.1. **India: The role of policies in the sugar production cycle**

The potential for expanding sugar production in India exists and can be fully exploited if adjustments were introduced to ensure a market driven relationship between sugar and sugarcane prices. Also, relaxing some of the existing measures, such as the monthly releases, could provide sugar factories with some cash flow flexibility. The use and valorisation of sugarcane by-products, such as ethanol, electric power, and other derivatives, can cushion against low sugar prices and other market risks. Clearly, the liberalisation of the sugar industry can only be undertaken within the context of broader domestic reforms, because of the linkages on both demand and supply sides that prevail in agricultural commodity markets.

* Beginning 2009/10, the SMP was replaced by the concept of Fair and Remunerative Price (FRP), which takes into account "reasonable margins" for growers of sugarcane.

References

McConell, Michael, Dohlman, Erik and Haley, Stephen, (2010), "World Sugar Price Volatility Intensified by Market and Policy Factors", *Amber Waves*, The Economics of Food, Farming, Natural Resources, and Rural America, Economic Research Service, USDA, September 2010.

International Sugar Organization, Quarterly Market Outlook, (2011), Mecas (11)02, February 2011, London.

ANNEX 6.A

Statistical tables: Sugar

Table 6.A.1. World sugar projections

Crop year

		Avg 08/09-10/11est	11/12	12/13	13/14	14/15	15/16	16/17	17/18	18/19	19/20	20/21
OECD[1]												
SUGAR BEET												
Production	mt	155	145	144	147	149	152	154	156	156	157	157
Biofuel use	mt	17	18	19	20	23	26	28	29	30	30	30
SUGAR CANE												
Production	mt	110	113	116	115	116	118	120	123	126	127	128
SUGAR												
Production	kt rse	36 554	35 104	35 636	36 092	36 259	36 730	37 119	37 664	38 139	38 376	38 576
Consumption	kt rse	43 529	43 860	44 538	44 889	45 140	45 380	45 686	46 019	46 372	46 684	47 039
Closing stocks	kt rse	14 167	12 830	12 179	11 920	11 967	11 988	12 086	12 408	12 798	13 101	13 364
HFCS												
Production	kt	12 734	12 993	12 819	12 885	12 977	13 096	13 199	13 303	13 384	13 492	13 580
Consumption	kt	12 763	12 756	12 604	12 650	12 721	12 811	12 902	12 981	13 018	13 091	13 150
NON-OECD												
SUGAR BEET												
Production	mt	67	75	76	77	78	80	83	85	85	85	86
SUGAR CANE												
Production	mt	1 518	1 546	1 619	1 642	1 686	1 723	1 765	1 828	1 867	1 926	1 981
Biofuel use	mt	340	380	409	444	482	509	538	560	589	630	670
SUGAR												
Production	kt rse	122 370	138 235	144 650	143 366	144 523	147 574	155 712	161 507	163 405	167 358	170 832
Consumption	kt rse	117 928	124 726	129 447	132 633	135 911	138 473	142 984	147 399	151 534	156 011	160 442
Closing stocks	kt rse	45 120	48 087	53 624	54 401	52 669	51 682	54 329	58 343	60 174	61 493	61 740
HFCS												
Production	kt	1 181	1 456	1 495	1 537	1 574	1 611	1 645	1 678	1 708	1 742	1 777
Consumption	kt	1 142	1 547	1 565	1 627	1 684	1 750	1 797	1 855	1 927	1 997	2 061
WORLD												
SUGAR BEET												
Production	mt	221	220	220	224	227	232	237	240	241	242	244
Area	mha	4	4	4	4	4	4	4	5	5	5	5
Yield	t/ha	51	51	51	51	52	52	53	53	53	54	54
Biofuel use	mt	17	18	19	20	23	26	28	29	30	30	30
SUGAR CANE												
Production	mt	1 627	1 659	1 734	1 757	1 802	1 841	1 885	1 951	1 993	2 054	2 109
Area	mha	23	24	25	25	26	26	26	27	28	28	29
Yield	t/ha	69	68	69	69	70	71	71	72	72	73	74
Biofuel use	mt	340	380	409	444	482	509	538	560	589	630	670
SUGAR												
Production	kt rse	158 925	173 339	180 286	179 458	180 783	184 304	192 831	199 170	201 544	205 733	209 408
Consumption	kt rse	161 457	168 586	173 985	177 522	181 051	183 853	188 670	193 418	197 906	202 695	207 481
Closing stocks	kt rse	59 286	60 917	65 802	66 321	64 637	63 671	66 415	70 750	72 972	74 594	75 104
Price, raw sugar[2]	USD/t	492.8	509.5	365.4	383.2	478.8	525.9	451.3	406.6	408.8	410.9	408.1
Price, white sugar[3]	USD/t	550.2	614.2	464.1	472.4	550.1	608.7	543.5	503.3	506.7	509.6	507.8
Price, HFCS[4]	USD/t	528.1	500.3	534.0	533.6	536.3	531.2	539.6	542.6	538.9	534.2	535.9

Note: Crop year: Beginning crop marketing year - see the Glossary of Terms for definitions.

rse : raw sugar equivalent.

HFCS: High fructose corn syrup

1. Excludes Iceland but includes EU6 members that are not members of the OECD (Bulgaria, Cyprus, Latvia, Lithuania, Malta and Romania).
2. Raw sugar world price, ICE Inc. No11 f.o.b, bulk price, October/September.
3. Refined sugar price, White Sugar Futures Contract No. 407, Euronext market, Liffe, London, Europe, October/September.
4. US wholesale list price HFCS-55 , October/September.

Source: OECD and FAO Secretariats.

StatLink http://dx.doi.org/10.1787/888932427987

Chapter 7

Meat

Market situation

The meat sector is adjusting to the supply and demand imbalances in the feed sector of the past three years, which has incited swings in feed prices. Beef and sheep meat farmers are enjoying a period of higher prices, but those producing white meats, require supply adjustment to avoid further financial difficulties. Faced with high production costs, restricted access to credit, high energy costs and a subdued demand during the financial crisis, cattle farmers culled their herds. This initially resulted in a sustained supply of meat products, and prices fell sharply. Prices started to recover as economies pulled out of recession. The red meats sector had liquidated breeding animals and was unable to rapidly satisfy the increasing post-recession demand. As a result, prices recovered strongly in 2010. The supply of pig and particularly poultry meat responded more quickly to the higher demand and, as a result, prices recovered at a slower pace than those of red meats.

Projection highlights

- The meat market outlook for the decade ahead reflects the response to sustained high feed costs in a context of firm demand, particularly from developing countries. High price signals in the first half of the Outlook are expected to result in the expansion of livestock inventories, and a subsequent expansion of trade during the second half (Figure 7.1).

- World meat production growth is anticipated to slow to 1.8% p.a. dampened by higher costs during the Outlook period, which compares to 2.1% p.a. for the previous decade. The growth is primarily driven by productivity gains from both larger economies of scale and technical efficiency gains, notably for poultry and pigmeat in developing countries (Figure 7.2).

- Relative to the previous decade, meat consumption growth in the Outlook period will decelerate due to high meat prices and a slowing of population growth. Demand growth will mostly stem from large economies in Asia, Latin America and oil exporting countries.

- Driven mostly by an expansion of poultry and beef shipments, world meat exports in 2020 are projected to increase by 1.7% p.a, in the Outlook period, which compares to 4.4% p.a. in the previous decade. Slower growth is largely attributable to reduced import demand by the Russian Federation which is seeking to expand its livestock sector. The bulk of the growth in meat exports will originate from South and North America, which together account for 84% of the world increase in exports.

Figure 7.1. **World meat prices adapt to high feed costs and firmness of demand
(c.w.e or r.t.c.)**

Nominal *vs.* real meat prices[1]

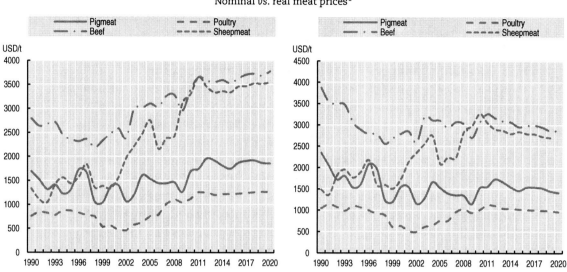

1. US Choice steers, 1100-1300 lb dressed weight, Nebraska. New Zealand lamb schedule price dressed weight, all grade average. US Barrows and gilts, No. 1-3, 230-250 lb dressed weight, Iowa/South Minnesota. Brazil average chicken producer price ready to cook.

Source: OECD and FAO Secretariats.

StatLink http://dx.doi.org/10.1787/888932427056

Figure 7.2. **Meat production growth dominated by developing countries**

Production growth: by region and meat type, 2020 vs. base period (c.w.e. or r.t.c.)

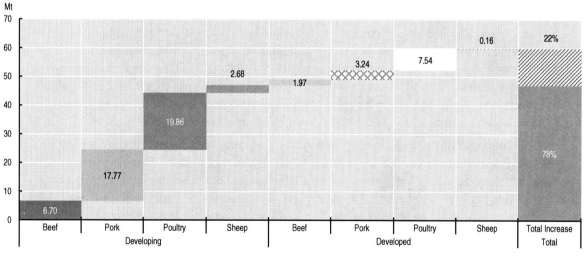

Source: OECD and FAO Secretariats.

StatLink http://dx.doi.org/10.1787/888932427075

Market trends and prospects

Prices

Meat prices, which in 2011 are at record high levels, will remain firm during the Outlook period. The current price peak, due to the combined effect of a tight supply situation from low livestock numbers and high feed costs, will trigger a modest increase in supply in the short run and price pressures may ease somewhat. However, prices will remain firm in the second half of the projection under persistently high production costs due not only to high feed prices, but also the assumption of ongoing introduction over the years of more stringent food safety, environmental, and animal welfare regulations (housing, transportation) and traceability by major meat producing countries. These collective preferences are likely to play a role in the future international trading system. Nominal prices for beef and sheep meat increase by 18% and 20% by 2020 relative to the 2008-2010 base period, whereas pigmeat and poultry prices are expected to be 26% and 16% higher (Figure 7.1). Sheepmeat prices have seen a substantial increase in its prices in the recent past due to a lower supply as well as a currency appreciation in Australia and New Zealand. In real terms, all meat prices are expected to remain firm and on a higher plateau for the Outlook period.

Production

Annual world meat production growth is projected to slow, averaging 1.8% p.a. during the Outlook period. Complying with the new housing regulations for sows, due to be implemented in January 2013, will increase costs for EU producers and may reduce production. High feed prices, inefficient road transport infrastructure in key regions richly endowed with natural resources (Brazil, the Russian Federation and Sub Saharan Africa) as well as increasing constraints on natural resources in other, will hamper the full potential for production growth that could be realised through higher livestock numbers, economies of scale and technical efficiency gains. The increase is expected to occur predominantly in developing countries, which will be responsible for about 78% of the additional output. Meat production growth will be originating mostly from the poultry and pigmeat sectors which, relative to the more expensive red meats, benefit from shorter production cycles and have higher feed-to-meat conversion rates (Figure 7.2). Sheep breeding stocks are expected to stop declining in Oceania as the increase in import demand from Middle East countries stimulates markets.

The Outlook period will be characterised by sustained high feed prices. This will lead to technological changes towards a more efficient use of this input. In intensive feed based production systems, this is likely to result in the development of more efficient feed to meat conversion technologies, notably in the poultry and pig industries. In the case of beef, grass based production systems should expand and will lead to a more strategic use of feed concentrate.

Consumption

Meat consumption growth in the Outlook period will be curbed relative to the previous decade by high meat prices and slowing population growth. Consumer aging, coupled with an increasing awareness of the impact of meat production on the environment are expected to exert some adverse effect on demand, particularly in developed countries. Moreover, occurrences of meat-based diseases like E. coli and salmonella, combined with recent episodes of meat and milk contamination with chemical compounds (dioxin and melamine), have served to lowered consumer confidence in some instances. Nevertheless, higher meat consumption brought about by income growth and urbanisation will strengthen the intake of animal proteins at the expense of foods of vegetal origin in emerging economies. It is expected that demand growth will mostly stem from large economies in Asia, Latin America and the oil exporting countries (Figure 7.3).

Figure 7.3. Increase in meat demand, by region between 2020 and the base period (c.w.e. or r.t.c.)

Consumption growth of 60 Mt is projected by 2020; predominantly in Asia

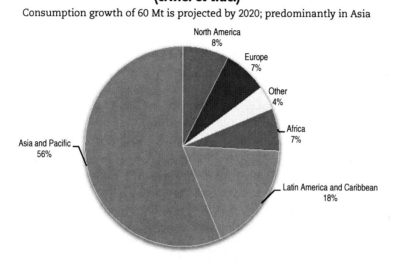

Source: OECD and FAO Secretariats.

StatLink ⬛⬛ http://dx.doi.org/10.1787/888932427094

Trade

Growth in meat trade for the next decade is anticipated to slow due to the combined effect of slowing production and firm world prices that discourage imports. An expansion of poultry and beef shipments will lead world meat exports to increase 16% by 2020 relative to the base period (see Figure 7.4). The bulk of the growth in meat trade is expected to originate largely from North and South America, which will account for nearly 84% of the total increase in all meat exported by 2020. US meat exports are expected to benefit from a lower import tariff applied in the new free trade agreement with Korea (KORUS) as well as the progressive easing of BSE-related import restrictions imposed by high income trading partners. Meat exports from the EU are anticipated to decline over the decade due to reduced domestic output following policy reforms, coupled with a growing domestic consumption brought about by the EU enlargement. The anual meat import quotas also increased as new countries joined the EU (see Box 7.1). Japan is projected to remain the leading meat importing country by 2020, followed by Mexico and Korea. The Russian Federation remains one of the largest net meat importers but TRQs will hamper meat imports as will China's self-sufficiency policy.

Box 7.1. **Evolution of EU tariffs' quotas (TRQs) for red meat**

Following the 2004 and 2007 EU enlargements, some quotas, both available for all (*erga omnes*) and country-allocated, have increased as a result of negotiations under Article XXIV.6 of the WTO Agreement on Agriculture. Moreover, from 1st January 2008, the former quotas for African, Caribbean and Pacific (ACP) countries were replaced with unlimited duty-free market access as a provisional application of the EPA (European Partnership Agreements), replacing the former Cotonou agreement.

Box 7.1. **Evolution of EU tariffs' quotas (TRQs) for red meat** (cont.)

Beef

The current beef TRQ can be divided into several GATT quotas comprising: country-allocated, *erga omnes*, live animals and meat products. There are also three bilateral quotas for baby beef (Balkans, Switzerland and Chile) and an *erga omnes* quota of 20 kt of high quality beef. The latter was instituted in 2009, following the conclusion of an US-EU memorandum of understanding, intended to resolve the long standing hormones dispute on EU meat imports from the United States. Moreover, in 2009 the EU concluded an agreement with Brazil (in the context of WTO Article XXIV.6), which increased the import quota for Brazilian high quality beef, as well as the *erga omnes* frozen beef quota for processing. Live animals and different meat products, defined by specific product categories, qualities and/or end uses are included in these TRQs. Duty-free in-quota imports can enter from all countries under the general high quality beef quota and from Chile (fresh, frozen) and Switzerland (live, dried), while a 4-6% *ad valorem* tariff is applied on live animal imports from all countries. In addition to some combined rates, a 20% *ad valorem* tariff is also applied on Hilton beef, frozen meat and frozen meat destined for processing.

Beef TRQ import licenses are allocated after reviewing all applications from different origins. Alternatively, for some country-specific, high quality beef quotas, import licenses are issued after certificates of authenticity are provided by qualified authorities in a third-party country. Import license applicants must be established operators in the EU Member State in which they apply and must have been engaged in international trade in the related sector in the previous two years. For meat processing-specific quotas, the latter requirement is replaced by proof of processing activity.

Table 7.1. **EU beef TRQs for 2006-2011**

Import tariff quota	Origin	Volume 2010-2011	Duty	Allocated per calendar year or GATT year (July-June)					
				2006-2007		2009-2010		2010-2011	
				Volume	%	Volume	%	Volume	%
High-quality beef	7 country allocations:	65 250 t pw	20%	49 493 t	82	36 208 t	56		
				–					
	Argentina	28 000 t		27 995 t	100	18 338 t	66		
	USA&Canada	11 500 t		1 785 t	16	1 336 t	12		
	Australia	7 150 t		7 149 t	100	7 147 t	100	Not yet available	
	Uruguay	6 300 t		6 299 t	100	6 299 t	100		
	Brazil	10 000 t		4 990 t	100	792 t	7.90		
	New Zealand	1 300 t		1 274 t	98	1 300 t	100		
	Paraguay	1 000 t		0 t	0	997 t	100		
	Australia (buffalo)	2 250 t		0 t	0	0 t	0		
	erga omnes[1]	20 000 t pw	0%			9 822 t	49		
Frozen beef	*erga omnes*	53 000 t pw	20%	53 000 t	100	53 000 t	100	53 000 t	100
Frozen beef for processing	*erga omnes*	63 703 t cw	20%*	54 703 t	100	44 350 t	70	43 447 t	68
Frozen thin skirt	*erga omnes*	800 t pw	4%	923 t	62	800 t	100	800 t	100
	Argentina	700 t pw				51 t	7.20	Not yet available	
Fresh&Frozen	Chile	1 750 t pw	0%	1 350 t	100	1 650 t	100	Not yet available	
Baby beef	Country allocated Balkans	22 525 t cw	20% av + 20% spec.	3 117 t	14	3 633 t	16	3 563 t	16
Dried boneless	Switzerland	1 200 t pw	0%	237 t	20	1 200 t	100	1 200 t	100
Live bovines	Switzerland	4 600 head	0%	4 600 h	100	1 610 h	35	1 380 h	30
Young males for fattening	*erga omnes*	24 070 head	16%+ 582[euro]/t	3 255 h	14	0	0	Not yet available	
Live mountain and Alpine breeds	*erga omnes*	1 421 head	4% or 6%	900 h	63	0	0	Not yet available	

1. According to the Memorandum of Understanding between the EU and Canada and that between the EU and US, the quantity of this erga omnes TRQ will be increased in two steps, first to 21 500 t (date of application to be determined) and from 2012 to 48 200 t.

* Higher duty for B-products. Under A-products: you have meat intended to produce cooked beef products and under B-products: meat intended to be used for producing smoked ans salted product. *StatLink* ᵇᵍᵇ http://dx.doi.org/10.1787/888932427531

Box 7.1. **Evolution of EU tariffs' quotas (TRQs) for red meat** (cont.)

Sheep and goat meat

EU sheep and goat meat imports are subject to TRQs totalling 284 651 t c.w.e., filled mostly (282 660 t c.w.e.) by both fresh and frozen sheep and goat meat imports (Harmonized System code 0204) that are mainly allocated to New Zealand. All TRQs, with the exception of the live animal quota, have a 0% in-quota duty rate. The TRQs have been relatively constant overtime, apart from small increases resulting from the GATT Article XXVIII negotiations and bilateral agreements. The Chilean quota (6 600 t in 2011) is scheduled to increase by 200 t annually, based on a bilateral agreement negotiated in 2003. Only 92 t (c.w.e.) of live animals can enter the EU at a 10% duty rate, regardless of origin. The quota allocated to Iceland (1 850 t) covers fresh and frozen meat, as well as certain processed products (e.g. smoked sheep meat). All sheep and goat meat TRQs are allocated on a calendar year, "first come first served" basis.

Table 7.2. **EU sheep and goat meat TRQs for 2004-2010**

Country group	Product, CN code	Ad valorem duty %	Specific duty	Origin	Annual volume (t cw)	Quota use, % 2010	Quota use, % 2007	Quota use, % 2004
1 Fresh& Frozen	0204 fresh and frozen sheep and goat meat	Zero	Zero	New Zealand	227 854	86	99	93
				Argentina	23 000	25	24	24
				Australia	18 786	98	97	98
				Chile[1]	6 600	89	78	54
				Uruguay	5 800	77	99	87
				Norway	300	0	2	90
				Turkey	200	0	0	0
				Others	200	26	60	0
				Greenland	100	0	0	0
				Faroes	20	0	0	0
2 Iceland Fresh-Frozen & processed	204 0210 99 21 0210 99 29 0210 99 60	Zero	Zero	Iceland[2]	1 850	99	41	79
3 Live animals	0104 10 30 0104 10 80 0104 20 90	10%	Zero	Erga omnes	92	0	3	0
TOTAL					**284 651**	**82**	**92**	**87**

1. Chile TRQ: 6 400 t in 2010, 5 800 t in 2007 and 5 200 t in 2004.
2. Iceland TRQ: 1 725 t in 2007 an 1 350 t in 2004.
Source: European Commission.

StatLink http://dx.doi.org/10.1787/888932427550

Beef exports during the Outlook period will expand at 1.8% p.a. compared to 2.9% p.a. in the past decade. The expansion will be led by the United States, Brazil and Canada. Brazil exported record volumes in the mid 2000s, following the sharp drop in US and Canadian beef exports after the BSE incidences. Brazilian exports have since declined, but will grow during the Outlook period despite increasing domestic consumption induced by growing income, with the country taking advantage of its extensive grasslands for rearing cattle in times of expensive feed. Brazil will establish its position as the leading world exporter, with volumes in 2020 reaching 2 Mt. As mentioned above, the United States will continue expanding from improved market access to the Pacific market. By 2020 US export volumes are anticipated to be higher than those recorded before the BSE crisis emerged. The expansion of exports by the US, in volume terms, will be more than offset by larger imports, and the country will see a continuation of its negative trade balance in beef.

By 2020 Canadian beef exports will also steadily increase, prompted by productivity gains and changes in feeding practice. Shipments from Australia will stagnate from reduced herds and expensive feeds, exports from New Zealand will marginally increase from an enlarged dairy herd, while in Argentina export restrictions will continue to limit trade.

The expansion of world pigmeat trade will be relatively modest during the Outlook period, but this outcome masks some significant changes in the composition of trade. North and South American pork shipment are expected to increase. Exports from Brazil are expected to expand, but its rapid growth of the last decade will be curbed during the projection period by a strong domestic demand. Net trade in China, where half of the world's output is produced and consumed, is not expected to change during the Outlook period. Government policies will continue to support the pork industry through the scaling up of production and the modernisation of its markets. These include buying into intervention stocks, setting up futures markets, and support for large scale production facilities and genetic improvements.

Figure 7.4. Evolution of world exports of beef, pigmeat, poultry and sheep (c.w.e. or r.t.c.)

Overall meat export to reach nearly 30 Mt by 2020 a 16% increase from the base period

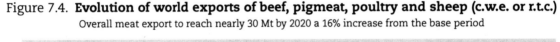
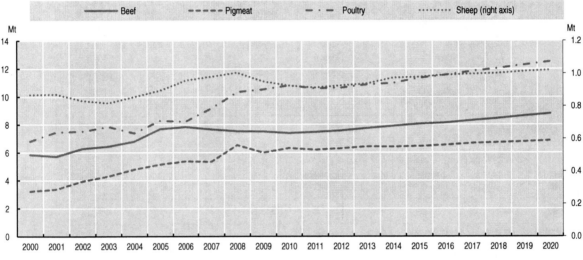

Source: OECD and FAO Secretariats.

StatLink ⬛🖳 http://dx.doi.org/10.1787/888932427113

A slowing down of trade growth in poultry products is anticipated, from an annual rate of 4.7% in last decade to 2% during the Outlook period. The largest contributors to projected export growth are the US and Brazil, both of which are expected to strengthen their dominance of world trade. During the first part of the projection, their exports will stagnate due to the demand response to high poultry product prices, as well as a tight supply situation created by expensive feeds. Nevertheless, the adaptation of producers to higher feed and energy costs is expected to induce structural changes in the industry, boosting production and exports, most notably during the second half of the projection period. By 2020, US and Brazilian exports would account for nearly half of the additional export supply in world markets. Growth in Argentinean exports to the South American market continuously increases, given ample feed, a depreciating peso and no export restrictions.

Thailand exports are also anticipated to expand slightly, mainly for processed products. Exports from the EU will decline due to growing domestic demand, a strong euro and animal welfare regulations limiting stocking density.

Import growth will be led by countries in the Middle East, Southeast Asia and Latin America. Expansion in Mexico's food processing industry is expected to boost the country's import demand, while purchases by Russia, once the world's largest importer, will significantly decline following higher domestic production. In the EU, the decline in exports during the projection period will be accompanied by a sustained, albeit moderate, expansion of imports. As a result, the EU, a traditional net exporter, will see a constant deterioration of its terms of trade, with a balanced account by 2020. The EU will nevertheless continue to play a major role in world markets, both as an exporter and an importer of poultry products.

Oceania sheepmeat exports will increase slightly, mainly due to supply response from Australia, as pasture based meat production will compete well against an increasingly grain intensive meat production. The destination of those exports will continue to be traditional markets combined with increased demand for sheepmeat from the Middle East. The European market will continuously lower their imports (which will remain below quota level) due to the tight world supplies, relatively high prices and a weaker domestic demand.

Main issues and uncertainties

Animal disease outbreaks have shown to have potential radical effects on supply, demand and trade. For diseases such as FMD and BSE, the impacts vary significantly depending on whether the region is an importer or exporter, the importance of market share and the ability to contain the outbreak within an intra-country region. Any outbreak in a major exporting country, such as Australia, Canada, US and Brazil, which could not be regionalised will affect domestic and international markets. The incidences of BSE in the US and Canada and resulting trade restrictions, altered world markets for a considerable period of time. For importers, the impacts are generally much less severe. Other potential disease outbreaks which may have zoonotic scope, such as H1N1, still loom as potential factors that could impact significantly meat markets, not only for trade, but also for global consumption.

A number of key market drivers and macroeconomic events could alter the meat market projections in this outlook. The Russian Federation has traditionally been a top meat importer, but the pigmeat and poultry sectors have experienced in recent years sustained growth. The outlook assumes that this trend will continue during the Outlook period, with the Russian Federation achieving a certain degree of self-sufficiency and having exportable surpluses. China's net trade position *vis-à-vis* pigmeat remains a key uncertainty that overhangs world markets. Due to its extraordinary volumes both in terms of production and consumption, unforeseen events in China which could result in import surges of pigmeat have the potential to severely impact international markets. In North Africa and the Middle East, large importers of sheep meat, poultry and beef, changes in oil prices, or the fallout from civil unrest have the potential to impact world meat trade.

The world meat market is highly fragmented due to sanitary restrictions, and therefore changes in the architecture of market access pose a significant risk to the validity of the projections. For example, the beef market is divided into Foot and Mouth free trade routes, and the rest of the world. Large exporters such as the US and Brazil belong to different circuits, and their prices do not always follow the same patterns. The US grants meat market access to the

Brazilian State of Santa Catarina, this is likely to intensify price arbitration between the Atlantic and Pacific markets. In the case of beef, the impact of opening this market would result in Brazilian farmers competing with producers located as far away as Australia.

Finally, environmental costs are rising for the production of virtually all meats, and the implementation of new legislation that conditions production to environmental protection may affect the growth of the sector. Livestock production is recognised as a key contributor to anthropogenic greenhouse gas (GHG) emissions (see Box 7.2). These emissions are expected to increase in the future, as population and income growth increase the global demand for livestock products. It remains uncertain to what extent over the next decade livestock production may be subject to carbon mitigation constraints in some countries. Pricing emissions from livestock production could potentially result in substantial shifts in production and relative meat prices, thus affecting not only the geography of production but also the consumer preference for cheaper meats that are associated with lower GHG emissions, notably poultry. Moreover, as mentioned earlier in the chapter, additional consumer concerns related to such issues as animal welfare, food quality, and production and processing methods may further introduce segmentation in the meat trade, for more information see the documents "Policy responses to societal concerns in food and agriculture: proceedings of an OECD workshop", OECD 2010 and Tothova, M. (2009), "The Trade and Trade Policy Implications of Different Policy Responses to Societal Concerns", OECD Food Agriculture and Fisheries, Working Pamers, No. 20, OECD publishing.

Box 7.2. **Greenhouse gas emissions from livestock production in the European Union**

With increased prosperity, people are consuming more meat and dairy products every year. Global meat production is projected to more than double from 229 mt in 1999-2001 to 465 mt in 2050, while milk output is set to climb from 580 to 1 043 mt.

Past studies have evaluated GHG emissions from animal production following a Life Cycle Assessment (LCA). The 2006 FAO study livestock's long shadow[1] as well as a follow-up report published in 2010[2] concluded that both livestock and the dairy sectors significantly contribute to global human-related GHG emissions.

Recently, a detailed regional analysis of total GHG emissions using an LCA approach, for the 27 countries of the European Union has also been carried out by the EC Joint Research Centre[3] using the CAPRI model. Total net GHG emissions of EU livestock production was estimated at 661 mt of carbon dioxide equivalents (CO_{2-eq}), which represent between 9 to 13% of total GHG emissions estimated for the EU agricultural sector, depending if emissions from land use and land use change are excluded or not. Of those emissions, 23% are emitted as methane, 24% as nitrous oxide (including cultivation of feed crops) and the industrial production of mineral fertilisers), 21% as CO_2 from direct and indirect energy use and 29% as CO_2 from land use and land use change. As presented in the figure below, ruminants (cows, sheep and goats) have the highest carbon footprint per kg produced, with beef production as the most-emitting activity.

The EC study has assessed some policy options to mitigate livestock emissions namely an emission standard applied across the EU, tradable emission permits and livestock emission taxes, pointing out that without a global policy framework any policy options put in place to mitigate livestock emissions will result in a considerable reduction in their effectiveness through emissions leakage (i.e. as a result of higher net imports of feed and meat products).

Box 7.2. **Greenhouse gas emissions from livestock production in the European Union** (*cont.*)

Figure 7.5. **Total GHG emissions of beef, pork, poultry and sheep and goat meat produced in EU27 in 2004, calculated with a cradle-to-gate life-cycle analysis with CAPRI**

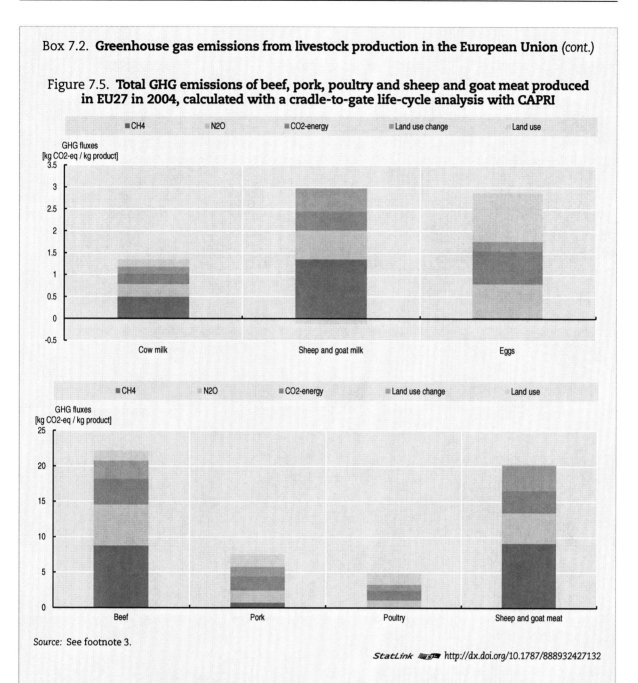

Source: See footnote 3.

StatLink http://dx.doi.org/10.1787/888932427132

1. FAO (2006), Livestock's long shadow – environmental issues and options, Food and Agriculture Organization of the United Nations, Rome.
2. FAO (2010), Greenhouse Gas Emissions from the Dairy Sector. A Life Cycle Assessment, Food and Agriculture Organization of the United Nations.
3. Leip A., F. Weiss, T. Wassenaar, I. Pérez Domínguez, T. Fellmann, P. Loudjani, F. Tubiello, D. Grandgirard, S. Monni and K. Biala (2010), The GGELS Project: European Greenhouse Gases Emissions from Livestock Production Systems (LPS), Dictus Publishing, 108pp.

ANNEX 7.A

Statistical tables: Meat

7.A.1.   World meat projections   *http://dx.doi.org/10.1787/888932428063*

Tables available online :

7.A.2.1.Beef and veal projections: production and trade   *http://dx.doi.org/10.1787/888932428082*
7.A.2.2. Beef and veal projections: consumption, per capita   *http://dx.doi.org/10.1787/888932428101*
7.A.3.1. Pig meat projections: production and trade   *http://dx.doi.org/10.1787/888932428120*
7.A.3.2. Pig meat projections: consumption, per capita   *http://dx.doi.org/10.1787/888932428139*
7.A.4.1. Poultry meat projections: production and trade   *http://dx.doi.org/10.1787/888932428158*
7.A.4.2. Poultry meat projections: consumption, per capita   *http://dx.doi.org/10.1787/888932428177*
7.A.5.1. Sheep meat projections: production and trade   *http://dx.doi.org/10.1787/888932428196*
7.A.5.2. Sheep meat projections: consumption, per capita   *http://dx.doi.org/10.1787/888932428215*
7.A.6.   Main policy assumptions for meat markets   *http://dx.doi.org/10.1787/888932428234*

Table 7.A.1. World meat projections

Calendar year

		Avg 2008-10	2011	2012	2013	2014	2015	2016	2017	2018	2019	2020
OECD[1]												
BEEF AND VEAL												
Production	kt cwe	27 537	27 009	26 651	27 012	27 426	27 806	28 084	28 227	28 450	28 632	28 749
Consumption	kt cwe	27 211	26 699	26 487	26 732	27 110	27 469	27 791	27 983	28 242	28 463	28 570
PIG MEAT												
Production	kt cwe	39 548	38 882	39 406	39 857	40 088	40 149	40 539	41 148	41 408	41 537	42 067
Consumption	kt cwe	37 104	36 568	37 101	37 460	37 747	37 803	38 164	38 746	39 054	39 138	39 628
POULTRY MEAT												
Production	kt rtc	40 205	41 095	41 766	42 385	42 984	43 622	44 345	45 064	45 736	46 378	47 093
Consumption	kt rtc	37 899	38 975	39 508	40 132	40 752	41 428	42 144	42 802	43 444	44 040	44 706
SHEEP MEAT												
Production	kt cwe	2 605	2 513	2 519	2 516	2 534	2 547	2 548	2 558	2 560	2 569	2 579
Consumption	kt cwe	2 151	2 052	2 040	2 027	2 014	2 012	1 994	1 995	1 983	1 984	1 986
TOTAL MEAT												
Per capita consumption	kg rwt	65.6	64.9	65.1	65.5	65.9	66.3	66.8	67.4	67.8	68.0	68.5
NON-OECD												
BEEF AND VEAL												
Production	kt cwe	37 921	38 224	39 040	39 867	40 688	41 418	42 149	42 924	43 681	44 542	45 378
Consumption	kt cwe	37 410	37 997	38 671	39 551	40 346	41 081	41 835	42 597	43 287	44 117	45 019
PIG MEAT												
Production	kt cwe	66 739	70 606	72 550	73 636	75 374	76 616	78 663	79 889	81 849	83 445	85 232
Consumption	kt cwe	68 601	72 488	74 252	75 408	77 098	78 362	80 438	81 677	83 589	85 225	87 051
POULTRY MEAT												
Production	kt rtc	54 814	59 020	60 436	62 172	63 841	65 852	67 749	69 640	71 491	73 490	75 317
Consumption	kt rtc	57 257	61 160	62 666	64 397	66 065	68 063	69 995	71 937	73 840	75 880	77 784
SHEEP MEAT												
Production	kt cwe	10 227	10 614	10 894	11 159	11 418	11 675	11 958	12 215	12 522	12 794	13 094
Consumption	kt cwe	10 615	11 011	11 304	11 585	11 870	12 143	12 446	12 712	13 034	13 313	13 621
TOTAL MEAT												
Per capita consumption	kg rwt	25.0	25.7	25.9	26.2	26.5	26.7	27.1	27.4	27.7	28.0	28.3
WORLD												
BEEF AND VEAL												
Production	kt cwe	65 458	65 233	65 691	66 878	68 114	69 224	70 233	71 151	72 130	73 173	74 127
Consumption	kt cwe	64 620	64 696	65 158	66 283	67 456	68 550	69 626	70 580	71 529	72 580	73 589
Price, EU[2]	USD/t dw	4 417	4 328	4 414	4 442	4 744	4 800	4 901	4 864	4 873	4 814	4 788
Price, USA[3]	USD/t dw	3 211	3 656	3 579	3 554	3 593	3 531	3 631	3 710	3 727	3 689	3 779
Price, Brazil[4]	USD/t dw	2 716	2 914	2 757	2 751	2 709	2 808	2 819	2 845	2 828	2 883	2 857
PIG MEAT												
Production	kt cwe	106 287	109 487	111 956	113 492	115 462	116 765	119 203	121 038	123 257	124 982	127 299
Consumption	kt cwe	105 705	109 055	111 353	112 868	114 845	116 165	118 603	120 424	122 643	124 363	126 679
Price, EU[5]	USD/t dw	2 098.0	2 264.8	2 525.4	2 575.9	2 439.8	2 354.6	2 483.7	2 535.6	2 562.5	2 647.9	2 557.5
Price, Brazil[6]	USD/t dw	1 410	1 558	1 575	1 597	1 479	1 462	1 522	1 606	1 595	1 675	1 617
Price, USA[7]	USD/t dw	1 471	1 743	1 958	1 916	1 811	1 748	1 871	1 911	1 921	1 869	1 860
POULTRY MEAT												
Production	kt rtc	95 019	100 115	102 202	104 557	106 826	109 473	112 094	114 704	117 228	119 868	122 411
Consumption	kt rtc	95 156	100 135	102 174	104 529	106 817	109 491	112 140	114 739	117 284	119 920	122 489
Price, EU[8]	USD/t pw	2 456.9	2 640.6	2 588.6	2 555.0	2 547.2	2 521.9	2 545.0	2 577.1	2 593.5	2 616.6	2 614.6
Price, Brazil[9]	USD/t rtc	1 090	1 261	1 256	1 200	1 218	1 221	1 231	1 247	1 258	1 271	1 266
Price, USA[10]	USD/t rtc	1 062	1 153	1 221	1 251	1 240	1 201	1 222	1 220	1 254	1 231	1 250
SHEEP MEAT												
Production	kt cwe	12 832	13 126	13 413	13 676	13 952	14 221	14 506	14 772	15 082	15 363	15 673
Consumption	kt cwe	12 766	13 063	13 345	13 612	13 883	14 155	14 440	14 706	15 018	15 297	15 607
Price, New Zealand[11]	USD/t dw	2 948	3 659	3 452	3 336	3 364	3 338	3 460	3 468	3 526	3 515	3 548
TOTAL MEAT												
Per capita consumption	kg rwt	32.6	32.9	33.1	33.3	33.6	33.8	34.2	34.5	34.8	35.0	35.4

Note: Calendar Year: Year ending 30 September for New Zealand.
1. Excludes Iceland but includes EU6 members that are not members of the OECD (Bulgaria, Cyprus, Latvia, Lithuania, Malta and Romania).
2. EU average beef producer price.
3. Choice steers, 1100-1300 lb lw, Nebraska - lw to dw conversion factor 0.63.
4. Brazil average beef producer price.
5. EU average pig meat producer price.
6. Brazil average pig meat producer price.
7. Barrows and gilts, No. 1-3, 230-250 lb lw, Iowa/South Minnesota - lw to dw conversion factor 0.74.
8. EU average chicken producer price.
9. Brazil average chicken producer price.
10. Wholesale weighted average broiler price 12 cities.
11. Lamb schedule price, all grade average.
Source: OECD and FAO Secretariats.

StatLink http://dx.doi.org/10.1787/888932428063

Chapter 8

Fish*

---

*   The term "fish" indicates fish, crustaceans, molluscs and other aquatic animals, but excludes aquatic mammals, crocodiles, caimans, alligators and aquatic plants.

Market situation

After a difficult 2009, characterised by a sharp decline of fish prices and a contraction in demand and trade, the seafood sector expanded again in 2010 and early 2011. This recovery was partly due to higher average fish prices as well as to growing demand. Consumer demand has been particularly strong in developing countries supported by the faster than expected economic upturn.

The average world apparent *per capita* fish consumption was stable in the period 2008-09, at about 17 kg/year (live weight equivalent), and slightly increased in 2010 due to growing demand. During the base period, fish accounted for about 15.7% of world population intake of animal protein and 6.1% of all protein consumed.

Fish prices have been on the rise in domestic markets as well as in export markets. The FAO Fish Price Index indicates that current fish prices, on average, are higher than ever, in particular for farmed fish. In early 2011, prices of aquaculture products were 23% more than in September 2008. On the other end, capture prices, after a sharp drop during the crisis, have only recently regained pre-crisis price levels.

In 2009, total fish production reached a record 145 Mt, with a slight decline of capture fisheries and an increase in aquaculture production. In 2010, capture fisheries further decreased due to lower catches of anchoveta in Latin America, while aquaculture production continued to increase its share in total fish production.

Projection highlights

- World fisheries production is projected at 164 Mt in 2020, a growth of about 15% above the average level for 2008-2010. Major increases in the quantity of fish produced will originate from aquaculture. However, for the projection period, the annual growth rate of aquaculture is estimated at 2.8%; a reduction compared to the rate of 5.6% of the previous decade (Figure 8.1).

- Fish prices (capture, aquaculture and trade) will increase over the medium term (Figure 8.2). With the growing price of fish meal and the high price of other feeds, the spread between the price of farmed and wild fish will grow over the medium term.

- Total fish and fishery products will continue to be highly traded, with about 38% of world fish production exported in 2020. World *per capita* fish food consumption is projected to reach 17.9 kg *per capita* in 2020, from 17.1 kg *per capita* of the average 2008-2010.

Figure 8.1. **Declining growth rate of fish production**

Growth rate of capture and aquaculture fish production by decades

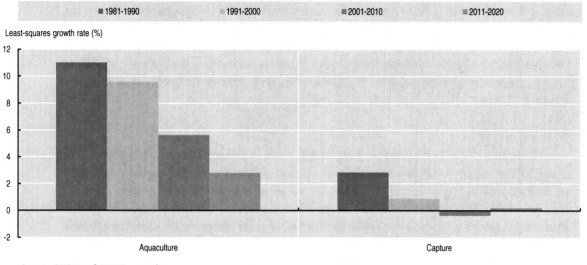

Least-squares growth rate (%)

Source: OECD and FAO Secretariats.

StatLink ⊞ http://dx.doi.org/10.1787/888932427151

Figure 8.2. **Rising world prices, with those for farmed fish increasing more than wild fish**

World fish price development in nominal terms between 2000 and 2020

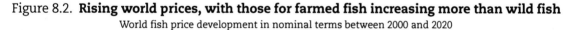

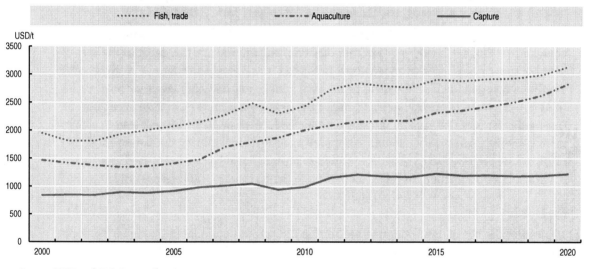

Source: OECD and FAO Secretariats.

StatLink ⊞ http://dx.doi.org/10.1787/888932427170

Market trends and prospects

This chapter illustrates the main results of the new dynamic policy specific partial equilibrium model on fish. At present, this is a standalone model, containing links to the Aglink-Cosimo model used for the agricultural projections, but not integrated into it (see Box 8.1 for more detailed information). The fish model has been developed also due to the significant importance of the fishery sector from the economic point of view, as well as for the major role played by fish in the human diet and, through fishmeal, in animal feed rations.

Prices

World fish prices will continue the growing trend experienced in 2010 and early 2011. They will be affected by income and population growth, stagnant capture fisheries production, increasing feed cost, a weaker US dollar and higher crude oil prices. All these factors will contribute to the rise in fish prices over the medium term. However, there will be different scenarios for capture fisheries production and for aquaculture. With the growing price of fishmeal and the higher price of other feeds, the spread between the average price of output from aquaculture and capture will grow over the medium term. In addition, the average price for wild fish should increase less than farmed ones due to expected changes in fish composition, with more catches of lower value fish. The average world price for captured species is expected to increase by 23 % and for aquaculture species by a significant 50% by 2020 compared to the average 2008-10. In addition to the need to compensate for the higher cost of fish meal, prices of aquaculture will also grow due to strong domestic demand. In 2020, the price of fish products traded will be 30% higher from 2008-10.

Due to stagnant capture fisheries, the increasing demand for fish will be met by aquaculture. Since it is not foreseen that oilseed meal will replace fish meal in the diet of many of the species raised in aquaculture, demand for fish meal will continue to grow. With a rather stable production, fish meal prices, which have reached high levels since 2009, are therefore expected to further increase during the next decade, up 43% in 2020 from 2008-10. During the same period, fish oil prices are projected to grow by 19%. This will lead to a large increase in the price ratio of fishmeal compared to oilseed meal. During the same period, fish oil prices are projected to grow by 19%. Although most of fish oil produced is used as an input in aquaculture production, the equivalent ratio in the oil market will increase only slightly.

Production

Under the set of assumptions used in this *Outlook* and stimulated by higher demand for fish, world fisheries production will continue to expand over the course of the projection period, reaching 164 Mt in 2020 (Figure 8.3). This represents an increase of about 15% above the average level for 2008-10. Growth in aquaculture production will offset rather stable world capture fisheries production in the forecast period. Capture fisheries should remain at around 90 Mt, with a slight increase in the medium term due to higher prices. However, there will be years (forecasted in the model as 2015 and 2020), when capture production will be affected by the El Niño phenomenon (see Glossary for more information on the El Niño). This effect will reduce catches in South America, in particular, of anchoveta caught by Peru and Chile.

Aquaculture production is projected to continue to increase, reaching nearly 74 Mt in 2020. This represents a 34.8% growth compared to the average level for 2008-10.

Figure 8.3. **World fish utilisation and consumption projections**
Development of utilisation of world fish production and per capita fish consumption between 2000-20

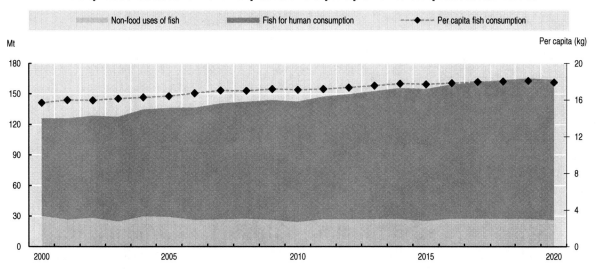

Note: Non-food uses of fish include utilisation of aquatic products for reduction to meal and oil, for feed and bait, for ornamental purposes, withdrawals from markets and any other non-food uses of fish production (*e.g.* fertilisers, medical uses, etc.).

Source: OECD and FAO Secretariats.

StatLink http://dx.doi.org/10.1787/888932427189

However, the annual growth rate for the projection period is estimated at 2.8%; a reduction compared to the increase of 5.6% in the previous decade. Notwithstanding the slower growth rate, aquaculture will still remain one of the fastest growing sectors when compared to other food-producing systems. The share of aquaculture in total fish production should grow from an average 38% for 2008-10 to 45% in 2020. In 2015, for the first time in history, fish for human consumption originating from aquaculture are expected to surpass those from capture fisheries. The share of farmed fish in total fish for human consumption was 47% on average during the 2008-10 period and is projected to reach 51% in 2015 and almost 54% by 2020 (Figure 8.4).

Aquaculture will continue to expand in all continents in terms of new areas and species, as well as intensifying and diversifying the product range for species and product forms that respond to consumer needs. Asian countries, and in particular China, will continue to dominate aquaculture production. In 2020, Chinese aquaculture production is projected to represent 61% of world production. Projections indicate a growth in Latin America, in particular in Brazil due to consistent economic investment in the sector. African production should also increase over the next decade by an expected 70% (reaching 1.7 Mt) due to private sector capacity put in place in the 2000s, in response to economic growth, rising local demand and local policies promoting aquaculture.

Fishmeal and fish oil production are projected to remain rather stable during the next decade. In 2020, their estimated production should be 5.9 Mt and 1.0 Mt, respectively, in product weight. In 2020, fish meal production should be only slighter higher (+2%) compared to the average for 2008-10. Due to growing demand for fish for human consumption, the share of capture fisheries utilised for the production of fish meal will gradually decline from about 23% in 2008-2010 to around 21% by the end of the forecast period. That share will be slightly smaller in the years of El Niño, projected in 2015

Figure 8.4. **Increasing role of aquaculture in fish consumption**
Share of fish originating from capture and aquaculture in total fish for human consumption by decades

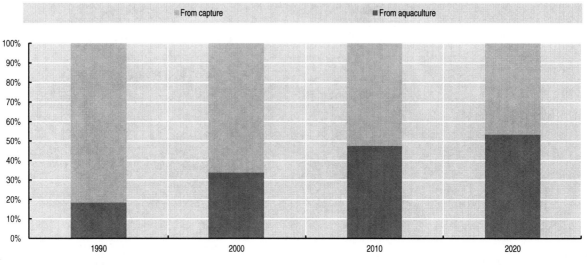

Source: OECD and FAO Secretariats.

StatLink http://dx.doi.org/10.1787/888932427208

and 2020, which diminishes catches of anchoveta, fish mainly reduced into fish meal and fish oil. In a view of stronger demand for fishmeal, a growing share of fish meal production should originate from fish residue. With growing income, people will consume an increasing share of fish in fillets or in other value added forms, thus creating more residues to be used for fish meal. Therefore, the share of the main producers of fish meal (Peru and Chile) in total production will be reduced (28% in 2020, against 30% in 2008-10).

Consumption

World *per capita* apparent fish consumption is projected to reach 17.9 kg in 2020, from 17.1 kg *per capita* of the average 2008-10. The cyclical decline in the price of other meats with no further feed price explosion, combined with higher prices of fish and fishery products will eventually stabilise consumption. *Per capita* fish consumption will increase in all continents (Figure 8.5), with Oceania and Europe showing the highest growth rates. Fish consumption will continue to be higher in more developed economies, even if decreasing in Japan and Canada. *Per capita* consumption in LDCs will increase, but will continue to be rather low (11.5 kg in 2020).

Fish consumption will continue to be affected by complex interactions of several factors, including rising living standards, growing emphasis on fish as a healthy and nutritious food, population growth, rapid urbanisation, increased trade and transformations in the food distribution and retail sectors. The total amount of fish consumed will continue to vary according to regions and countries, reflecting the different levels of availability of fish and other foods, including the accessibility of aquatic resources in adjacent waters, as well as diverse food traditions, tastes, income levels, prices and seasons. Annual *per capita* apparent fish consumption will vary from less than 1 kg in one country (*e.g.* Ethiopia) to more than 100 kg (*e.g.* Maldives) in another.

Figure 8.5. **General growth of fish consumption**

Comparison of per capita fish consumption by continent in 2008-2010 and 2018-2020

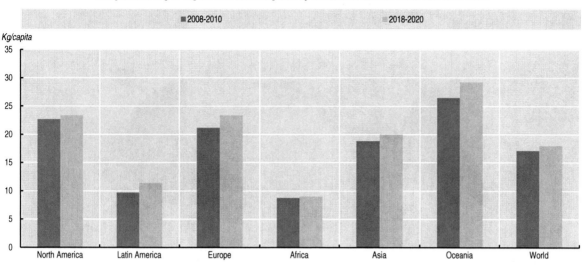

Source: OECD and FAO Secretariats.

StatLink http://dx.doi.org/10.1787/888932427227

Trade

According to the projections, total fish and fishery products (fish for human consumption, fish meal and fish oil) will remain highly traded, with about 38% of world fish production exported in 2020. In quantity terms, world trade of fish for human consumption is expected to increase at an annual growth rate of 2.3% in the period 2011-20, a decline in respect to the level experienced in the previous decade (+3.5%). Developed countries will account for about 60% of world imports of fish for human consumption, while developing countries will continue to be the main exporters, although with a decreasing share in world export quantities (63% in 2020 against 67% in 2008-10). In 2020, 51% of world fish exports for human consumption will originate from Asia, with China maintaining its position of the world's leading fish exporter (Figure 8.6).

The fishery industries of developing countries will continue to rely heavily on developed countries, not only as markets for their exports, but increasingly as a source of imports for local consumption and as suppliers of raw material for their processing industries. A growing share of exports from developing countries will continue to consist of processed fish products prepared from imports of unprocessed fish to use as raw material for further processing.

Developing countries will remain the primary importers of fish meal (63% of the total in 2020), also due to their importance in aquaculture production, having a share of 94% of world aquaculture fisheries production in 2020. China alone should represent 61% of world aquaculture production in 2020, with a share of about 36% of world fish meal imports. European countries will continue to be the major importers of fish oil, with a share of 63% of the total in 2020.

Figure 8.6. **Trade of fish for human consumption by major exporters and importers in 2020 (share in quantity)**

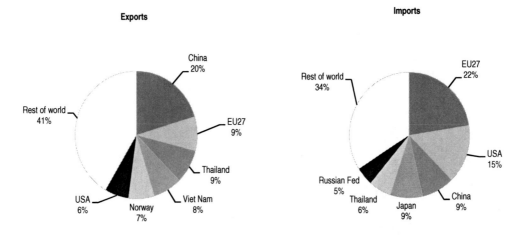

Source: OECD and FAO Secretariats.

StatLink http://dx.doi.org/10.1787/888932427246

Main issues and uncertainties

The fish projections reported in this chapter are based on specific assumptions regarding the future macroeconomic environment, international trade rules and tariffs, frequency and effects of El Niño phenomenon, absence of abnormal fish related disease outbreaks, fishery quotas, longer term productivity trends and the absence of market shocks. Should one of these assumptions change, the resulting fish projections would be affected. A number of uncertainties remain.

In the projections, overall capture fisheries production is reported to remain rather stable. However, according to recent FAO estimates (FAO SOFIA 2010*), about half of the stock groups monitored by FAO are estimated to be fully exploited. In addition, 32% of the stocks are estimated to be either overexploited, depleted or recovering from depletion, and 15% being underexploited or only moderately exploited. The latter is the lowest percentage recorded since the mid-1970s. Notwithstanding this rather critical status of stocks in some fishing areas, scientists indicate that in the near future there should be compensation between increases of catches in some fisheries and areas and decreases in others and with the overall catches remaining rather stable. However, in order to obtain these results, effective fisheries management policies that maintain stocks and productivity from fisheries should be implemented.

The majority of future growth in fish production will come from aquaculture. However, the prospects of this sector will depend on several factors, including the availability, sustainability and cost of fishmeal and fish oil and of other alternative sources of feeding; access and availability to areas and water; environmental impacts; availability of technology and finance; effects on biodiversity; climatic changes; governance; food safety and traceability issues as well as policy decisions in producing systems.

* FAO, The State of Fisheries and Aquaculture 2010, Rome, FAO. 2010. p. 197.

Fish is widely traded and it is particularly important as a source of foreign currency for many developing countries, including small island States. Future expansion of trade will be affected by several issues:

- development of new technologies, *e.g.* aquaculture breeding technology;
- changes in fish species and product forms, *e.g.* growth in farmed species and in the use of fillets and other value added forms;
- competitiveness with other food products, *e.g.* relative prices, in particular for chicken and other meat;
- prices and margins throughout the fisheries value chain, *e.g.* margins to producers;
- rising commodity prices in general and the impact on producers as well as on consumers, *e.g.* soybean prices influencing the price of fish feed and the price of farmed fish;
- energy prices and the impact on fisheries, *e.g.* growing energy prices can lead to higher costs, in particular in the more energy intensive fishing practises in capture fisheries;
- perceived risks and benefits for human health from fish consumption, *e.g.* focus on fish as a healthy and nutritious food;
- concern about overexploitation of certain fish stocks, *e.g.* increase consumer awareness could force government to implement stricter management measures;
- introduction of private standards, including for environmental and social purposes, and their endorsement by major retailers, *e.g.* the ability of countries to implement private standards could affect sourcing;
- certification and traceability requirements, *e.g.* sourcing will be affected if companies and countries are not able to comply;
- trade disputes related to selected fish species, *e.g.* trade disputes may affect bilateral trade;
- multilateral trade negotiations in the WTO, including the focus on fisheries subsidies, *e.g.* further trade liberalisation will stimulate international fish trade; improved subsidies rules may reduce overcapacity and overfishing;
- climate change, carbon emissions and their impacts on the fisheries sector, *e.g.* rising temperatures will change the composition of species in many fishing areas.

Box 8.1. **The Fish and Seafood Model**

For the first time, fish and seafood markets (both capture and aquaculture) are included in the OECD-FAO medium term outlook projections using a new dynamic policy specific partial equilibrium model, which has links to, but is not integrated into, the Aglink-Cosimo model used for the agricultural projections. It contains 1 100 equations and covers the same 56 countries/regions as Aglink-Cosimo with forty-two of these countries endogenous as well as five continents and a world total. There are three world market clearing price identities: one for aggregate fish and seafood, one for fish meal and one for fish oil. An approximation of the world price of captured fish and seafood is also endogenous as is a weighted average price of all the species raised in aquaculture.

Box 8.1. **The Fish and Seafood Model** (*cont.*)

There are two types of supply functions: captured species and aquaculture. Supply of captured species are either exogenous, endogenous but only affected by El Nino (climatic pattern that affects the Pacific Ocean) and endogenous but responding to price. As captures are tightly controlled by fishing quotas in many countries, only about 13% of the world capture is responding to the price in the model. For aquaculture, 99% of the world total is endogenous and responding to the price of output and the price of feed.

Fish meal and oil supply are composed of two components: from crushed whole fish (reduction) and from fish residue. Crushed whole fish is modeled like oilseed crush for those countries that are not subject to fishing quotas. Producers are responding to the weighted average output price and to the price of whole fish. The weighted average price is calculated using the fish meal and oil prices multiplied by their respective yield. Fish meal and oil production from fish residue is tied to production of fish for food consumption.

Demand is for aggregate fish and seafood but it is split according to three end uses: food, processed into fish meal and oil, and other uses (kept exogenous). In general, the own price and income elasticities imposed in the food demand functions are relatively high since these products are luxury goods in many countries of the world. Because of fishing quotas, the price of fish influences only 37% of the crush demand in the model. Demand for fish meal and oil responds to the need of aquaculture, the own price and the price of the respective oilseed products. The estimated elasticities show strong substitution between the fish and the oilseed products.

The price of aggregate fish and seafood is calculated in each country market clearing identity. The weighted average price of aquaculture species is tied to this domestic fish price and to the ratio of aquaculture production to total production (with an estimated negative sign). Domestic fish meal and oil price is the world price adjusted for tariff and transport cost (for importing countries). Consumer prices are a function of the fish price and of the GDP deflator used as an approximation for other costs.

Imports and exports of fish and seafood are either exogenous or a function of domestic and world prices adjusted for tariffs and transport costs. The elasticities were estimated or chosen to insure a transmission between these two prices consistent with the historical correlation coefficient. Fish meal and oil exports or imports are calculated in the market clearing identity.

Tariffs are the main policy instrument included in the model and they are, in general, lower than those for agricultural products. There are three links between the fish and the agriculture markets; on the demand side through the substitution between fish and other animal products, through the amount of feed demanded by aquaculture and through the interaction between fish meal and oil and their respective oilseed substitutes.

ANNEX 8.A

Statistical tables: Fish

Table 8.A.1. World fish projections

Calendar year

		Avg 2008-2010	2011	2012	2013	2014	2015	2016	2017	2018	2019	2020
FISH												
OECD												
Production	kt	31 884	32 025	32 318	32 744	32 980	32 349	33 126	33 390	33 507	33 639	33 311
of which aquaculture	kt	5 420	5 505	5 607	5 862	6 091	6 321	6 485	6 624	6 773	6 978	7 266
Consumption	kt	39 323	39 732	40 096	40 507	40 786	40 200	40 958	41 294	41 523	41 675	41 282
of which for food	kt	31 791	31 992	32 415	32 884	33 272	33 280	33 655	34 045	34 351	34 596	34 615
of which for reduction	kt	6 844	6 826	6 768	6 709	6 601	6 006	6 390	6 335	6 259	6 165	5 753
Non-OECD												
Production	kt	111 194	115 414	117 553	120 079	122 876	122 620	126 205	128 118	129 898	131 655	130 782
of which aquaculture	kt	49 228	51 773	53 842	55 864	58 150	60 076	61 040	62 713	64 277	65 826	66 418
Consumption	kt	103 670	107 836	109 802	112 292	114 996	114 644	118 271	120 112	121 779	123 516	122 709
of which for food	kt	85 043	88 226	90 351	92 702	95 239	96 142	98 113	100 085	101 604	103 070	103 150
of which for reduction	kt	12 642	13 473	13 255	13 344	13 461	12 156	13 762	13 580	13 679	13 724	12 737
World												
Production	kt	143 077	147 439	149 870	152 822	155 856	154 969	159 331	161 508	163 405	165 294	164 094
of which aquaculture	kt	54 647	57 278	59 449	61 726	64 241	66 397	67 525	69 337	71 049	72 803	73 683
Consumption	kt	142 993	147 568	149 898	152 799	155 782	154 844	159 230	161 406	163 302	165 191	163 991
of which for food	kt	116 834	120 219	122 766	125 586	128 511	129 422	131 768	134 130	135 955	137 666	137 765
of which for reduction	kt	19 486	20 299	20 022	20 054	20 061	18 162	20 151	19 916	19 937	19 889	18 490
Price												
Aquaculture[1]	USD/t	1 884.5	2 091.1	2 156.7	2 174.7	2 174.3	2 315.2	2 357.4	2 429.6	2 505.3	2 622.4	2 825.3
Capture[2]	USD/t	992.0	1 158.9	1 212.6	1 180.2	1 172.8	1 228.3	1 196.0	1 201.4	1 186.3	1 191.7	1 223.1
Trade[3]	USD/t	2 406.2	2 734.4	2 839.5	2 790.1	2 769.6	2 904.7	2 878.6	2 917.1	2 927.9	2 989.4	3 131.9
FISH MEAL												
OECD												
Production	kt	1 961.6	2 029.4	2 029.0	2 036.0	2 030.4	1 906.6	2 018.4	2 025.3	2 020.0	2 011.1	1 922.5
from whole fish	kt	1 464.3	1 491.4	1 482.4	1 471.9	1 449.7	1 311.3	1 407.1	1 399.6	1 379.8	1 356.3	1 253.2
Consumption	kt	2 299.9	2 354.4	2 286.2	2 281.6	2 285.5	2 134.9	2 173.8	2 224.3	2 213.0	2 193.2	2 127.2
Variation in stocks	kt	-77.9	28.0	23.2	17.6	-4.3	-55.6	54.4	1.9	1.8	1.8	-50.4
Non-OECD												
Production	kt	3 783.9	3 832.6	3 827.0	3 888.3	3 947.5	3 649.8	4 079.4	4 069.2	4 125.2	4 165.6	3 934.2
from whole fish	kt	2 950.5	3 175.7	3 143.4	3 182.7	3 228.4	2 922.4	3 335.7	3 310.6	3 352.5	3 381.8	3 149.2
Consumption	kt	3 732.8	3 481.6	3 505.6	3 614.1	3 695.7	3 615.1	3 729.6	3 867.2	3 929.4	3 980.7	3 922.9
Variation in stocks	kt	-209.4	-2.0	41.0	11.0	1.0	-138.0	140.0	1.0	1.0	1.0	-143.0
World												
Production	kt	5 745.5	5 862.0	5 856.0	5 924.2	5 977.9	5 556.4	6 097.8	6 094.4	6 145.2	6 176.7	5 856.6
from whole fish	kt	4 414.8	4 667.0	4 625.8	4 654.6	4 678.1	4 233.8	4 743.4	4 710.2	4 732.3	4 738.1	4 402.4
Consumption	kt	6 032.7	5 836.0	5 791.8	5 895.7	5 981.2	5 750.0	5 903.4	6 091.5	6 142.4	6 173.9	6 050.1
Variation in stocks	kt	-287.2	26.0	64.2	28.6	-3.3	-193.6	194.4	2.9	2.8	2.8	-193.4
Price[4]	USD/t	1 355.7	1 675.1	1 666.5	1 622.2	1 614.6	1 841.7	1 773.6	1 721.8	1 758.7	1 807.9	1 940.2
FISH OIL												
OECD												
Production	kt	570.4	582.8	584.9	594.2	599.0	573.6	596.3	595.0	593.7	591.3	574.5
from whole fish	kt	327.0	328.1	330.3	332.7	332.3	303.5	322.8	318.9	315.0	310.2	290.8
Consumption	kt	859.6	896.9	886.3	905.6	910.5	873.4	885.3	901.7	900.2	900.0	893.1
Variation in stocks	kt	-35.3	20.0	22.7	2.0	1.6	-27.2	26.4	2.0	1.8	1.6	-31.6
Non-OECD												
Production	kt	442.3	494.5	487.1	487.8	489.9	416.6	497.2	491.2	493.1	493.6	442.5
from whole fish	kt	380.0	438.3	430.9	431.5	433.6	359.9	439.9	433.5	434.9	434.9	383.3
Consumption	kt	194.0	157.8	164.9	175.2	180.1	160.9	170.5	182.3	186.1	186.2	169.6
Variation in stocks	kt	-5.7	2.6	-1.9	-0.8	-3.2	-16.9	11.4	0.2	-1.4	-2.8	-14.0
World												
Production	kt	1 012.7	1 077.3	1 072.1	1 082.0	1 089.0	990.2	1 093.4	1 086.2	1 086.8	1 084.9	1 017.1
from whole fish	kt	707.0	766.5	761.2	764.2	765.9	663.4	762.7	752.4	749.8	745.1	674.1
Consumption	kt	1 053.7	1 054.7	1 051.2	1 080.8	1 090.6	1 034.3	1 055.7	1 084.0	1 086.3	1 086.1	1 062.7
Variation in stocks	kt	-41.0	22.6	20.8	1.2	-1.7	-44.1	37.7	2.2	0.4	-1.2	-45.6
Price[5]	USD/t	1 161.7	1 060.5	1 034.6	1 036.2	1 053.7	1 243.8	1 218.8	1 186.5	1 212.0	1 258.8	1 382.0

Note: The term "fish" indicates fish, crustaceans, molluscs and other aquatic animals, but excludes aquatic mammals, crocodiles, caimans, alligators and aquatic plants.
1. World unit value of aquaculture fisheries production (live weight basis).
2. FAO estimated value of world ex vessel value of capture fisheries production.
3. World unit value of trade (sum of exports and imports).
4. Fish meal, 64-65% protein, Hamburg, Germany.
5. Fish oil, any origin, N.W. Europe.
Source: OECD and FAO Secretariats.

StatLink http://dx.doi.org/10.1787/888932428253

Chapter 9

Dairy

Market situation

After sharply increasing (2007), dramatically falling (2008) and quickly rebounding (2009), international dairy prices remained at relatively high but stable levels over much of 2010. Toward the end of the year and early 2011, global prices strengthened rapidly but stayed well below the peak levels of 2007/08 with the exception of record high butter prices (Oceania). Much of the strength in the dairy markets could have been attributed to a combination of strong demand in the Russian Federation and South East Asia, and constrained supplies from Oceania. Imports of milk powders to China have soared, fuelled by rising income but also food safety concerns, in the aftermath of the milk adulteration incidents. Steep increases in grain and energy prices have put upward pressure on feed costs, curtailed supply expansion and have been additional factors underpinning prices. The global dairy sector is entering into a decade of relatively high prices, continuing strong demand for milk and dairy products but also higher production costs and possibly continued market variability. The outlook period starts amid geopolitical turmoil in North Africa and Middle East, the uncertain impact of the earthquake tragedy in Japan, and a global economy adjusting to higher energy costs.

Projection highlights

- After a downward correction from peak 2011 levels, international dairy prices are expected to rise in nominal terms while remaining relatively flat in real terms (Figures 9.1 and 9.2). On average, world market prices in real terms are expected to be 10% (SMP) to 40% (butter) higher over the projection period compared with the previous decade.

- Popularity of dairy products, westernisation of diets and the increasing range of dairy products continue to be the key drivers underpinning dairy markets worldwide. The dairy sector remains among the fastest growing sectors covered in the *Outlook*. In the next 10 years, world milk production is projected to increase by 153 Mt. The majority of the growth is anticipated to come from developing countries. The average growth rate for the projection period is estimated at 1.9%, slightly below the 2.1% level witnessed in the last decade.

- World production of WMP, butter and fresh dairy products (FDP) is expected to grow 26% by 2020, while cheese and SMP would gain 19% and 15% as compared to the base period, 2008-10. After years of stagnation, the recent return of SMP and butter trade growth is expected to continue and SMP and butter trade is projected to increase by 30% and 10% respectively. Cheese and WMP powder trade is anticipated to grow by more than 20%.

- The magnitude of potential Chinese imports remains an important uncertainty in this *Outlook*. Dairy product imports to China are projected to stay above historical averages, stimulated by domestic food safety concerns in the short run, growing incomes and a strengthening yuan over the projection period.

Figure 9.1. **After a downward correction prices continue rising in nominal terms**

World dairy prices in nominal terms

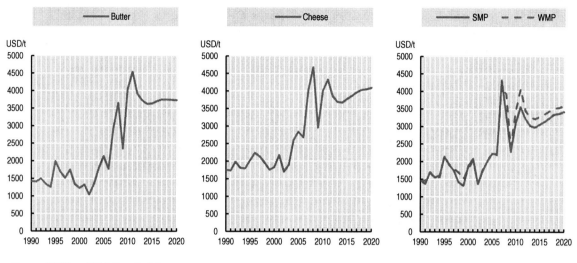

Source: OECD and FAO Secretariats.

StatLink ⟨⟨ http://dx.doi.org/10.1787/888932427265

Figure 9.2. **Prices in real terms are expected to stay relatively flat**

World dairy prices in real terms (2005 USD)

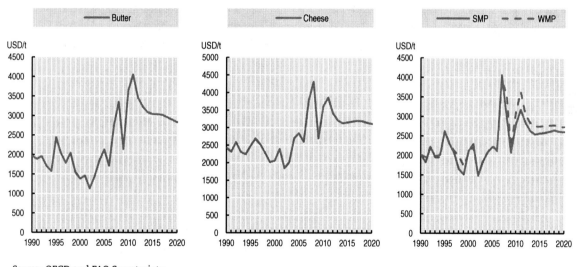

Source: OECD and FAO Secretariats.

StatLink ⟨⟨ http://dx.doi.org/10.1787/888932427284

Market trends and prospects

Prices

After peaking in 2011, global dairy product prices are expected to ease as demand adjusts and as supply responds, particularity in Oceania. High production costs are expected to moderate the price fall despite the fact that feed prices are likely to decrease over the short run and dairy producers are expected to further adjust their practices to mitigate impact of higher costs.

The projected decline in international prices is expected to be short lived, and followed by a subsequent rise in nominal terms of about 2% p.a. on average (Figure 9.1). Prices in real terms are anticipated to stay relatively flat, although at levels well above those of the previous decade (Figure 9.2). Growing demand stimulated by rising population and income, especially in developing countries, underlines the firmness in prices over the medium term. Over the Outlook period, prices in real terms are expected to average between 10% (SMP) and 40% (butter) higher than the last decade. The relative strength in prices stems, not only from continuing strong demand, but also from higher feed prices and other production costs, such as energy, labour and land.

Butter prices, for decades typically below other dairy price quotations, strengthened with the structural shift in energy prices and corresponding increase in other fats and oils prices. The relative strength in butter prices is expected to adjust only slowly over the projection period as emerging exporters concentrate more on milk powders.

The outlook price projections reflect the usual assumptions of stability in weather and in economic and policy conditions. Under these "normal" conditions, prices are not expected to surpass the peak levels of 2007/08 or 2011 by the end of the projection period. However, actual price outcomes are likely to exhibit significant annual variations around the projected trend.

Production

Milk production

After stagnating in 2009, milk production rebounded in 2010 and is expected to grow initially in excess of 2% annually for the next three years, causing prices to decline. As prices adjust downward, the growth in milk production after 2013 is expected to be less vigorous. The average annual growth for the next ten years is projected at 1.9%, compared with the 2.1% average annual growth experienced in the past decade.

Between 2010 and 2020, world milk production is projected to increase by 153 Mt. The majority, 73%, of the additional milk production is anticipated to come from developing countries. India and China alone account for 38% of global gains. The global milk production share of developed countries is expected to fall below 50% while the milking animals share drops below 10% by 2020. In contrast, the share of LDCs in global milk production will remain at only 4% while their share in global animal inventories is nearly 30%. The large disparity between the share of milk production and inventories between developing and developed countries is, to a large extent, a consequence of an enormous gap in milk yields, but also the reliance on sheep, goats and camels as milk animals, which have inherently lower yields than milk cows.

Regional differences in production growth depend on the market and policy context, the milk-feed price ratio, competition for land and water and environmental constraints (Figure 9.3). In the context of higher energy and feed prices, pasture based milk producing

Figure 9.3. **Substantial regional differences in production growth remain**
Milk production growth (2008/10 – 2020)

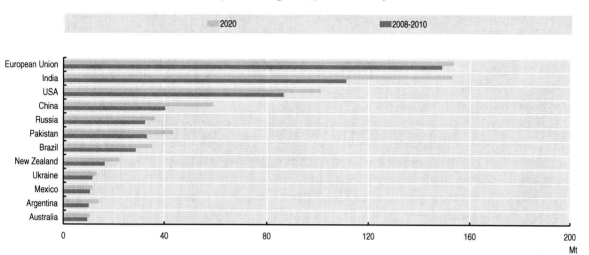

Source: OECD and FAO Secretariats.

StatLink ᴤᴤᴨ http://dx.doi.org/10.1787/888932427303

systems, such as those of Oceania and Latin America, are expected to strengthen their comparative advantage relative to grain fed systems, although they would remain heavily conditioned by weather patterns. Some of these regional differences are noted below.

New Zealand: following the weather related slowdown in 2010, milk production is expected to rebound and increase rapidly in the next few years. After 2013, production expansion is expected to decelerate. The conversion of sheep and beef farms to dairy farms is expected to continue, mainly in the South Island. The annual growth rate is projected to average 2.3% over the Outlook period – such growth is, however, dependent on normal weather and pasture growth.

Australia: milk production is expected to increase as water availability for irrigation has substantially improved. In the second half of the projection period, the growth is expected to slow down bringing the average annual growth over the projection period to 1.2%. Although farmers continue to adopt management strategies to alleviate water constraints – water availability remains a key factor for the medium term prospects.

European Union: with increasing producer prices, farm returns improved and the tense "milk crisis" situation on the domestic market has calmed. However, despite higher producer prices, increased costs will hinder the supply response. As a result, milk deliveries are not expected to keep pace with the annual increase in production quota over the quota phasing out period. After the announced 2015 quota abolition, milk production is expected to continue growing by 0.3% annually but EU milk deliveries are projected to remain below the expired quota level even in 2020.

United States: the milk price to feed ratio improved from the depressed 2009 levels and helped to reverse the decline in cow inventories. Despite a short run increase, the trend in cow numbers is expected to continue and decline moderately over the medium term. Production is expected to grow by 1.4% annually as yield gains more than offset the modest reductions in cow numbers.

Latin America: milk production in Argentina is expected to reach record levels. Investment and improved management efficiency are expected to drive milk production gains in the future. Milk production is expected to grow by nearly 3% p.a. The potential for even higher growth is hindered by high land prices and competition mainly from the soybeans sector. Brazil's milk production is projected to grow by 1.7% p.a., stimulated by increased domestic consumption. Profit margins, currently squeezed by high feed prices and a strong real, are expected to improve over the medium term on the assumptions of a weakening real, some reduction of feed costs, and increased productivity gains.

China: after years of double digit growth, the dairy industry is still struggling in the aftermath of its 2008 melamine crisis. A higher incidence of animal disease and recent alerts on milk adulteration with leather protein are factors adding to the malaise. The government is stepping up efforts to prevent further milk adulteration and to improve consumer confidence in domestically produced products. Milk production is expected to grow at 3.3% annually on average. This is much slower growth than that seen in the last decade as the focus moves increasingly from milk quantity to milk quality.

The growth in milk production in other developing countries is anticipated to be relatively strong. Milk production in India, the world's largest milk producer, will slow somewhat compared to the past decade but still grow by almost 3 % p.a. Other countries in Asia, which are not traditional milk producing countries, will also continue to expand, but will also expand imports of dairy products to sustain growing domestic demand. Growth in yields, from a low base will continue to account for most of milk production gains. More milk production will originate from milk cows, as opposed to other sources, such as goat, sheep, camel and buffalo milk which are important sources of milk production in many countries.

Dairy products production

After a decline in production related to reductions in China, global WMP production rebounded in 2010 and is expected to be one of the fastest growing products along with butter and FDP. As compared to the base period, 2008-10, WMP, butter and FDP are expected to grow by 26%, while cheese and SMP would gain 19% and 15%.

Nearly three-quarters of all additional butter produced globally is expected to come from India and Pakistan. New Zealand and the US would contribute another 10%. Most of the additional global production of SMP is expected from New Zealand (33%), the US (24%) and India (18%). The global SMP gains are heavily tempered by lower production in the EU, which is to be overtaken by the US as the largest SMP producer.

The EU and the US continue to dominate global cheese production with a two-thirds share of the total. Together they are responsible for 55% of expected additional global cheese output. Despite the projected lower annual growth, China is expected to remain the largest WMP supplier, producing more than a quarter of global quantities. New Zealand WMP production is projected to expand following the gains in New Zealand milk production. China and New Zealand together account for two-thirds of all WMP production expansion.

Consumption

Increasing population and income, together with the growing popularity of dairy products, particularly among developing country consumers is a key factor behind strong demand in the medium term. Demand continues to be encouraged by the growing influence of retail chains and multinational companies in these countries, which is facilitating improved consumer access to dairy products. Also, in many countries consumption is enhanced by government programmes (*i.e.* school milk).

The demand for milk and dairy products is expected to remain particularly strong in important developing dairy markets such as North Africa, the Middle East and East Asia, but also in more mature markets such as those in the European Union, the United States and Russia. The rate of growth and *per capita* consumption of milk and milk products remains significantly different among regions (Figure 9.4). LDC countries consume less than 50 kg per person per year on average, compared with 100 kg per person for developing countries, while the developed regions of North America and Europe consume well in excess of 200 kg per person (in milk equivalent). Such a *per capita* consumption disparity represents an investment potential and future opportunities for both the domestic and global dairy sectors.

Figure 9.4. **Large disparity in consumption levels and growth**

Left panel: Index of milk and dairy products consumption growth (in milk equivalent, 2002=1)
Right panel: Levels of milk and dairy products per capita consumption growth (in milk equivalent)

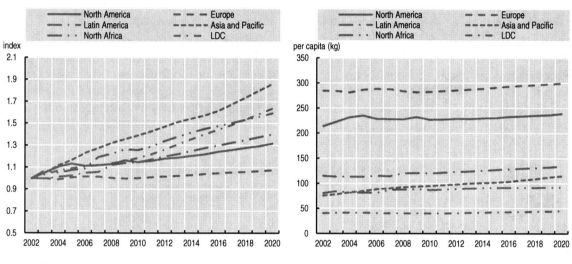

Source: OECD and FAO Secretariats.

StatLink http://dx.doi.org/10.1787/888932427322

Dairy product consumption in developed countries may increase only modestly, with the exception of cheese, for which growth may be 16% by 2020 as compared to the 2008-10 base period. New packaging technology, more convenience and possible substitutability with meats help boosting cheese consumption. In developing regions the consumption of all products increases vigorously at around 30% from the base period, driven by increasing population and income levels. Strong growth for butter comes primarily from increased demand for butter and ghee in India and Pakistan. A modest increase in butter consumption in developed countries results from a recovery of butter consumption in the Russian Federation and steady growth in the US. Developing countries dominate consumption of WMP, with an 80% of global WMP consumption share, and will account for nearly all additional WMP consumption over the Outlook period.

Trade

Oceania (New Zealand and Australia) is expected to remain the most significant exporter region, with a more than 40% share of the global export market. The dominant market position of New Zealand and Australia will, however, keep global markets under the influence of the region's weather and production conditions (Box 9.1).

The situation of stable trade volumes for SMP and declines for butter over much of the last decade changed recently as both categories showed remarkable growth. This growth is expected to continue and SMP trade is projected to increase by 30% over the base period, mainly the result of more exports from Oceania and the US, and of importers substituting away from higher priced WMP. Global butter exports are expected to increase by 10% while

---

Box 9.1. **Production patterns in Oceania – impacts on global dairy markets**

New Zealand and Australia (Oceania) presence on the international dairy markets has increased considerably after the elimination of domestic support and deregulation, but also after reduced market participation of some traditional exporters (notably from the EU).[1] The global export market share of Oceania has risen from 20% in the 1980s to more than 40% today. The region has become an important driver of global dairy markets with milk production predominantly based on lower cost pasture systems that are less influenced by movements in feedstock prices but more dependent on weather conditions.

The baseline underlying the medium term outlook is deterministic and assumes normal weather and production conditions. A stochastic analysis, using the Aglink-Cosimo model, was applied to illustrate the uncertainties around production levels, based on historical experiences, and the resulting impacts on global dairy markets.[2] The analysis clearly indicates that Oceania production conditions can have a substantial influence on global dairy markets. Although dairy farmers in Oceania are constantly learning to mitigate the impacts of adverse weather (i.e. better water management), the weather swings in the region will continue to inflict uncertainties on the global dairy markets.[3]

Figure 9.5. **Oceania production levels – Monte Carlo draws**

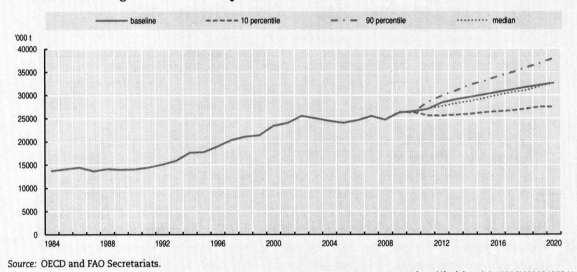

Source: OECD and FAO Secretariats.

StatLink http://dx.doi.org/10.1787/888932427341

The results of 500 Monte Carlo simulations, inputs into 500 scenario model runs, show Oceania milk production ranging from 27.4 Mt(10th perc.) to 37.9 Mt (90th perc.) by 2020. The median values of the production distribution are slightly below the baseline, which reflects an expected recovery in New Zealand production and strong short-run growth prospects in Australia following the plentiful rain that replenished reservoirs, ending the 7-year drought.

Box 9.1. **Production patterns in Oceania – impacts on global dairy markets** (cont.)

Figure 9.6. **Simulation results for world butter prices**

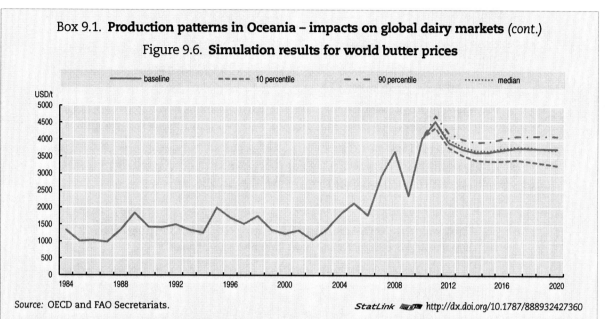

Source: OECD and FAO Secretariats.

StatLink http://dx.doi.org/10.1787/888932427360

The results of the model simulations illustrate a relatively wide range of plausible values for world butter prices, from USD 3 250/t (10th perc.) to USD 4 100/t (90th perc.) by 2020. The baseline and median are nearly identical at the end of the projection period but baseline values are slightly below the median in the short run, consistent with the assumption of strong supply response and more favourable hydrologic situation in the Oceania region.

Figure 9.7. **Results for world dairy prices in 2020**

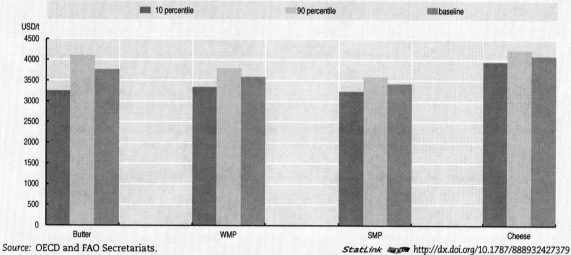

Source: OECD and FAO Secretariats.

StatLink http://dx.doi.org/10.1787/888932427379

The impacts on world dairy prices differ considerably by product. The most affected commodity (from the right to the left) and the widest possible range of results is for butter which stems from the dominant butter export position of New Zealand. Cheese is affected the least as Oceania has a lower export market share.

1. In Australia, structural adjustments after the deregulation in year 2000 coincided with series of droughts which, in fact, resulted in the reduction of domestic milk output.
2. Variance/covariance matrices were constructed to build multivariate distributions based on annual historical milk production levels in Australia and New Zealand between 1970 and 2010 in order to account for correlated impacts of extreme weather events on both countries. The 10th and 90th percentiles do not represent low and high extremes but rather plausible alternatives based on past variations in Oceania production patterns.
3. It is important to note that the historical production variation is determined by various factors, not only by weather, but weather conditions are among the most important ones.

the traditional leaders in export growth, cheese and WMP, are both expected to record solid growth of 22% and 21% respectively (Figure 9.8).

The recent dramatic increase in imports of milk powders by China is expected to ease only slowly. Rebuilding of consumer confidence in domestic products will likely take several years. Modernisation of the dairy industry will gradually improve the situation, but, despite the quality improvement in the medium term, growing income and a strengthening yuan will keep dairy product imports above historical averages (Figure 9.9).

Large quantities of EU dairy intervention stocks accumulated during the 2009 EU milk crisis have not put pressure on global prices as they have been only gradually released, to a large extent, under the domestic *food programme for the most deprived persons*. Over the

Figure 9.8. **The declining trend in trade for butter and SMP is to reverse**

Global dairy product exports and major dairy products exporters

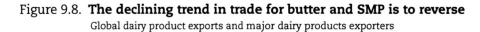

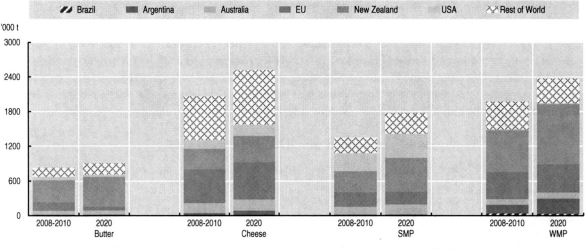

Source: OECD and FAO Secretariats.

StatLink ᴬᴵᴾ http://dx.doi.org/10.1787/888932427398

Figure 9.9. **Rising importance of China imports on global milk powder markets**

China imports of milk powders and the global milk powder import share

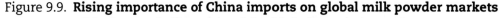

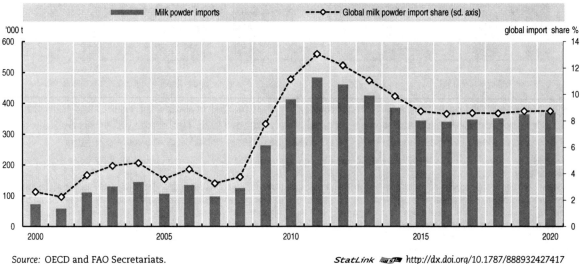

Source: OECD and FAO Secretariats.

StatLink ᴬᴵᴾ http://dx.doi.org/10.1787/888932427417

projection period, export shares of the EU on the international dairy markets are expected to stagnate for cheese and WMP and continue to decline for butter and SMP.

The seven largest importing countries of dairy products continue to account for less than 50% of the world market (Figure 9.10). The Russian Federation remains the key importer of butter and cheese. In the 1990s, Russian Federation dairy product production and consumption contracted by more than 60%. Driven by increased income over the last decade, consumption started to rise but dairy production lagged behind thus propelling higher imports. An increase in Russian domestic milk production, stimulated by government efforts (*i.e.* subsidies for purchase of pedigree bulls), has narrowed the gap and has limited butter imports. This situation is likely to prevail over the projection period, although cheese imports are expected to continue a steady 1.6% annual growth (Figure 9.11).

Figure 9.10. Imports remain fragmented and import product mix continues to vary by country

Major dairy products importers

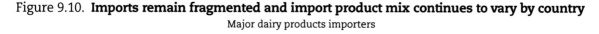

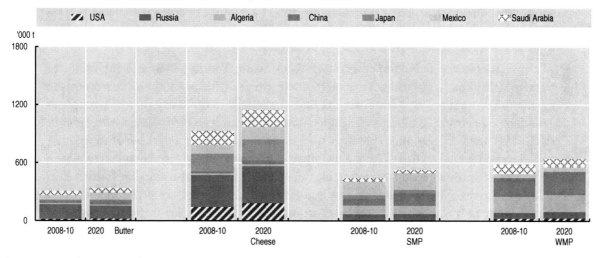

Source: OECD and FAO Secretariats.

StatLink http://dx.doi.org/10.1787/888932427436

Figure 9.11. Russian Federation growth in butter imports limited but cheese imports continue rising

Russian Federation milk production and dairy products imports

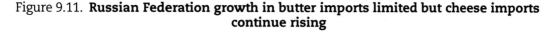

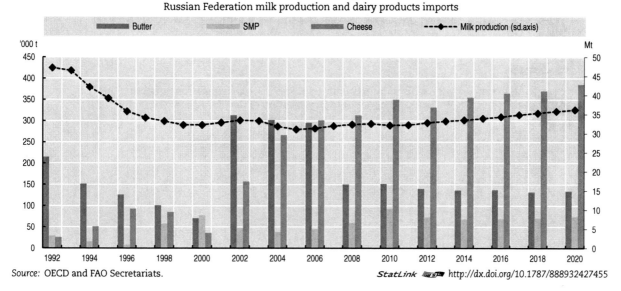

Source: OECD and FAO Secretariats.

StatLink http://dx.doi.org/10.1787/888932427455

Main issues and uncertainties

The dairy industry globalisation, together with domestic and trade policy reforms, have shifted international dairy markets from a supply driven paradigm, characterised by excess production and depressed world prices, to a more demand driven paradigm, responsive to market signals and changing consumer preferences. The sector is increasingly shaped by the prospects of sustained high prices for dairy products. Higher international prices are creating incentives for investment, expansion and restructuring in local dairy industries. Higher prices and a correspondingly higher value of milk production have also set the dairy sector among the highest gross value sectors in agriculture. However, high prices can also have negative consequences for the dairy industry. Under very high prices, demand may retreat and dairy ingredients can be replaced by cheaper substitutes in food manufacturing. Changing production formulas and recipes can have a long lasting impact as there would be a certain resistance to reverse the process. The "higher price" *Outlook* for dairy may also mask that the global dairy sector is increasingly confronted with higher production costs and what appears to be more unstable market environment; more extreme weather patterns, rapidly changing macroeconomic situation, input prices and, consequently, increased price variability.

The increased concerns of consumers about health and nutrition and the trends of tightening food law legislations are expected to continue. This is another important issue for the future, bringing opportunities but also challenges to the dairy sector. A couple of examples concerning labelling and debate related to health can be noted here. In order to strengthen transparency, an EU proposal asks for an indication on a package as to whether a product had ever been frozen (this may impact butter and cheese). In the search to reduce incidents of cardiovascular diseases and obesity, a tax on saturated fat (which also concerns certain dairy products) will be implemented in Denmark as of 1st October 2011. Recent joint FAO/WHO expert consultation on fats and fatty acids in human nutrition notes that there is no probable or convincing evidence for significant effects of total dietary fats on coronary heart disease or cancer (FAO, 2010). The probiotics sector is among the fastest growing dairy business, propelled by perceived benefits of various bacteria strains. In several countries certain health claims on the probiotics products are being revisited. The impacts of various labelling and health claims on dairy products consumption are uncertain, but it seems certain that the debate over nutrition and health is likely to intensify among products but also between the industry and food safety authorities.

Reference

FAO (2010), "Fats and fatty acids in human nutrition. Report of an expert consultation", FAO *Food and Nutrition Paper, No. 91*, Food and Agriculture Organization of the United Nations, Rome, 2010.

ANNEX 9.A

Statistical tables: Dairy

Table 9.A.1. World dairy projections (butter and cheese)

Calendar year

		Avg 2008-10est.	2011	2012	2013	2014	2015	2016	2017	2018	2019	2020
BUTTER												
OECD[1]												
Production	kt pw	3 703	3 667	3 720	3 755	3 785	3 831	3 854	3 869	3 902	3 934	3 974
Consumption	kt pw	3 252	3 239	3 259	3 270	3 300	3 331	3 360	3 387	3 418	3 443	3 471
Stock changes	kt pw	-18	-5	4	22	4	4	-5	-16	-13	-11	3
Non-OECD												
Production	kt pw	6 081	6 533	6 711	6 898	7 039	7 150	7 340	7 609	7 879	8 186	8 485
Consumption	kt pw	6 634	7 120	7 315	7 499	7 655	7 780	7 971	8 237	8 505	8 814	9 109
WORLD												
Production	kt pw	9 784	10 200	10 430	10 653	10 824	10 981	11 194	11 478	11 781	12 120	12 459
Consumption	kt pw	9 887	10 359	10 573	10 769	10 956	11 112	11 331	11 624	11 922	12 257	12 580
Stock changes	kt pw	-23	-17	-3	22	4	4	-5	-16	-13	-11	3
Price[2]	USD/t	3 347	4 540	3 918	3 723	3 626	3 635	3 702	3 751	3 749	3 741	3 729
CHEESE												
OECD[1]												
Production	kt pw	15 239	15 572	15 806	16 026	16 265	16 512	16 798	17 022	17 234	17 453	17 689
Consumption	kt pw	14 538	14 846	15 071	15 247	15 460	15 676	15 941	16 148	16 353	16 555	16 812
Stock changes	kt pw	31	-12	-12	-6	-7	-3	-5	2	3	5	6
Non-OECD												
Production	kt pw	4 431	4 683	4 843	4 938	5 071	5 185	5 290	5 398	5 528	5 656	5 811
Consumption	kt pw	5 094	5 480	5 655	5 792	5 946	6 087	6 214	6 333	6 468	6 611	6 743
WORLD												
Production	kt pw	19 670	20 255	20 648	20 964	21 336	21 697	22 088	22 420	22 762	23 109	23 499
Consumption	kt pw	19 632	20 326	20 726	21 038	21 406	21 763	22 155	22 481	22 822	23 166	23 556
Stock changes	kt pw	37	-8	-15	-11	-7	-3	-5	2	3	5	6
Price[3]	USD/t	3 882	4 325	3 861	3 696	3 673	3 770	3 865	3 970	4 038	4 056	4 093

Note: Calendar year: Year ending 30 June for Australia and 31 May for New Zealand in OECD aggregate.

1. Excludes Iceland but includes EU6 members that are not members of the OECD (Bulgaria, Cyprus, Latvia, Lithuania, Malta and Romania).
2. F.o.b. export price, butter, 82% butterfat, Oceania.
3. F.o.b. export price, cheddar cheese, 39% moisture, Oceania.
Source: OECD and FAO Secretariats.

StatLink ⬛🖅🖎 http://dx.doi.org/10.1787/888932428310

Table 9.A.2. World dairy projections (powders and casein)

Calendar year

		Avg 2008-10est.	2011	2012	2013	2014	2015	2016	2017	2018	2019	2020
SKIM MILK POWDER													
OECD[1]												
Production	kt pw	2 745	2 750	2 755	2 811	2 842	2 918	2 937	2 951	2 983	3 001	3 020
Consumption	kt pw	1 753	1 716	1 721	1 727	1 740	1 759	1 765	1 762	1 757	1 766	1 779
Stock changes	kt pw	54	-65	-78	-58	-55	-16	-12	-3	-3	-5	-1
Non-OECD												
Production	kt pw	693	721	759	777	815	839	869	888	882	907	945
Consumption	kt pw	1 579	1 774	1 826	1 876	1 930	1 973	2 012	2 040	2 074	2 110	2 152
WORLD												
Production	kt pw	3 438	3 470	3 514	3 589	3 658	3 757	3 805	3 839	3 866	3 908	3 965
Consumption	kt pw	3 332	3 489	3 547	3 603	3 670	3 731	3 777	3 802	3 830	3 876	3 931
Stock changes	kt pw	54	-65	-78	-58	-55	-16	-12	-3	-3	-5	-2
Price[2]	USD/t	2 908	3 559	3 220	3 020	2 975	3 064	3 142	3 239	3 348	3 366	3 421
WHOLE MILK POWDER												
OECD[1]												
Production	kt pw	1 989	2 113	2 168	2 195	2 216	2 221	2 240	2 270	2 292	2 332	2 353
Consumption	kt pw	754	740	754	758	760	765	772	776	778	780	782
Stock changes	kt pw	0	1	1	1	1	1	1	1	1	1	1
Non-OECD												
Production	kt pw	2 156	2 280	2 357	2 429	2 470	2 521	2 593	2 660	2 736	2 800	2 881
Consumption	kt pw	3 529	3 725	3 843	3 938	3 998	4 049	4 133	4 226	4 322	4 424	4 523
WORLD												
Production	kt pw	4 144	4 393	4 525	4 624	4 686	4 742	4 833	4 930	5 028	5 132	5 234
Consumption	kt pw	4 284	4 465	4 597	4 696	4 758	4 814	4 905	5 002	5 100	5 204	5 306
Stock changes	kt pw	0	1	1	1	1	1	1	1	1	1	1
Price[3]	USD/t	3 264	4 068	3 452	3 263	3 215	3 277	3 355	3 437	3 514	3 534	3 589
WHEY POWDER												
Wholesale price, USA[4]	USD/t	672	994	906	827	822	834	870	901	932	949	981
CASEIN												
Price[5]	USD/t	8 038	8 395	7 604	7 830	7 863	7 850	7 888	7 963	8 219	8 274	8 420

Note: Calendar year: Year ending 30 June for Australia and 31 May for New Zealand in OECD aggregate.

1. Excludes Iceland but includes EU6 members that are not members of the OECD (Bulgaria, Cyprus, Latvia, Lithuania, Malta and Romania).
2. F.o.b. export price, non-fat dry milk, 1.25% butterfat, Oceania.
3. F.o.b. export price, WMP 26% butterfat, Oceania.
4. West Region.
5. Export price, New Zealand.

Source: OECD and FAO Secretariats.

StatLink http://dx.doi.org/10.1787/888932428329

Glossary of terms

A-H1N1

This is an influenza virus that had never been identified as a cause of infections in people before the current H1N1 pandemic. Genetic analyses of this virus have shown that it originated from animal influenza viruses and is unrelated to the human seasonal H1N1 viruses that have been in general circulation among people since 1977.

Average Crop Revenue Election (ACRE) program

A new programme introduced with the 2008 US FCE Act allowing farmers to choose revenue-based protection against yield and market fluctuations.

AMAD

Agricultural Market Access database. A co-operative effort between Agriculture and Agri-food Canada, EU Commission-Agriculture Directorate-General, FAO, OECD, The World Bank, UNCTAD and the United States Department of Agriculture, Economic Research Service. Data in the database is obtained from countries' schedules and notifications submitted to the WTO.

Aquaculture

The farming of aquatic organisms including fish, molluscs, crustaceans and aquatic plants, etc. Farming implies some form of intervention in the rearing process to enhance production, such as regular stocking, feeding and protection from predators. Farming also implies individual or corporate ownership of the stock being cultivated. For statistical purposes, aquatic organisms that are harvested by an individual or corporate body that has owned them throughout their rearing period contribute to aquaculture, while aquatic organisms that are exploitable by the public as a common property resource, with or without appropriate licenses, are the harvest of capture fisheries.

ASEAN

The Association of Southeast Asian Nations, or ASEAN, was established on 8 August 1967 in Bangkok, Thailand, with the signing of the ASEAN Declaration (Bangkok Declaration) by the Founding Fathers of ASEAN, namely Indonesia, Malaysia, Philippines, Singapore and Thailand. Brunei Darussalam then joined on 8 January 1984, Vietnam on 28 July 1995, Laos PDR and Myanmar on 23 July 1997, and Cambodia on 30 April 1999, making up what is today the ten Member States of ASEAN.

Australia-US Free Trade Agreement (AUSFTA)

A Bilateral Agreement negotiated between the United States and Australia that came into force on 1 January 2005. AUSFTA covers goods, services, investment, financial services, government procurement, standards and technical regulations, telecommunications, competition-related matters, electronic commerce, intellectual property rights, labour and the environment.

Avian influenza

Avian influenza is an infectious disease of birds caused by type A strains of the influenza virus. The disease, which was first identified in Italy more than 100 years ago, occurs worldwide. The quarantining of infected farms, destruction of infected or potentially exposed flocks, and recently inoculation are standard control measures.

Atlantic beef/pigmeat market

Beef/pigmeat trade between countries in the Atlantic Rim.

Baseline

The set of market projections used for the outlook analysis in this report and as a benchmark for the analysis of the impact of different economic and policy scenarios. A detailed description of the generation of the baseline is provided in the chapter on Methodology in this report.

Biofuels

In the wider sense defined as all solid, fluid or gaseous fuels produced from biomass. More narrowly, the term biofuels comprises those that replace petroleum-based road-transport fuels, i.e. bioethanol produced from sugar crops, cereals and other starchy crops that can be used as an additive to, in a blend with or as a replacement of gasoline, and biodiesel produced mostly from vegetable oils, but also from waste oils and animal fats, that can be used in blends with or as a replacement of petroleum-based diesel.

Biomass

Biomass is defined as any plant matter used directly as fuel or converted into other forms before combustion. Included are wood, vegetal waste (including wood waste and crops used for energy production), animal materials/wastes and industrial and urban wastes, used as feedstocks for producing bioproducts.

Bovine Spongiform Encephalopathy (BSE)

A fatal disease of the central nervous system of cattle, first identified in the United Kingdom in 1986. On 20 March 1996, the UK Spongiform Encephalopathy Advisory Committee (SEAC) announced the discovery of a new variant of Creutzfeldt-Jacob Disease (vCJD), a fatal disease of the central nervous system in humans, which might be linked to consumption of beef affected by exposure to BSE.

BRIICs

Refers to the emerging economies of Brazil, the Russian Federation, India, Indonesia and China.

Capture fisheries

Capture fisheries refer to the hunting, collecting and gathering activities directed at removing or collecting live wild aquatic organisms (predominantly fish, molluscs and crustaceans) including plants from the oceanic, coastal or inland waters for human consumption and other purposes by hand or more usually by various types of fishing gear such as nets, lines and stationary traps. The production of capture fisheries is measured by nominal catches (in live weight basis) of fish, crustaceans, molluscs and other aquatic animals and plants, killed, caught, trapped or collected for all commercial, industrial, recreational and subsistence purposes.

Cereals

Defined as wheat, coarse grains and rice.

CAFTA

CAFTA is a comprehensive trade agreement between Costa Rica, the Dominican Republic, El Salvador, Guatemala, Honduras, Nicaragua, and the United States.

Common Agricultural Policy (CAP)

The European Union's agricultural policy, first defined in Article 39 of the Treaty of Rome signed in 1957.

Coarse grains

Defined as barley, maize, oats, sorghum and other coarse grains in all countries except Australia, where it includes triticale and in the European Union where it includes rye and other mixed grains.

Country of Origin Labelling (COOL)

A provision of the 2008 US Farm Act that requires retailers to inform consumers of country of origin of different commodities, among them meats.

Conservation Reserve Program (CRP)

A major provision of the United States' Food Security Act of 1985 and extended under the Food and Agriculture Conservation and Trade Act of 1990, the Food and Agriculture Improvement and Reform Act of 1996, and the Farm Security and Rural Investment Act of 2002 is designed to reduce erosion on 40 to 45 million acres (16 to 18 million hectares) of farm land. Under the programme, producers who sign contracts agree to convert erodable crop land to approved conservation uses for ten years. Participating producers receive annual rental payments and cash or payment in kind to share up to 50% of the cost of establishing permanent vegetative cover. The CRP is part of the *Environmental Conservation Acreage Reserve Program*. The 1996 FAIR Act authorised a 36.4 million acre (14.7 million hectares) maximum under CRP, its 1995 level. The maximum area enrolled in the CRP was increased to 39.2 million acres in the 2002 FSRI Act.

Commonwealth of Independent States (CIS)

The heads of twelve sovereign states (except the Baltic states) have signed the Treaty on establishment of the Economic Union, in which they stressed that the Azerbaijan Republic, Republic of Armenia, Republic of Belarus, Republic of Georgia, Republic of Kazakhstan, Kyrgyz Republic, Republic of Moldova, Russian Federation, Republic of Tajikistan, Turkmenistan, Republic of Uzbekistan and Ukraine on equality basis established the Commonwealth of Independent States.

Common Market Organisation (CMO) for sugar

The common organisation of the sugar market (CMO) in the European Union was established in 1968 to ensure a fair income to community sugar producers and self-supply of the Community market. At present the CMO is governed by Council Regulation (EC) No. 318/2006 (the basic regulation) which establishes a restructuring fund financed by sugar producers to assist the restructuring process needed to render the industry more competitive.

Crop year, coarse grains

Refers to the crop marketing year beginning 1 April for Japan, 1 July for the European Union and New Zealand, 1 August for Canada and 1 October for Australia. The US crop year begins 1 June for barley and oats and 1 September for maize and sorghum.

Crop year, oilseeds

Refers to the crop marketing year beginning 1 April for Japan, 1 July for the European Union and New Zealand, 1 August for Canada and 1 October for Australia. The US crop year begins 1 June for rapeseed, 1 September for soyabeans and for sunflower seed.

Crop year, rice

Refers to the crop marketing year beginning 1 April for Japan and Australia, 1 August for the United States, 1 September for the European Union, 1 November for Korea and 1 January for other countries.

Crop year, sugar

A common crop marketing year beginning 1 October and extending to 31 September, used by ISO (International Sugar Organization).

Crop year, wheat

Refers to the crop marketing year beginning 1 April for Japan, 1 June for the United States, 1 July for the European Union and New Zealand, 1 August for Canada and 1 October for Australia.

Decoupled payments

Budgetary payments paid to eligible recipients who are not linked to current production of specific commodities or livestock numbers or the use of specific factors of production.

Direct payments

Payments made directly by governments to producers.

Doha Development Agenda

The current round of multilateral trade negotiations in the World Trade Organisation that were initiated in November 2001, in Doha, Qatar.

Domestic support

Refers to the annual level of support, expressed in monetary terms, provided to agricultural production. It is one of the three pillars of the Uruguay Round Agreement on Agriculture targeted for reduction.

Eastern Europe

Refers to Russia, Ukraine and Kazakhstan.

Economic Partnership Agreements (EPAs)

Free trade agreements currently being negotiated between the EU and the African, Caribbean Pacific (ACP) group of developing countries to replace the Cotonou Agreement which expired in 2007.

El Niño

In this publication, El Niño is used to indicate a broader term of quasi-periodic ocean climate conditions including La Niña, Southern Oscillation, or ENSO, which are characterized by anomalies in the temperature of the surface of eastern coast of Latin America (centred on Peru) warming or cooling known as *El Niño* and *La Niña* respectively – and air surface pressure in the tropical western Pacific (the Southern Oscillation), often around Christmas time. The abnormal warm ocean climate conditions are accompanied by dramatic changes in species abundance and distribution, higher local rainfall and flooding, massive deaths of fish and their predators (including birds).

Energy Independence and Security Act (EISA) 2007

US legislation passed in December 2007 that is designed to increase US energy security by lessening dependence on imported oil, to improve energy conservation and efficiency, expand the production of renewable fuels, and to make America's air cleaner for future generations.

Ethanol

A biofuel that can be used as a fuel substitute (hydrous ethanol) or a fuel extender (anhydrous ethanol) in mixes with petroleum, and which is produced from agricultural feed-stocks such as sugar cane and maize.

Everything-But-Arms (EBA)

The Everything-But-Arms (EBA) Initiative eliminates EU import tariffs for numerous goods, including agricultural products, from the least developed countries. The tariff elimination is scheduled in four steps from 2006/07 to 2009/10.

Export credits (with official support)

Government financial support, direct financing, guarantees, insurance or interest rate support provided to foreign buyers to assist in the financing of the purchase of goods from national exporters.

Export restitutions (refunds)

EU export subsidies provided to cover the difference between internal prices and world market prices for particular commodities.

Export subsidies

Subsidies given to traders to cover the difference between internal market prices and world market prices, such as for example the EU *export restitutions*. Export subsidies are now subject to value and volume restrictions under the *Uruguay Round Agreement on Agriculture*.

FCE Act, 2008

Officially known as the Food, Conservation and Energy Act of 2008. This US farm legislation replaces the FSRI Act of 2002 and covers the period 2008 – 2013.

FSRI Act, 2002

Officially known as the Farm Security and Rural Investment Act of 2002. This US farm legislation replaces the FAIR Act of 1996, covering a wide range of commodity programmes and policies for US agriculture for the period 2002-2007.

Gur, jaggery, khandasari

Semi-processed sugars (plantation whites) extracted from sugarcane in India.

Health Check Reform of the Common Agricultural Policy

On 20 November 2008 the EU agriculture ministers reached a political agreement on the Health Check of the Common Agricultural Policy. Among a range of measures, the agreement abolishes arable set-aside, increases milk quotas gradually leading up to their abolition in 2015, and converts market intervention into a genuine safety net. Ministers also agreed to increase modulation, whereby direct payments to farmers are reduced and the money transferred to the Rural Development Fund.

High Fructose Corn Syrup (HFCS)

Isoglucose sweetener extracted from maize.

Historical Price Volatility

Historical price volatility is calculated following the method used by the Chicago Board of Trade (CBOT) from the following formula:

$$\sigma = \sqrt{\sum_{i=1}^{n} [r_t - \mu]^2 / n - 1}$$

Where r_t are the logarithmic returns on prices P_t: $r_t = ln(P_t) - ln(P_{t-1})$ and μ is the average return, and n is the number of sample observations. In annualized terms, multiplied by the inverse of the square root of time, $1/\sqrt{T}$, where T represents the frequency of the observation (*e.g.* daily, monthly, etc).

Implied volatility

The concept of implied volatility is based on the Black-Scholes option pricing formula. Given the exercise price, current price, risk free rate and maturity of an option, there is some value for volatility that makes the price determined by the Black Scholes formula equal to the current price. This is called implied volatility. For further reference, refer to Mayhew, S. (1995), "Implied volatility", *Financial Analysts Journal* 51 (4): 8–20.

Industrial oilseeds

A category of oilseed production in the European Union for industrial use (*i.e.* biofuels).

Intervention purchases

Purchases by the EC Commission of certain commodities to support internal market prices.

Intervention purchase price

Price at which the European Commission will purchase produce to support internal market prices. It usually is below 100% of the intervention price, which is an annually decided policy price.

Intervention stocks

Stocks held by national intervention agencies in the European Union as a result of *intervention* buying of commodities subject to market price support. Intervention stocks may be released onto the internal markets if internal prices exceed intervention prices; otherwise, they may be sold on the world market with the aid of *export restitutions*.

Inulin

Inulin syrups are extracted from chicory through a process commercially developed in the 1980s. They usually contain 83% fructose. Inulin syrup production in the European Union is covered by the sugar regime and subject to a production quota.

Isoglucose

Isoglucose is a starch-based fructose sweetener, produced by the action of glucose isomerase enzyme on dextrose. This isomerisation process can be used to produce glucose/fructose blends containing up to 42% fructose. Application of a further process can raise the fructose content to 55%. Where the fructose content is 42%, isoglucose is equivalent in sweetness to sugar. Isoglucose production in the European Union is covered by the sugar regime and subject to a production quota.

Least squares growth rate

The least-squares growth rate, r, is estimated by fitting a linear regression trend line to the logarithmic annual values of the variable in the relevant period, as follows: $Ln(x_t) = a + r * t$.

Live weight

The weight of finfish and shellfish at the time of their capture or harvest. Calculated on the basis of conversion factors from landed to nominal weight and on rates prevailing among national industries for each type of processing

Loan rate

The commodity price at which the *Commodity Credit Corporation* (CCC) offers *non-recourse loans* to participating farmers. The crops covered by the programme are used as collateral for these loans. The loan rate serves as a floor price, with the effective level lying somewhat above the announced rate, for participating farmers in the sense that they can default on their loan and forfeit their crop to the CCC rather than sell it in the open market at a lower price.

Market access

Governed by provisions of the *Uruguay Round Agreement* on *Agriculture* which refer to concessions contained in the country schedules with respect to bindings and reductions of tariffs and to other minimum import commitments.

Marketing allotments (US sugar program)

Marketing allotments designate how much sugar can be sold by sugar millers and processors on the US internal market and were established by the 2002 FSRI Act as a way to guarantee the US sugar loan program operates at no cost to the Federal Government.

Marketing year, oilseed meals

Refers to the marketing year beginning 1 October.

Marketing year, vegetable oils

Refers to the marketing year beginning 1 October.

Market Price Support (MPS) Payment

Indicator of the annual monetary value of gross transfers from consumers and taxpayers to agricultural producers arising from policy measures creating a gap between domestic market prices and *border prices* of a specific agricultural commodity, measured at the farm gate level. Conditional on the production of a specific commodity, MPS includes the transfer to producers associated with both production for domestic use and exports, and is measured by the price gap applied to current production. The MPS is net of financial contributions from individual producers through producer levies on sales of the specific commodity or penalties for not respecting regulations such as production quotas (*Price levies*), and in the case of livestock production is net of the market price support on domestically produced coarse grains and oilseeds used as animal feed (*Excess feed cost*).

Methyl Tertiary Butyl Ether (MTBE)

A chemical gasoline additive that can be used to boost the octane number and oxygen content of the fuel, but can render contaminated water undrinkable.

Milk quota scheme

A supply control measure to limit the volume of milk produced or supplied. Quantities up to a specified quota amount benefit from full *market price support*. Over-quota volumes may be penalised by a levy (as in the European Union, where the "super levy" is 115% of the target price) or may receive a lower price. Allocations are usually fixed at individual producer level. Other features, including arrangements for quota reallocation, differ according to scheme.

North American Free Trade Agreement (NAFTA)

A trilateral agreement on trade, including agricultural trade, between Canada, Mexico and the United States, phasing out tariffs and revising other trade rules between the three countries over a 15-year period. The agreement was signed in December 1992 and came into effect on 1 January 1994.

Oilseed meals

Defined as rapeseed meal (canola), soyabean meal, and sunflower meal in all countries, except in Japan where it excludes sunflower meal.

Oilseeds

Defined as rapeseed (canola), soyabeans, sunflower seed, peanuts and cotton seeds in all countries, except in Japan where it excludes sunflower seed.

Pacific beef/pigmeat market

Beef/pigmeat trade between countries in the Pacific Rim where foot and mouth disease is not endemic.

Payment-In-Kind (PIK)

A programme used in the US to help dispose of public stocks of commodities. Under PIK, government payments in the form of Commodity Credit Corporation (CCC)-owned commodities are given to farmers in return for additional reductions in harvested acreage.

PROCAMPO

A programme of direct support to farmers in Mexico. It provides for direct payments per hectare on a historical basis.

Producer Support Estimate (PSE)

Indicator of the annual monetary value of gross transfers from consumers and taxpayers to agricultural producers, measured at farm gate level, arising from policy measure, regardless of their nature, objectives or impacts on farm production or income. The PSE measure support arising from policies targeted to agriculture relative to a situation without such policies, i.e. when producers are subject only to general policies (including economic, social, environmental and tax policies) of the country. The PSE is a gross notion implying that any costs associated with those policies and incurred by individual producers are not deducted. It is also a nominal assistance notion meaning that increased costs associated with import duties on inputs are not deducted. But it is an indicator net of producer contributions to help finance the policy measure (e.g. producer levies) providing a given transfer to producers. The PSE includes implicit and explicit payments. The percentage PSE is the ration of the PSE to the value of total gross farm receipts, measured by the value of total production (at farm gate prices), plus budgetary support. The nomenclature and definitions of this indicator replaced the former Producer Subsidy Equivalent in 1999.

Purchasing Power Parity (PPP)

Purchasing power parities (PPPs) are the rates of currency conversion that eliminate the differences in price levels between countries. The PPPs are given in national currency units per US dollar.

Non-Recourse loan programme

Programme to be implemented under the US FAIR Act of 1996 for butter, non-fat dry milk and cheese after 1999 in which loans must be repaid with interest to processors to assist them in the management of dairy product inventories.

Renewable Energy Directive (RED)

EU directive legislating binding mandates of 20% for the share of renewable energy in all Member States' energy mix by the year 2020, with a specific mandate of 10% for the renewable energy share in transport fuels.

Renewable Fuel Standard (RFS and RFS2)

A standard in the United States for the use of renewable fuel use in the transport sector in the Energy Act (EISA). RFS2 is a revision of the RFS program for 2010 and beyond.

Saccharin

A low calorie, artificial sweetener used as a substitute for sugar mainly in beverage preparations.

Scenario

A model-generated set of market projections based on alternative assumptions than those used in the baseline. Used to provide quantitative information on the impact of changes in assumptions on the outlook.

Set-aside programme

European Union programme for cereal, oilseed and protein crops that both requires and allows producers to set-aside a portion of their historical base acreage from current production. Mandatory set-aside rates for commercial producers are set at 10% until 2006.

Single Farm Payment

With the 2003 CAP reform, the EU introduced a farm-based payment largely independent of current production decisions and market developments, but based on the level of former payments received by farmers. To facilitate land transfers, entitlements are calculated by dividing the reference amount of payment by the number of eligible hectares (incl. forage area) in the reference year. Farmers receiving the new SFP are obliged to keep their land in good agricultural and environmental condition and have the flexibility to produce any commodity on their land except fruits, vegetables and table potatoes.

SPS Agreement

WTO Agreement on Sanitary and Phyto-sanitary measures, including standards used to protect human, animal or plant life and health.

Stock-to-use ratio

The stock-to-use ratio for cereals is defined as the ratio of cereal stocks to its domestic utilisation.

Stock-to-disappearance ratio

The stock-to-disappearance ratio for wheat and coarse grains is defined as the ratio of stocks held by the traditional exporters (Argentina, Australia, Canada, the European Union, and the United States) to their disappearance (i.e. domestic utilisation plus exports). For rice the major exporters considered in the calculation are India, the United States, Pakistan, Thailand and Vietnam.

Support price

Prices fixed by government policy makers in order to determine, directly or indirectly, domestic market or producer prices. All administered price schemes set a minimum guaranteed support price or a target price for the commodity, which is maintained by associated policy measures, such as quantitative restrictions on production and imports; taxes, levies and tariffs on imports; export subsidies; and public stockholding.

Tariff-rate quota (TRQ)

Resulted from the Uruguay Round Agreement on Agriculture. Certain countries agreed to provide minimum import opportunities for products previously protected by non-tariff barriers. This import system established a quota and a two-tier tariff regime for affected commodities. Imports within the quota enter at a lower (in-quota) tariff rate while a higher (out-of-quota) tariff rate is used for imports above the concessionary access level.

Uruguay Round Agreement on Agriculture (URAA)

The terms of the URAA are contained in the section entitled the "Agreement on Agriculture" of the Final Act Embodying the Results of the Uruguay Round of Multilateral Trade Negotiations. This text contains commitments in the areas of *market access*, domestic support, and *export subsidies*, and general provisions concerning monitoring and continuation. In addition, each country's schedule is an integral part of its contractual commitment under the URAA. There is a separate agreement entitled the Agreement on the Application of Sanitary and Phyto-sanitary Measures. This agreement seeks establishing a multilateral framework of rules and disciplines to guide the adoption, development and the enforcement of sanitary and phyto-sanitary measures in order to minimise their negative effects on trade.

Vegetable oils

Defined as rapeseed oil (canola), soyabean oil, sunflower seed oil, coconut oil, cotton oil, palm kernel oil, peanut oil and palm oil, except in Japan where it excludes sunflower seed oil.

Voluntary Quota Restructuring Scheme

Established as part of the reform of the European Union's Common Market Organisation (CMO) for sugar in February 2006 to apply for four years from 1 July 2006. Under the scheme, sugar producers receive a degressive payment for permanently surrendering sugar production quota, in part or in entirety, over the period 2006-07 to 2009-10.

WTO

World Trade Organisation created by the Uruguay Round agreement.

Methodology

This section provides information on the methodological aspects of the generation of the present *Agricultural Outlook*. It discusses the main aspects in the following order: First, a general description of the agricultural baseline projections and the *Outlook* report is given. Second, the compilation of a consistent set of the assumptions on macroeconomic projections is discussed in more detail. A third part presents an important model element that has been improved for last year *Outlook*, *i.e.*, the representation of production costs in the model's supply equations. Then the 4th part presents the methodology developed for the stochastic analysis conducted with the AGLINK-COSIMO model.

The generation of the OECD-FAO Agricultural Outlook

The projections presented and analysed in this document are the result of a process that brings together information from a large number of sources. The use of a model jointly developed by the OECD and FAO Secretariats, based on the OECD's Aglink model and extended by FAO's Cosimo model, facilitates consistency in this process. A large amount of expert judgement, however, is applied at various stages of the Outlook process. The Agricultural Outlook presents a single, unified assessment, judged by the OECD and FAO Secretariats to be plausible given the underlying assumptions, the procedure of information exchange outlined below and the information to which they had access.

The starting point of the outlook process is the reply by OECD countries (and some non-member countries) to an annual questionnaire circulated at mid-year. Through these questionnaires, the OECD Secretariat obtains information from these countries on future commodity market developments and on the evolution of their agricultural policies. The starting projections for the country modules handled by the FAO Secretariat are developed through model based projections and consultations with FAO commodity specialists. External sources, such as the World Bank and the UN, are also used to complete the view of the main economic forces determining market developments. This part of the process is aimed at creating a first insight into possible market developments and at establishing the key assumptions which condition the outlook. The main economic and policy assumptions are summarised in the Overview chapter and in specific commodity tables of the present report. The main macroeconomic variables assumed for the outlook period are based on the December 2010 medium term projections of the OECD's Economics Department for OECD countries, and on the Global Economic Prospects of January 2011 of the World Bank for other countries. While sometimes different from the macroeconomic assumptions provided through the questionnaire replies, it has been judged preferable to use just two consistent sources for these variables. The sources and assumptions for the macroeconomic projections are discussed in more detail further below.

As a next step, the modelling framework jointly developed by the OECD and FAO Secretariats is used to facilitate a consistent integration of this information and to derive an initial set of global market projections (baseline). In addition to quantities produced, consumed and traded, the baseline also includes projections for nominal prices (in local currency units) for the commodities concerned. Unless otherwise stated, prices referred to in the text are also in nominal terms. The data series for the projections is drawn from OECD and FAO databases. For the most part information in these databases has been taken from national statistical sources. For further details on particular series, enquiries should be directed to the OECD and FAO Secretariats.

The model provides a comprehensive dynamic economic and policy specific representation of major world producing and trading countries for the main temperate-zone commodities as well as rice and vegetable oils. The Aglink and Cosimo country and regional modules are all developed by the OECD and FAO Secretariats in conjunction with country experts and, in some cases, with assistance from other national administrations. The initial baseline results for the countries under the OECD Secretariat's responsibility are compared with those obtained from the questionnaire replies and issues arising are discussed in bilateral exchanges with country experts. The initial projections for individual country and regional modules developed by the FAO Secretariat are reviewed by a wider circle of in-house and international experts. In this stage, the global projection picture emerges and refinements are made according to a consensus view of both Secretariats and external advisors. On the basis of these discussions and of updated information, a second baseline is produced. The information generated is used to prepare market assessments for biofuels, cereals, oilseeds, meats, dairy products and sugar over the course of the outlook period, which is discussed at the annual meetings of the Group on Commodity Markets of the OECD *Committee for Agriculture*. Following the receipt of comments and final data revisions, a last revision is made to the baseline projections. The revised projections form the basis of a draft of the present *Agricultural Outlook* publication, which is discussed by the *Senior Management Committee* of FAO's Department of Economic and Social Development and the OECD's *Working Party on Agricultural Policies and Markets of the Committee for Agriculture*, in May 2011, prior to publication. In addition, the *Outlook* will be used as a basis for analysis presented to the FAO's *Committee on Commodity Problems* and its various *Intergovernmental Commodity Groups*.

The *Outlook* process implies that the baseline projections presented in this report are a combination of projections developed by collaborators for countries under the OECD Secretariat's responsibility and original projections for the 42 countries and regions under the FAO Secretariat's responsibility. The use of a formal modelling framework reconciles inconsistencies between individual country projections and forms a global equilibrium for all commodity markets.. The review process ensures that judgement of country experts is brought to bear on the projections and related analyses. However, the final responsibility for the projections and their interpretation rests with the OECD and FAO Secretariats.

Sources and assumptions for the macroeconomic projections

Population estimates from the 2008 Revision of the United Nations Population Prospects database provide the population data used for all countries and regional aggregates in the *Outlook*. For the projection period, the medium variant set of estimates was selected for use from the four alternative projection variants (low, medium, high and constant fertility). The UN Population Prospects database was chosen because it represents a comprehensive source of reliable estimates which includes data for non-OECD developing countries. For consistency reasons, the same source is used for both the historical population estimates and the projection data.

The other macroeconomic series used in the AGLINK-COSIMO model are real GDP, the GDP deflator, the private consumption expenditure (PCE) deflator, the Brent crude oil price (in US dollars per barrel) and exchange rates expressed as the local currency value of USD 1. Historical data for these series in OECD countries (except Turkey, Chile and Israel) as well as Brazil, Argentina, China and Russia are consistent with those published in the *OECD Economic Outlook No. 88*, December 2010 and in the OECD Main Economic Indicators. Assumptions made about the future paths of all these variables apart from exchange rates, are based on the recent (December 2010) medium-term macroeconomic projections of the OECD Economics Department.

For non-member economies, projections from the World Bank (Global Economic Perspectives, January 2011) have been extended to 2020 using its longer term poverty projections.

The model uses indices for real GDP, consumer prices (PCE deflator) and producer prices (GDP deflator) which are constructed with the base year 2005 value being equal to 1. The assumption of constant real exchange rates implies that a country with higher (lower)inflation relative to the United States (as measured by the US GDP deflator) will have a depreciating (appreciating) currency and therefore an increasing (decreasing) exchange rate over the projection period, since the exchange rate is measured as the local currency value of 1 USD. The calculation of the nominal exchange rate uses the percentage growth of the ratio "country-GDP deflator/US GDP deflator".

The oil price used to generate the *Outlook* is based on information from the *OECD Economic Outlook No. 88* until 2010 and from the Energy Information Administration for 2011, then it has been kept constant in real term for the projection period.

The representation of production costs in AGLINK-COSIMO

Changes in production costs are an important variable for farmers' decisions on crop and livestock production quantities, in addition to output returns and, if applicable, policy measures.

While supply in AGLINK-COSIMO is largely determined by gross returns, production costs are represented in the model in the form of a cost index used to deflate gross production revenues. In other words, supply equations in the model in most cases depend on gross returns per unit of activity (such as returns per hectare or the meat price) relative to the overall production cost level as expressed by the index. Consequently, equations for harvested areas in crop production and for livestock production quantities take the following general forms:

$$AH = f\left(\frac{RH}{CPCI}\right); \quad QP = f\left(\frac{PP}{CPCI}\right)$$

with:

AH	area harvested (crop production)
RH	returns per hectare (crop production)
CPCI	commodity production cost index
QP	production quantity (livestock production)
PP	producer price (livestock production)

Among others, energy prices, increased by rising crude oil prices, have fostered attention to agricultural production costs in agricultural commodity models. Energy prices can significantly impact on international markets for agricultural products as production costs for both crops and livestock products are highly dependent on energy costs. Fuels for tractors and other machinery, as well as heating and other forms of energy are directly used in the production process. In addition, other inputs such as fertilisers and pesticides have high energy content, and costs for these inputs are driven to a significant extent by energy prices. It is therefore important to explicitly consider energy prices in the representation of production costs.

The production cost indices employed in AGLINK-COSIMO for livestock products is constructed from three sub-indices representing non-tradable inputs, energy inputs, and other tradable inputs, respectively. While the non-tradable sub-index is approximated by the domestic GDP deflator, the energy sub-index is affected by changes in the world crude oil price and the country's exchange rate. Finally, the tradable sub-index is linked to global inflation (approximated by the US GDP deflator) and the country's exchange rate. This relationship is shown in the following equation:

$$
\begin{aligned}
CPCI_{r,t} = &\ CPCS_{r,t}^{NT} * GDPD_{r,t} \big/ GDPD_{r,bas} \\
&+ CPCS_{r,t}^{EN} * \left(XP_{t}^{OIL} * XR_{r,t} \right) \big/ \left(XP_{bas}^{OIL} * XR_{r,bas} \right) \\
&+ \left(1 - CPCS_{r,t}^{NT,I} - CPCS_{r,t}^{EN,I} \right) * \left(XR_{r,t} * GDPD_{USA,t} \right) / \left(XR_{r,bas} * GDPD_{USA,bas} \right)
\end{aligned}
$$

with:

CPCI   commodity production cost index for livestock

$CPCS^{NT}$ share of non-tradable input in total base commodity production costs

$CPCS^{EN}$ share of energy in total base commodity production costs

GDPD   deflator for the gross domestic product

XP^{OIL} world crude oil price

XR   nominal exchange rate with respect to the US Dollar

r,t   region and time index, respectively

bas   base year (2000 or 2005 or 2008) value

The production cost index is different for each *crop products* and is constructed from five sub-indices representing seeds inputs, fertiliser inputs, energy inputs, other tradable inputs and non-tradable inputs, respectively.

$$
\begin{aligned}
CPCI_{r,t}^{c} = &\ CPCS_{r,t}^{NT} * GDPD_{r,t} \big/ GDPD_{r,bas} \\
&+ CPCS_{r,t}^{EN} * \left(XP_{t}^{OIL} * XR_{r,t} \right) \big/ \left(XP_{bas}^{OIL} * XR_{r,bas} \right) \\
&+ CPCS_{r,t}^{FT} * \left(XP_{t}^{FT} * XR_{r,t} \right) \big/ \left(XP_{bas}^{FT} * XR_{r,bas} \right) \\
&+ CPCS_{r,t}^{TR} * \left(XR_{r,t} * GDPD_{USA,t} \right) / \left(XR_{r,bas} * GDPD_{USA,bas} \right) \\
&+ CPCS_{r,t}^{SD} * PP_{r,t}^{c}(-1) \big/ PP_{r,bas}^{c}
\end{aligned}
$$

with:

$CPCI^{C}$ commodity production cost index for crop product c

$CPCS^{NT}$ share of non-tradable input in total base commodity production costs

$CPCS^{EN}$ share of energy in total base commodity production costs

$CPCS^{FT}$ share of fertiliser in total base commodity production costs

CPCS^{TR}	share of other tradable input in total base commodity production costs
CPCS^{SD}	share of seeds input in total base commodity production costs
GDPD	deflator for the gross domestic product
XP^{OIL}	world crude oil price
XP^{FT}	world fertiliser price
PP^c	producer price for crop product c
XR	nominal exchange rate with respect to the US Dollar
c	Crop product
r,t	region and time index, respectively
bas	base year (2000 or 2005 or 2008) value

The shares of the various cost categories are country specific. They were estimated based on historic cost structures in individual countries. Shares vary depending on the development stages of the countries and regions. Developed countries tend to have higher shares of energy, fertiliser and tradable inputs than developing nations.

The fertiliser price is constructed by FAO fertiliser analysts as following:

$$XP^{FT} = 0.2 * DAP + 0.16 * MOP + 0.02 * TSP + 0.62 * Urea$$

With:

US Diammonium Phosphate (DAP)

Can Potassium Chloride (MOP)

Triple superphosphate (TSP)

Urea (Black Sea)

And is represented by an equation in the AGLINK-COSIMO model:

$$\log(XP_t^{FT}) = CON + elas_{FT}^{OIL} * \log(XP_t^{OIL})$$
$$+ elas_{FT}^{crop} * \log(0.5 * XP_{t-1}^{CG} + 0.2 * XP_{t-1}^{WT} + 0.2 * XP_{t-1}^{OS} + 0.1 * XP_{t-1}^{RI})$$

With:

XP^{OIL}	world crude oil price
XP^{FT}	world fertiliser price
XP^{CG}	world coarse grain price
XP^{WT}	world wheat price
XP^{OS}	world oilseed price
XP^{RI}	world rice price

Procedures used to conduct partial stochastic simulations with AGLINK-COSIMO

The AGLINK-COSIMO model is designed and developed as a tool to perform analysis of agricultural markets and forward looking analysis of agricultural and trade policies. The baseline projections generated for the annual *OECD-FAO Agricultural Outlook* constitute a key application of the AGLINK-COSIMO model.

On an annual basis, data are updated and the model is rolled forward dynamically year-by-year to generate a ten-year baseline reflecting how markets could evolve given an extension of current policy (or known changes), normal weather, trend yield growth, assumed stable macroeconomic settings, and certain other factors, such as petroleum prices.

Policy analysis is usually conducted by changing a single or a set of assumptions about policy or macroeconomic variables solving the model for these new given data, and comparing the new simulation output to the baseline.

Stochastic simulations provide useful insight into uncertainties surrounding AGLINK-COSIMO baseline projections by providing multiple alternative scenarios while not implying that one of these scenarios will be the "real" outcome.

This methodology was used for studying price variability as part of a study on risk management. It also contributes to different pieces of work on price volatility that have been undertaken recently by the Secretariat with an analysis of the contribution of different exogenous risk factors to price volatility using the AGLINK-COSIMO model (OECD, 2011).

Yields

The deterministic benchmark projections presented in the 2010 *Agricultural Outlook* are based on a "normal" weather assumption, *i.e.* no shock in crop yield due to weather shocks is taken into account and no assumption is made on possible climate change (*i.e.* variation from average weather). For the partial stochastic analysis, a number of different sets of crop yields for coarse grains, wheat and rice* and all countries studied in the *Agricultural Outlook* over the coming ten years have been simulated. The methodology developed for the present analysis does not allow price effects on yields. This differs from the standard modelling of yields within AGLINK-COSIMO where market prices have an impact on yield evolutions in some countries. The stochastic framework mainly focuses on reproducing observed yield variability:

Six independent geographic zones have been defined. In each of the zones, variance/covariance matrices were constructed to build the multivariate distributions based on annual historical yield data between 1970 and 2009. Yields have been assumed to follow truncated multivariate normal distributions. This allows replicating over the projection period the variability of yields that has been observed over the past 40 years. There is some scope for improving the modelling of yields within the partial stochastic framework. It is envisaged to use empirical multivariate distributions instead of truncated multivariate normal distributions in future versions of the stochastic work.

Crude oil, fertiliser prices and macroeconomic variables

Crude oil prices are also simulated using a truncated normal distribution that has been calibrated on past historical trends. The international fertiliser price is modeled as a function of the crude oil price calibrated on historical data. A simple macroeconomic model of GDP changes and consumer price index for leading economies (Brazil, China, European Union, India, Japan, Russia and the United States) was also developed and calibrated over historical data. The crude oil price being one of the variables of this simple model, random draws for macroeconomic data are obtained by solving this macroeconomic model on random draws for the crude oil price.

---

* 150 in OECD (2011), 500 in the stochastic scenarios presented in the overview.